Renew Ritual Return

Native America Afresh

Jay Miller, PhD, ed

© 2020

Renew Ritual Return

Spring brings renewal, a greening, leafing, and birthing out of nature. Humans recognize this very dynamic process in rituals celebrating revivified life, and the nurturing and sustaining of it. The very word in English evokes this upward thrust, conveyed in flickering flames, sprouting corn, and leaping salmon.

Assembled herein are classic but obscure works comparing instances of such vital rituals, beginning with the rekindling of a tribal fire in the Americas, followed by a comparison of rites before the harvest of the New World staple – maiz, maize, corn – at the core of seasonal farming observances, and for the welcoming of the first salmon of the new year. Also included are updated clarifications of the record for the Lenape Delaware and Eastern Cherokee.

Such marking of events and stages in the cycles of life, and of death, is in keeping with Native American senses of time as repeating itself, at various intensities and fates, with the hopes and prayers that proper observances, public and private, of key rituals will keep these renewals on a safe and healthy cyclical course.

Of these authors, Gilbert went on to work with Eastern Cherokee for his PhD and a career in federal service. John Witthoft long worked for the Pennsyvania state museum, and enganged in intensive work with Eastern Cherokee, who curate his fieldnotes and archives. Erna Gunter was a key member of the Boasan cohort, the only woman to lead the fourth of major anthropology departments in the US, at Washington, along with Columbia, Harvard, and Berkeley. At a time when comparative studies based in library research was the rule, she chose First Salmon, as Irving Hallowell did bears, TT Waterman and Robert Lowie did folklore themes, and her husband by contract Leslie Spier, did Plains Sun Dance and kinship systems.

As academic and social conventions change, as natives themselves engage in scholarly dialog and analysis, certain terms have been judged offensive, if not racist. Rather than expunge them from the record, to highlight these changes, they appear ~~herein~~ crossed out or stricken through. Wherever possible, punctuation has been simplified, sometimes reducing multiple punctuations to a single main one that does not cause confusion. Editorial decisions are intended to "free up" text for greater topographic flexibility, as, for example, a space after the colon : in a citation instead of jamming together date and page, hence (1900: 20).

Contents

THE UNIVERSITY OF CHICAGO
NEW FIRE CEREMONIALISM IN AMERICA

A DISSERTATION
SUBMITTED TO THE GRADUATE FACULTY
IN CANDIDACY FOR THE DEGREE OF
MASTER OF ARTS
DEPARTMENT OF ANTHROPOLOGY
BY
WILLIAM HARLEN GILBERT, JR.
CHICAGO. ILLINOIS
JUNE 1930

CONTENTS

New Fire Ceremonialism in America

Introduction

By the term "New Fire Ceremonialism" we designate the kindling at customary intervals or on habitual occasions of a sacred flame to the accompaniment of ritualistic formulae and taboos. The flame thus kindled is used either to renew perpetual fires or for other ceremonial purposes and is disposed of at the end of the rites in a prescribed manner. Under this definition we will exclude the kindling of a new flame on incidental occasions such as epidemic prevalence or witchcraft manias which comes under the term of the "Need Fire".

The New Fire is a culturally central trait in the focal areas of both Hemispheres. In the Old World it occurs widespread over the Classical Mediterranean Area in Greece and Home and survives in some Easter Rites of various branches of Christianity. It is a characteristic trait of the East African Cattle Area and reaches culmination in the Herero Fire Rites of South Africa. In Asia it was common in Persia and in parts of India as well as appearing strongly in China, Formosa, and Japan.[1]

In the New World the New Fire Rite is, except in the case of the Karok, confined to the maize growing areas: the southern part of the Eastern Woodlands, the Southeast, the [2] Southwest, Mexico, Yucatan, Central America, and Peru. It thus appears to be an outcome of the ceremonial elaboration characteristic of sedentary agricultural communities.

Assuming that the American New Fire Rites are an independent development, with which the Old World New Fire has no direct connections, a background must be sought in the general mental outlook of the New World Aborigines. The chief means of expressing this outlook was thru ceremony and myth. In both of these the position of fire was one of extraordinary importance.

A chance remark dropped by Dr. Eustace Haydon, that the position of fire in Primitive Religion would make an excellent topic for investigation furnished the germ from which has sprung this study. Out of the rather rich material on fire rites of the New World we have selected the New Fire for topical treatment since, occurring as a prominent and important feature of the advanced nations, it seems to furnish a unifying threat. Moreover the New Fire, like Baptism in Europe, is a typical element of the type dubbed "Religious" and serves to illustrate the kind of problems which lie in this field of Anthropology. The field of Ethnological Religion is as yet a largely untrodden area.

The method of treatment used in this paper will be then, first, a preliminary survey of the facts of distribution and variation of the New Fire followed by a general view of its background in the Fire Cultus of the New World. A second section will deal with the theoretical consideration of the position [3] and significance of the New Fire in American Indian Life. This theoretical treatment will consider the relation of the New Fire to other cultural elements, its geographical distribution, and the possible theories such as Diffusion and Parallelism which may partially serve to explain the New Fire Ceremonies as we see them. A comparison of the various forms of these ceremonies may be expected to throw light on the question of whether the New Fire is an historical entity or a mere subjective category. The possibility of European influence will enter also as a factor both thru direct diffusive impingement on the ceremonies and thru

---

[1] Frazer, "The Fire Festivals of Europe", *The Golden Bough*, Vol. 10, Chap. IV. pp. 106-327. Published 1947 Gilbert, in English, in Argentina's *Revista del Instituto de Anthropología de la Universidad National de Tucumán* 3 (3): 233-317.

biasing the subjective interpretation of the observers who have recorded them. An additional glance at the time perspectives involved may also throw some light on the problem.

For invaluable assistance in preparing this monograph the author wishes to thank especially Dr. Edward Sapir and Dr. Robert Redfield of the Department of Anthropology of Chicago both for stimulus in ideas and for constructive criticism on form of treatment. Likewise aid of various kinds was kindly lent by Dr. Eric Thompson and Dr. Paul Martin of the Field Museum by Dr. Clark Wissler of the American Museum of Natural History by Dr. A.L Kroeber of the University of California by Dr. Walter Hough of the National Museum and by Dr. R.B Dixon of Harvard University. [4]

Peruvian New Fire

The only authorities which have been available on the New Fire Rite among the Incas are Garcilaseo de la Vega's *Royal Commentaries of Peru* and Juan de Velasco's *Histoire du Royaume de Quito*. We will give a brief summary of both accounts since they differ considerably.

According to Garcilaseo's account the New Fire was made at the winter solstice ceremony, called *Intip Raymi* held in June at Cusco. At this nine day ceremony the Incas commemorated their ancestors and particularly the sun. As it was esteemed a most solemn event every important official was required to be present including all the principal curacas or lords of provinces, the captains and army commanders and the Inca himself.[2]

It was a prerogative of the Inca to officiate at this festival as the first and eldest child of the sun. The curacas dressed in their finest clothes and gayest garments with gold and silver plated garland adornments and crowns of gold. Some dressed as birds, other, such as the Yuncas, appeared in odd costumes of all sorts and paraded in a fantastic manner to the accompaniment of musical instruments. Each curaca carried the ensign of his province, some of them bore weapons, and each strove to outdo the others in fineness of display. [5]

A three day fast preceded the festival and during this period only a little unbaked white raise and a few simple herbs were eaten. No fires were kindled in the whole city and the men abstained from their wives.

On the third day, which was the day before the sacrifice, along with other preparations the New Fire was made by the chief priest.

> It was necessary that the fire for the sacrifice should be new, and given by the hand of the Sun, as they expressed it. For this purpose they took a large bracelet, called *chipana* (like those they usually wear on the left thumb). This was held by the high priest. It was larger than usual, and had on it a highly polished concave plate, about the diameter of an orange. They put this toward the Sun, at an angle, so that the reflected rays might concentrate on one point, where they had placed a little cotton wool well pulled out, for they did not know how to make tinder; but the cotton was soon lighted in the natural way. With this fire, thus obtained from the hands of the Sun, they consumed the sacrifice, and roasted all the meat on that day. Portions of the fire were then conveyed to the temple of the Sun, and to the convent of virgins, where they were kept in all the year, and it was an evil omen if they were allowed to

---

[2] Garcilasso de la Vega *The Royal Commentaries of the Yncas*, translated by C.E Markham for the Hakluyt Society, vol. II (vol. 45 of the series), pp. 155-167 (Book VI Ch. 20-23).

go out. If on the eve of the festival, which was the time when they made the preparations for the sacrifice, there was no sun wherewith to light the new fire; they obtained it by means of two thin cylindrical sticks about the girth of a man's finger and half a <u>vara</u> long which they rubbed together.

They looked upon it as a bad omen to light the fire for the festival in this way, saying that as the Sun refused to kindle the flame with his own hand, he must be angry with them.[3] The Inca family prepared the sacrifices and drinks to be offered to the sun, making cakes called *canca* and other dishes, and in these all of the populace shared during the feast period. [6]

Assembling at break of day in the municipal market place called Huacaypata, the whole population of the city saluted the sunrise with genuflections and throwing empty kisses into the air. The Inca then poured out a libation and drank to the health of the Sun. Thence proceeding to the temple the celebrants kept silence while the Inca offered golden vessels to the Sun and the priests examined the vitals of slaughtered llamas for good or evil omens. Following this the flesh of a great number of llamas was given out to all and drink in plenty was distributed. There was a fixed order of drinking and honor and ranking were adjudged from the presentation of the cups one to another. Then dancing, songs and masquerades began and occupied the remainder of the festival.

Turning to Velasco's account we find that the renewal of the temple fire by the New Fire Rite is at a maize harvest festival of autumn This Ceremony was called *Pauca Huatay* and marked the beginning of the New Year in March.

La fête de ce mois, une de quatre principales, était la seule que fût précedée de trois jours de jeûne; on ne pouvait allumer de feu dans aucune maison, ne manger autre chose que des fruits et des légumes, pendant tout le temp que le soleil était sur l'horizon. Cette fête était marquée par trois cérémonees; la premiere, qui s'appelait Mushucnina, consistant a renouveler le feu sacré. C'était l'Inca en personne qui, au moyen d'une miroir de metal concave, nommé Inca-Viroo. prenait les premiers rayons du soleil au jour de l'equinox, et en allumait le feu sacré.[4]

Then the sun was offered bread, wine, perfumes, flowers and gold [7] and silver vases. Slaughtered llamas were also offered up. The Inca distributed wine and bread personally to his seigneurs.[5]

On envoyait aussi, dans chaque maison, une parcelle de feu sacré.[5]

The third part of the ceremony consisted in music and dancing.

It can be readily seen that the chief differences between the two descriptions lies in the time of the year at which the New Fire is said to have been made. Otherwise the general aspect of the two ceremonies is remarkably alike. In Velasco's account, however, the Inca himself is said to have kindled the fire and the sacred flame is distributed to private homes. Markham, in his writings on Inca ceremonies, seems to consider the Velasco account the more reliable.

Possibly then, the New Fire is connected with the maize harvest which would offer striking correlation with the New Fire Rites of North America. The principal emphasis seems to lie in having the sun renew the sacred fire for his temple and for the convent of the virgins. The

---

[3] Garcilasco, *op. cit*, pp. 162-153.
[4] Juan de Velasco Histoire du Royaume de Quito in H. Ternaux-Compan's Voyages, Relations et Memoires originaux pour servir a l'Histoire de la Decouverte de l'Amerique. XVIII p. 140.
[5] *Ibid.*

appearance of vestals of the fire in this area, substantiated by several authorities, offers an interesting parallel to similar institutions among the Mayas and Aztecs.[6] [8]

Talamanca New Fire

W.M Gabb travelled in Central America during the years preceding 1874 and recorded numerous observation on the life of the primitive tribes of Costa Rica and Panama. According to his descriptions the Talamancan tribes surrounding the Lagoon of Chiriqui have funeral feasts involving a New Fire Rite. The Bribri, Cabeçars, and Tiribis are tribes who carry on these rites.[7]

When a person of prominence died the body was put in a hammock, covered with a section of bark cloth and then chicha, chocolate, and food were collected for a feast.

A Fire was lighted amidst singing, by twirling a pointed stick in a socket on the face of another. This was the Sacred Fire, which was communicated to a small heap of wood placed in one side of the house. This (Fire) could be used for no common purpose whatever. No ordinary fire could be lighted from it; not even could one use a stick of it to light his pipe. It must burn continuously for nine days. In case of its accidental going out before that time, only a priest could extinguish it, and he only with a calabash of chocolate, and during, or at the end rather, of the suitable incantation.[8]

Anciently much property was buried but now during the feast one of the guests relates the biography of the departed placing meanwhile small seeds and shavings on the breast of corpse to illustrate objects involved in his achievements in war, in peace and in the hunt. The body is wrapped in leaves, secured by lashings, laid in a coffin and deposited on a bench in a concealed spot. [9]

At the end of a year the bones are cleaned by a professional "bone picker " then wrapped in a bundle which is placed on a rack in the house where the feast is held for a second time. Another New Fire is kindled. (Map I, p182)

The priest begins a low chant and two men started twirling the sticks to light the Fire. As fast as one tired, another took his place until the sparks glowed in the pit bored in the lower stick. A yell from the priest announced this, and a piece of cotton wool was ignited from the burning dust; with this the fire-wood, previously prepared, was lighted and the Fire placed under the remains. Here it was kept until the end of the feast. After the lighting of the Fire, singing and dancing began in earnest, interrupted occasionally by eating and drinking.[9]*

---

[6] Acosta, Natural and Moral History of the Indies, Bk. V Ch. 15 (vol. 60 in Hakluyt Series Markham transl. pp. 292-301 v. I).
Cieza de Leon, Travels p. 139 and the Second Part of the Chronicles of Peru, p. 85 ff, both in Markham's transl. for Hakluyt vols. 48 and 68.
Garcilasso, *op. cit*, part I Bk. IV. Chs. l to 3 pp. 292-299.

[7] W.M Gabb, "Of the Indian Tribes and Languages of Costa Rica," in Proceedings of the American Philosophical Society, vol. 1V no. 92, 1874, p. 483ff.

[8] *Ibid*, p. 497.

[9] Gabb, *op. cit.*

The soul wandering about in the neighborhood and subsisting on wild fruits, is attracted to the second funeral feast by the lighting of the New Fire. There it is given directions by the presiding medicine man on how to reach Sibu, the abode of the dead. At the end of a varying period the food begins to give out so the feast must come to an end. The Fire is carefully carried from its place under the corpse and piled almost between the feet of the principal priest. The leader then begins a long dirge again directing the soul on its journey to Sibu and, as he approaches the end of his recital, with a cry he suddenly pours chocolate over the Fire and totally extinguishes it, which act sends the soul off on its final pilgrimage. The bones are then carried to their last resting place, a pit four feet deep paved with stones and roofed with slabs.[10] [10]

There are three types of religious ministrants among these tribes, namely, *usekaras* or high priests *tsugurs* or ordinary priests and *awas* or shamans. It is the *tsugur* class who preside in the funeral feasts. It is possible that the neighboring colony of Nahuan Nicaraos vho dwell near the Chiriqui Lagoon may have transmitted the idea of the New fire to these tribes of Talamancas since

> The religion of the Nicaraos (Nahua of Lake Nicaragua vicinity} was in all essentials similar to that of the Aztec altho the ritual was not so elaborate .... [11]

It is also worth noting that the Talamancas are linguistically allied to the Chibchas of the Colombian Plateaux further south and this, if backed up by other cultural similarities, suggests the possibility of finding New Fire Rites among the latter on better investigation.

Possibly the nearest affinities to these funeral rites of the Bribri and their neighbors are to be sought in the grave fires kindled by various tribes of South America and of the West Indies and which seem to give rise to the Ossuary Sacred Fires of the lower Mississippi valley.

In fine then, the New Fire of the Bribri and their congeners appears to have been a flame lit purely for the purpose of magical control of the soul's activities. Why it was lit twice, once at death and once a year later (this is a rather dubious inference arising possibly from the vagueness of the description), does not appear. These tribes could bear much further investigation. [11]

Maya New Fire

Our sole authority on the ancient Mayas, the Bishop Diego de Landa, furnishes all of the references available on the New Fire in Yucatan Civilization save what can be inferred from interpretation of the codices in such studies as Long's <u>The Burner Period of the Mayas</u>. In recent years Tozzer's investigations of the Lacandone Incense Bowl Renewal Ceremony offers some interesting comparisons with the past in the matter of the New Fire.

Among the ancient Maya the New Fire was kindled on the occasion of New Year celebrations in the month <u>*Pop*</u>.[12] At this time all of the household utensils such as plates, cups, baskets, clothes and dresses of idols, were renewed. The houses were swept clean and everything old thrown on the rubbish pile where nobody dared to touch them, badly in need as

---

[10] *Ibid*, pp. 483 ff. Also see Thomas A Joyce, Central American and West Indian Archeology, pp. 104-105.

[11] Joyce, *op. cit*, p. 18.

[12] Diego de Landa, Relacion de las Cosas de Yucatan, cap. 40.

they might be. All of the participants fasted and were continent for at least 13 days before the New Year and meat was eaten unseasoned. Misfortune followed for whosoever broke his fast.

On the main day of the sacrifice the priest and his sleeted assistant prepared a number of little balls of fresh incense on small boards. These balls were of copal and were to be used in burning before the idols. All of the men assembled in the courtyard of the temple, women being excluded from the rites except for certain dances. All of the assembly were adorned with paint and cleaned from the grease acquired during [12] the penances and fast. Offerings of food and newly fermented wine were made to the idols. The priest then entered carrying a brazier and the balls of incense. First, the evil spirit was expelled from the vicinity and all present offered up a prayer. Then the priest's assistants kindled the New Fire for the year.[13] The priest cast balls of incense into the brazier and distributed other balls to the rest of the assembly in the order of their rank. Each worshiper then dropped the ball given him into his brazier and let it burn. Banquets and orgies of drinking terminated the proceedings, while some of the more devout repeated the ceremonies in their homes. This is all we know about the ancient rite of the New Fire.

There seem to have been perpetual fires in the temples of Yucatan tended by vestal virgins who were called "virgins of the fire." If these should let the fire go out or should violate their vows while in office they were shot to death with arrows. Possibly the New Fire was used to renew the temple fires yearly or oftener as Landa seems to imply. According to Long's interpretation the Fire rites of the Mayas were bound up with the calendrical repetition of a [13] series of four rites every sixty-five days.[14] The Tonalamatl was divided into four subdivisions of sixty-five days each, which were in turn subdivided into four lesser periods by the four fire ceremonies. A regular sixty-five day cycle was thus established thruout the year for incense rites. The four rites of the sixty-five day period were: −

1. U cha Kak ahtoc　　−　　The burner takes the Fire (Prepares it)
2. U hoppol u kak ahtoc −　　The Fire of the burner begins (New Fire)
3. U yalcab u kak ahtoc −　　The burner gives the Fire scope (Replenishes it)
4. U Tup kak ahtoc　　−　　The burner extinguishes the Fire.

The four burners are thought to be identified with the four Bacabs or deities of the cardinal points and also with the four Chacs or rain gods. Moreover there seem to be even further identifications with the Uinal time division and with four epochs in cosmogonic lore.

The New Fire or Virgin Fire was a Goddess called Suhuikak and had a glyph character of its own on the monuments.

---

[13] "'.'...Y abaxo en el patio tendian todos cada uno sus idolos sobre hojas de arboles que para ello avia, y sacada lumbre nueva, començavan a quemar en muchas partes de su encienso, y a hazer ofrendas de comida guisadas ...' " = " '(in month *Xul* or October) and again "Començavan todos sus oraciones devotas y los chaces sacavan lumbre nueva; quemavan el encienso al demonio y el sacerdote commençave a echar su encienso en el' " (in month *Pop* or July) Landa, cap. XL, quoted by Tozzer, A Comparative Study of the Mayas and Lacandones, pp. 133-134.

[14] R.C.E Long "The Burner Period of the Mayas" Man 108, Nov. 1923. See also C.P Bowditch, The Numeration, Calendar System and Astronomical Knowledge of the Mayas, pp. 248, 272- 274 and J.T Goodman, The Archaic Maya Inscriptions, pp. 28-35.

Passing over to the Lacandones, the culturally fossilized remnant of the Maya culture, we find that the ancient Chilan or priests have vanished and only the shaman-like chacs or men now survive. The functions of the ancient priests are carried on by the head of the family in each encampment. Women and children are excluded from the ceremonies. [14]

The Brazier Renewal Ceremony, called Alena after the name of the chief brazier used in the ceremonies, is a yearly event extending somewhat over a month from the middle of February to the middle of March. It consists in the renewal of the "life" of the incense bowls which are used in sacrifice to the gods. It is probably a direct survival of the Ocna Rites mentioned by Landa as being held in December and January in honor of the Chacs or Lords of the milpae (fields). In fact, incense vessels of types quite like the modern *braseros* of the Lacandones are found in ancient Maya ruins and help point to the relative antiquity of the ceremonies.[15] The time of the year at which the present festival is held is largely determined by the ripening of the products of the milpas. Thus it appears that the New Fire is here, as in Peru, bound up with the maize harvesting activities.

The Lacandones are a small group scattered in family units around the Lacantun and Lacanha tributaries of the upper Usumacinta River and near Lakes Petha, Anaite, and Peten. Each family or group of connected families living together is possessed of several of the braseros. A *brasero* is, in its essence, a bowl for burning incense, with a grotesque stone face mask on one side of the olla (bowl) and is made of native clay by the Lacandones. Incense is burned within the bowl but offerings of food and drink are placed on the protruding lip of the face [15] in behalf of one of the gods. All of the rites of this ceremony follow about the same pattern and consist of incense burning and offerings of food and drink to the accompaniment of chanting and prayers. Variation occurs only in regard to the nature of the articles offered. The face mask being removable from the edge of the olla, in the renewal of the incense bowls the idols of stone are simply taken from the old and placed in new ollas. To the head in the ollas offerings are made in behalf of the god. There are also smaller incense burners without idols used in the rites which are called *braseritos*. All of the incense bowls are housed in a special hut called the *hermita*, a sideless structure with a low hanging thatched roof. It is in the *hermita* that the sacred fire is kindled and kept during the ceremony.

In preparation for the ceremony besides the numerous new ollas and *braseritos* which are made, drums, consisting of clay jars with membranes stretched over them, are also prepared. Among other instruments used are conch shell trumpets, reed oboes and gourd rattles. Ceremonial ponchos are also made, that of the leader bearing special symbols, and are stained with the juice of the achiote berry. The chief offerings are

Posol   − a soup made of corn boiled with lye then ground moist and mixt thoroly with water;
Buliwa − a kind of corn bread with beans; and
Baltse − an intoxicating drink made from the bark of the Baltse tree.
Copal gum and rubber are burned as incense.

The purpose of the Renewal Ceremony is to supplicate the gods for life and health since above all things the Lacandones [16] fear disease and death. The extremely solemn character of the Rites are marked by the fact that all of the trails are stopped with brushwood during important sections of the Ceremony and all ingress to the encampment is denied to outsiders.

---

[15] Tozzer, A Comparative Study of the Mayas and Lacandones, p. 105 sqq.

The New Fire is kindled twice, once for the kindling of the incense in the rite of the last offering to the old *braseros* and once in the beginning of sacrifice to the new.

....new fire is kindled by the leader and his assistant working together. This is done by the simple two stick method, the wooden drill twisted between the palms and revolving in the notch of a horizontal stick of softer wood. The lower stick or 'hearth' has no gutter running from the notch to the edge, as is often the case in this form of fire-drill. By friction the tinder, placed beneath the horizontal stick, is heated and finally kindled. Among the Lacandones the tinder consists of shavings of logwood resting in a corn husk. As soon as the fire is kindled it is handed to the wife who enters at this time and whose duty is to light, by means of it, the wood already prepared. The whole ceremony of the new fire finds an interesting parallel in several of the rites mentioned by Landa.[16]

....during the operation of making the new fire, the leader hands to his assistant two palm leaves and to every other man and boy present a single leaf. In the camp fire kindled by the wife, the leader then lights two pine sticks and with them he sets fire to the nodules of copal in the incense burners. During the operation everyone turns his back to the altar where it is being done.[17]

Oddly enough the nodules of copal used in the offerings are divided into "male" and "female" nodules.

The New Fire for the New Braseros is lit on the third day of the "life" of the New Braseros. We are not told how the flames of the New Fire are finally disposed of. [17]

In summing up the New Fire of the Maya Area we may say that it is mainly connected, so far as we can ascertain, with incense sacrifices to the gods but that anciently it may have been used also in renewing perpetual temple fires. Whereas in modern times, as it survives among the Lacandones, it is kindled but once only in the year, in the ancient period it was probably kindled at least twice a year according to Landa (in months *Pop* and *Xul*), and possibly every sixty-five days if Long's interpretations should prove correct. The New Fire seems to be bound up with the maize harvest as in Peru. [18]

Mexican New Fire

There is a great profusion of references to the New Fire Rites of Ancient Mexico. The principal authorities which we have followed are Sahagun in his unrivalled account entitled *Historia de las Cosas de la Nueva Espana*. Torquemeda's *Monarquia Yndiana* and Clavigero's *Storia della Messico*. Bancroft's excellent summaries in English of the original authorities in his *Native Races of the Pacific Coast* have also proved serviceable. We have used several quotations from Bancroft after carefully checking up on his paraphrasing of the original authorities since his descriptions are rather striking.

----

[16] Tozzer, *op. cit*, pp. 133 ff.
[17] *Ibid*, pp. 133-134.

Mexico was by all odds the center wherein the New Fire Rites had their greatest development. There were at least three distinct ceremonies in which the New Fire figured and in addition New Fire making was resorted to at the birth of children and on setting forth to battle. New Fire was made annually at the second feast of the God of Fire, Xiuhtecutli, held in the eighteenth or last month, Yscalli, (our February) and annually at the feast of Camaxtli, father of Quetzalcoatl, held in the second month, Tlacaxipeoalistli. Every fifty-two years, at the close of a calendrical cycle. New Fire was made at the great Toxilraolpilia world renewal ceremony in mid-winter. Judging from the available evidence these ceremonies were shared by all of the advanced nations of Mexico; Astecs, Tarascans, Mixtecs, Zapotecs, Huastecs, Totonacs, and Olmecs. [19]

Celebrations were held yearly in honor of Camaxtli but the quadrennial rites were especially imposing. First a severe fast was undertaken by the priests which lasted for eight days. They spent the time in piling firewood in the Temple of Camaxtli. Succeeding the priestly fast another eight day fast was undergone by the laymen. During these fasts only unseasoned maize cakes were eaten. Fires must be kept alight for the whole period, the lives of the slaves attending being forfeited if the flames were extinguished. On the day of great penance the priests, amidst chanting and drum playing, cut holes in their tongues and inserted sticks for penitential bleeding.[18]

At the end of the fasting periods the temple was repaired and adorned and three days before the festival en all night dance was held in the temple yard. The image of Camaxtli was adorned as was that of Quetzalooatl his son.

At midnight the priest, dressed in the vestments of the idol lighted the New Fire.[19] This act was consecrated by slaying the principal captive of the occasion who was called "the son of the Sun." After this great numbers of other captives were slain and their bodies consumed in the fire together with other offerings of paper, quail and copal incense. [20]

Xiuhtecutli, the God of Fire as already noted, was represented as a naked man with ulli blackened chin, a lip jewel of red stone, and a parti-colored paper crown on his head having green plumes issueing from the top like flames of fire and feather tassels hanging down to the ears, on his ears were turquoise earrings wrought in mosaic. On his back was a dragon's head made of yellow feathers and some little marine shells. There were bells or rattles on his ankles. In his left hand he held a gold plated shield in which were set five chalchiutes in a cross shape. In his right hand he held a round plate of gold which was called "the looking plate " and with this he covered his face and peeped thru a hole in the center. Xiuhtecutli was called "father" by the people and was regarded with mingled emotions of love and fear. To him homage was rendered in the rite of "the throwing " in which when eating, a little section of the food was first cast into the fire, and in "the tasting" in which before drinking, a little *pulque* was spilt on the edge of the hearth.[20]

Xiuhtecutli had at least twelve minor names and being one of the outstanding deities was possessed of a particular calendar place, compass direction, a special temple called Tzomolco, a special priesthood called Ixcocauhqui Tzomolco and three important festivals: Xocohuetzi, Yzcalli, and Ce' itzcumtli, the last of which was a moveable feast. Xiuhtecutli is regarded [21] as

---

[18] Torquemada, Monarquia Yndiana, Tom. II, Lib. 10, cap. XXXI, pp. 288-290.

[19] *Ibid.* "Luego a la media noche venia un Ministro de los que alli servian, vestido con los ensignias de el Demonio, y sacabales Lumbre nueva, y esto hecho, sacrificaban un de los mas Principales de los Cautivos, que tenian para el Sacrificia de esta Fiesta." Also see Bancroft, Native Races, vol. II pp. 312-315.

[20] Bancroft, Native Races, vol. III, p. 384 basing on Sahagun lib. I, cap. 13.

the abstract pre-solar fire which existed before the creation of the sun or moon and is possessed of an extensive mythology. He quite overshadows Chantico and Quaxolotl, the lesser fire deities.[21]

At the Festival of the Fire God in the tenth month, Xocohuetzi, there is no record of a New Fire Rite but in the second Festival in the eighteenth month, Yzcalli, New Fire is made. This second feast is called Motlaxquiantota which means "our father the fire toasts his food"[22] and was celebrated in Mexico, Tlacopan, Coyuhuacan, Azcapuzalco, Quauhtitlan and Tlascala.

> An image of the god of fire was made, with a frame of hoops and sticks tied together as the basis or model to be covered with his ornaments. On the head of this image was put a shining mask of Turquoise mosaic, banded across with rows of green chalchiutes. Upon the mask was put a crown fitting to the head below, wide above and gorgeous with rich plumage as a flower; a wig of reddish hair was attached to the crown, so that the evenly cut locks flowed from beneath it, behind and around the mask, as if they were natural. A robe of costly feathers covered all of the front of the image, and fell over the ground before the feet, so light that it shimmered and floated with the least breath of air until the variegated feathers glittered and changed color like water. The back of the image seems to have been left unadorned, concealed by a throne on which it was seated, covered with a dried tiger skin, paws and head complete. Before the statue new fire was produced at midnight by boring rapidly by hand one stick upon another; the spunk or tinder so inflamed was put in a hearth by a fire lighter.[23] [22]

Clavigero's account of this ceremony differs slightly from Sahagun's. They agree in placing the time in February but Clavigero gives the date of the kindling of the New Fire as the fifteenth instead of the tenth. According to Clavigero, on the tenth day of the month the whole of the Mexican youth went out for a ceremonial hunt. On the fifteenth the fire in the temple and in the private houses was extinguished and kindled anew before the idol of the god. The hunters presented all of their spoils to the priests who threw a part on the fire as an offering to the god and dressed the rest for the tables of the nobility and themselves. Afterwards the old men drank pulque and sang before the image of the god. Every fourth year elaborate rites of human sacrifice graced the occasion of this feast.[24]

Every fifty-two years at the close of a calendric cycle the most important of all festivals was held, that of Renewing the World. This was the Toxilmolpilia or the "binding up of the years" in which all belongings were renewed, all statues of the gods renovated and old things cast away.

> ... en fin de los cincuenta y dos anos, hacian una muy solemne fiesta, y sacaban fuego nueva, y apagaban todo el viejo, y tomaban todas las provineias de ésta N.E fuego nuevo: entónces renovaba todas las estátuas de los Idolos, y todas las alhajas,

---

[21] Lewis Spence, The Gods of Mexico, pp. 268-234.

[22] Sahagun lib. 11, cap. 37 "nuestro padre el fuego tuesta para comer."

[23] Bancroft, *op. cit*, III, p. 30 basing on Sahagun, lib. II, cap. 18, 37. Of Yzcalli the latter says "A los diez dias de este mes sacaban fuego nuevo a la media noche delante de la imagen de Xiuhtecutli, muy curiosamente ataviada, y encendidos fuegos luego a la manana venian los mancebos y muchachos, y traian diversos animales que habian cazado en los dias pasados, ...

[24] Clavigero, The History of Mexico (transl. by C Cullen) vol. 11 p. 82 ff.

y el propósito de servir los otros cincuenta y dos anos, y tambien tenian profecia ú
oráculo del demonio, que en uno de estos periodos se habia de acabar el mundo.[25] [23]

The most important feature of this event was the successful production at midnight of the New fire amidst highly dramatic scenes. Here we reach the culmination of the New Fire, New Life, New Year Ceremonies of the Western Hemisphere. It was firmly believed by the natives that at the end of one of these cycles the whole world would come to an end and the universe plunged into primaeval chaos for an indefinite period.

> On the last night of their century, they extinguished the fires in all of their temples and houses, broke their vessels, earthen pots, and all other kitchen utensils, preparing themselves in this manner for the end of the world, which at the termination of the century they expected with terror.[26]

The five days preceding the New Century were accounted unlucky since they did not fit into the calendar and were spent by the unlucky natives in fear and anxious forebodings. If the New Fire should not be produced, it was believed that the dreaded *tztzimitliz* or night demons would descend to devour humanity and that children, if not hid away, would be transformed into mice and pregnant women into wild beasts. (Map II, p182)

About six miles from Mexico City stands Mt. Huixachtla on the boundary line between the cities of Xtztaplapa and Colhuacan and on the summit of this peak the New Fire of the Century must be lit so that it could be seen for miles around.

At the appointed hour, after sunset, the priests dressed in their robes of office, set out in stately procession for the mountain, walking at a rate calculated to bring them to the [24] summit a little before midnight. The priests wore the robes of the gods themselves for this solemn occasion. The populace awaited the event with trembling for, if the New Fire were not successfully kindled the light of the Sun would never be seen again. If the Pleiades reached the zenith then the omens were accounted excellent.

Finally the mountain peak was reached, a priest of the ward of Capolco whose duty it was to light the New Fire, carrying the fire sticks in his hands. At the proper moment the frictional method was applied and New Fire produced on the prostrate breast of a notable captive. The heart of the victim was immediately afterward torn out and flung on the newly kindled flame as a first sacrifice.[27]

From the crowded house-tops every eye was bent on *Vixachtlan* (*Huixachtla*). Suddenly a moving spark of light was seen by the nearest, then a great column of

---

[25] Sahagun, lib. IV appendix Tom 1, p. 339.

[26] Clavigero, *op. cit*, II, pp. 92-94.

[27] "On his bare breast the cedar boughs are laid;
On his bare breast dry sedge and odorous gums.
Laid ready to receive the sacred spark.
And blaze to herald the ascending Sun
Upon his living altar."

Part 2 Canto 26 of Southey's *Madoc* quoted by Prescott, History of the Conquest of Mexico, I, 125-127.

Sahagun describes the Toxilmolpilia in lib. VII cap. 9-12, pp. 259-264 Tom II.

flame shot up against the sky. The New Fire! and a great shout of joy went up from all the country round about. The stars moved on in their courses. Fifty and two years more had the universe to exist. Everyone did penance, cutting his ear with a splinter of flint, and scattering the blood toward the place where the fire was; even the ears of children in the cradle were so cut. And now from the blazing pile on the mountain, burning brands of pine candle wood were carried by the swiftest toward every quarter of the kingdom. In the city of Mexico, in the Temple of Huitzilopochtli, before the altar, there was a fire-place of stone and lime containing much copal; into this a blazing brand was flung by the first runner, and from this place fire was carried to all of the houses by the priests, and thence came again to all of the city. There soon blazed great central [25] fires in every ward, and it was a thing to be seen the multitude of people that came together to get light, and the general rejoicings.[28]

The New Fire having been obtained, the people began to renew all of their belongings, household goods and furniture, clothing and the like. Everything was made new as a sign of the new sheaf of years and sacrifices began, of quails and copal incense. After a meal of wild amaranth seed and honey a general fast was ordered until noon on the first day of the new century. Even the drinking of water during this period was forbidden. In the afternoon eating and drinking began and general festivities were initiated by the sacrifice of captives and slaves. These rejoicings lasted for thirteen days. Thus, counting the five unlucky days with the thirteen the total duration of this event was eighteen days. The Toxilmolpllia was an occurrence which, happening once in a lifetime, acquired especial importance for the individual. Moreover this Ceremony had the widest vogue, extending to the confines of the Mexican dominion and even into the neighboring states.[29]

In the temples of Mexico, as in those of Yucatan, sacred fires were kept burning perpetually, which were tended by a virgin order. It was accounted an evil omen if the fires went out and death was the penalty for incontinence on the part of a virgin while in office.[30] These sacred fires were probably always renewed from New Fire in the ceremonies just described. [26]

The Aztecs were also accustomed to light a New Fire on the occasion of setting forth on a military campaign. Again, at the birth of a child the mother was held to be unclean for four days and a fire was kindled and kept burning for a like period of time. On the fourth day the child was passed thru the flame which was then put out.[31]

Worship in Michoacan, the on a smaller scale, was very similar to that in Mexico. Curicaneri was the patron deity, having been adopted from the Chichimecs in place of Xaratanga, the former chief god.

Before setting out on the march, a fire was lighted before the idol, (of Curicaneri or Xaratanga) and as the incense rose to the heavens the priest addressed the God of Fire, imploring him to accept the offering and favor the expedition.[32]

---

[28] Bancroft, Native Races, III, p. 393 ff.
[29] Clavigero, *op. cit*, pp. 92-94.
[30] Fraser, The Golden Bough, II p. 245.
[31] Brinton, Myths of the New World, p. 90.
[32] Bancroft, Native Races III, p. 445.

Fire rites were also probably common in Oajaea where worship bore an even stronger resemblance to that of Mexico than did that of Michoacan.[33] The Zapotec position in regard to fire can be partially gleaned from the fact that the <u>Zapotec</u> word meaning fire, also denotes divinity, idol, everything sacred, the earth itself.[34]

In summing up the Mexican New Fire Rites we may say that they appear to be originally acts of worship at the time of the annual kindling of fresh sacrifices to the gods. Later the New [27] Fire came to take on other significances, especially in connection with the world renewal ceremony held at fifty-two year cycles. The New Fire of the Motlaxquiantota Ceremony, held in February (*Yzcalli*), seems to have calendric parallelism with the Maya Ocna and the Lacandone Akna Rites and the maize ripening. This would link up with the maize cycle significance of the Pueblo and Muskogian New Fires, as we shall see. Altho cremation was occasionally resorted to, there seems to be no evidence of the earlier strata of funeral fires which crops out in the Talamanca and Porto Rico Areas. The New Fire of Mexico then was essentially used to kindle special sacrifices and to renew temple fires and the fires of private houses. [28]

Pueblo New Fire

The Village Indians of the Southwest: Hopi, Zuni, Tanoan, and Keresan were and are in possession of New Fire Rites of extreme antiquity which possibly have connections with those of Mexico. Two of the New Fire Rites observed by the Hopi have been described in detail by J.W Fewkes. Miss M.C Stevenson has given some of the features of two other New Fire rites among the Zuni. E.S Curtis has also mentioned New Fires among the Keresan natives of Cochiti and Acoma.

There are some seven pueblos of the Hopi people but Fewkes has confined himself to the Walpi Pueblo, where he found a November New Fire and New Year Ceremony which, as ordinarily given, lasts five days but which every four years is extended to nine days due to elaborations involving the initiation of novices. The shorter form is called *Wüwütcimtû*, from one of the Religious societies prominent in its celebration and the extended form, *Naacnaiya*. Formerly the *Naacnaiya* was celebrated every year. The November New Fire rite is observed in all of the Pueblos of the Hopi except Sitomocovi and Hano (Tewa).[35]

Four societies of Priests, making up the bulk of the community, unite in the celebration of the Ceremony. These societies are the *Tataukyamu, Wüwütcimtû, Aaltû,* and *Kwakwantû.* [29] The first two conduct the phallic public dances and act as chorus in the kiva where New Fire is made but the sacred flame is actually handled only by the latter two societies. The chief of the *Kwakwantû* personifies the fire god, in whose honor the most important part of the ceremony is performed.

Four sacred rooms were occupied in this ceremony. The *Tataukyamû* met in the *Mong-kiva.* This was the chamber in which New Fire was kindled with the rotating fire-drills. The *Wüwütcimtû* society met in the *Wikwaliobi-kiva*: the *Aaltû* met in the *Al-kiva* and the *Kwakwantû* in the *Tcivato-kiva.* (Maps III, IV, p183)

Rites are conducted simultaneously in all of the kivas, especially on the last night, making it exceedingly difficult for a single observer to adequately follow the Ceremony. Sticks

---

[33] *Ibid.*

[34] *Ibid.*

[35] J.W Fewkes, "New Fire Ceremony at Walpi" (1898), p. 80 American Anthropologist N.S vol. II,1900; see also "The Na-ac-nai-ya: A Tusayan Initiation Ceremony" Journal of American Folklore, vol. V, 1892, pp. 189-221.

with attached feathers, called "*natci*" were displayed at the entrances of the kivas to indicate that ceremonies were in progress within and duplicates of the *natcis*, called *ketsakwa*, were used in the kiva rites and were carried by chiefs in several of the public dances as badges of office. Trails to the kivas were all closed by drawing a line of meal across them. In former times any one who ventured to cross the lines of meal was killed. This symbolic closing is not observed in the abbreviated rites. This trail closing is reminiscent of like practices of the *brasero* renewal of the Lacandones. Trails are opened by drawing a line along them.

For several days before the ceremonies began, large quantities of wood were piled near the kiva hatches, and after [30] the rites began this fuel was carried down into the room and fed to the flames of the New Fire by an old man who newer left his task. The flames of the New Fire were regarded with reverence and no one was allowed to light a cigarette from it, blow in it, or otherwise profane it.

The following is a brief synopsis of the events of the *Wüwütcimti*.

November 8: "Smoke Assembly" − *Tcotcoñyuñya* − Chiefs of the four societies assembled in an old kiva shortly after sunset and smoking ensued. The assembly then sent out a Town Crier to announce the New Fire. *Ensignia* (stringed feathers) were laid on the trail.

November 9: "The Announcement" − *Tiyuñava* − The Crier summoned in a loud voice the members of the societies to assemble and also invoked the gods to send the desired snow, ice, and rain to water the farms.

November 13: "The Assembly" − *Yuñya* − An altar to the six directions was built in the *Mong-kiva* at sunrise. A low pile of sand with six radiating lines of meal was next laid down near the fireplace. The *nakwipi* or medicine bowl was then set in the center and charm liquid poured in. Another altar to the six directions was built at noon in the *Tcivato-kiva*. The New Fire was made in the *Mong-kiva* as follows: A cubical fire stone was set in the center of the kiva and on this was set the fire board and stick. The fire stone was set on a bed of shredded cedar bark and two men relieved each other at intervals in twirling the fire stick. Singing accompanied the twirling of the fire [31] stick. Soon a smudge appeared In the cedar bark and this was used to ignite the greasewood whereupon the songs ceased. During this ceremony the fire god concealed himself behind a screen. Offerings of stringed pine needles were first dropped in the newly kindled flame. A cedar bark torch was then used to carry flame to other kivas. None of the sacred fire was allowed to be extinguisht until the end of the ceremony. The day of assembly was ended by visits to the shrines of *Tuwapontumsi, Talatumsi*, and old Walpi where sacrifices were kindled with the New Fire.

November 14: *Sockahimu* − "All Rest" − There was a Phallic Dance by the *Wüwütcimtû* and nocturnal rituals by the novices, with hazing.

November 15: *Komoktotokyu* − "Wood Gathering" − Songs and Dances were given by the Wüwütcimtû.

November 16: *Totokyu* − "Feast" − First there was a sweeping of the floors of all the kivas. Then the Altar of the *Al-kiva* was laid down with complicated rain cloud symbolism. Following this there were other ceremonies about the medicine bowl at in the *Tcivato-kiva* and another dance by the *Wüwütcimtû*. The Tataukyamû then danced, carrying phallic emblems and making lascivious gestures. In the Episode of the Meal Beggars, meal was begged from door to door by the societies and this was later used in making trails from kivas to shrines. Finally came the great nocturnal Feast in the kivas, in which there was much singing. The time for Important night ceremonies in the Tcivato-kiva [32] and also others is determined toy the position of the Pleiades and Orion which were closely watched at this time.

November 17: *Pigumnovi* or *Tihuni* − "Dispersal" − First there were visits of six youths with prayer offerings to the shrine of *Talatumsi*, the Earth Goddess and a distant spring. The New Fire was allowed to die out and the embers scraped carefully out of the fireplaces into watermelon rinds and thrown with meal over the cliffs. Most of the ceremonial paraphernalia was also thrown over the cliffs. The priests then vomited over the cliffs and returned to the kivas where further purificatory rites were performed. For several days after the conclusion of the festival rabbit hunts were indulged in by the several societies.

The *Naacnaiya* Ceremony differs from the *Wüwütcimti* in that at the former rite novices are initiated; the great snow pipe is smoked, a figurine of *Talatumsi*, the Dawn Woman, is brought into the village from her shrine, and in general there is a longer duration of the ceremonies. The New Fire is made in the *Mong-kiva* in the same manner as in the abbreviated rite. Large bonfires are made over which the priests leap in imitation of mountain sheep.[36]

From sun analysis of the societies that take part in the November rites Fewkes comes to the conclusion that the New Fire was brought to Walpi by clans formerly living in the Gila Valley and consists of Rain Making and Germination Magic or, in [33] effect, World Renewal Rites. [37]

The meaning of the New Fire Ceremony is obscure, but it seems to our present knowledge to be a prayer to the Germ God for fertility of human beings, animals, and crops. The Germ Gods, Earth Gods, and Fire Gods are to be placated and honored by these rites and no doubt the new fire ceremonies of all times and peoples were held with such intent, for the relation of life and fire are a philosophic observation of the remote past. With this ceremony the round of the year has been finished and the Hopi are ready to begin again.[38]

The Lesser New Fire Ceremonies, called Sumaicoli, are held at Tewa and Walpi in both March and July. The *Sumaicoli* rites were probably introduced into Hopiland by Tanoan Clans from the Rio Grande Valley and are the special property of a class of Fire Priests known as Yayawimpkia who specialise in the cure of disease by fire.[39]

As in the Greater New Fire Rites objects are placed at the entrances of the kivas to indicate that *Sumaicoli* rites are in progress but the latter rites are secret, not public like the others. The objects placed at the kiva entrances consist of two small ferruled sticks with spherical gourds attached. The duration of the Ceremony is one day only. *Sumaicoli* Masks are worn when the celebrants appear in public.

---

[36] Fewkes, "The Naacnaiya", Jour. Amer. Folkl, vol. V 1892, pp. 189-221.
[37] Fewkes, "New Fire at Walpi", A.A, 1900, p. 80 *op. cit.*
[38] Walter Hough, The Hopi Indians, pp. 163-7. Alexander, North American Mythology, p. 194.
[39] Fewkes, "The Lesser New Fire Ceremony at Walpi" American Anthrop. N.S 3 1901 pp. 438-453.

First, the *Sumaicoli Wimi* or paraphernalia are prepared. These are idols, painted slats, symbols and masks. Altars are [34] disc-like shields which are set side by side on the floor with edges touching. An object on the floor composed of many black sticks tied together like a *fascis*, ornamented with attached feathers, represents the Spider Woman.

The whole ceremony of the Sumaicoli consists in; first, making Fire by friction; second, manufacture of prayer offerings; and third, consecration of prayer offerings involving the ceremonial smoke, verbal prayers and an invocation of the Spider Woman.

Kindling the New Fire by friction is a means of directing the magic power of the Sumaicoli Wimi. The fire sticks are sexed, i.e, the twirler is termed "male" and the notched stick "female." Pollen is added and as soon as a spark of ignited dust falls on the shredded cedar bark it is fanned into flame and the fuel is thereby ignited.

Two kinds of prayer, one sensible and the other nonsensical, are employed. In the latter, archaic monosyllables are shouted into the floor. Prayer sticks, consisting of twigs with attached feathers, are carried, together with torches bearing the Sacred Fire, to the shrines. In the evening there are songs in the kiva. The *Sumaicoli* Masks help the priests to imitate ancient deities and are endowed with magic power. The gist of these rites is a sort of act of sympathetic magic by which the priest endeavors to insure the germination of corn thru the action of the spell on the Earth, Dawn, or Spider Woman who controls the crops. The New Fire is believed to create new [35] life in the corn and elsewhere.[40]

The Yaya priests perform, in addition to their homeopathic fire practices, many incredible feats of jugglery and legerdemain.

Passing from the Hopi to the Zuni we find two more New Fire Rites in somewhat different setting. The Zuni year is divided into two seasons of six months. At both the winter and summer solstices, culminations of the seasons, New Fire Ceremonies are held.[41]

The date for the Winter Solstice Ceremonies is set by the Sun Priest who gauges the time by the place where the sun rises. The maker of the Sacred Fire of the New Year is chosen by the chief and notified by a messenger. The latter, immediately after sunrise, carries a small quantity of prayer meal wrapped in corn husks to the home of the selected party. Clasping the latter's hand with both of his, the messenger, while still holding the meal, delivers his message and prays. The office of Fire maker is filled alternately by a member of the Badger Clan and a child of that Clan. He often becomes the personation of the God *Shúlaawi'si* in the *Shálläki* ceremonial in the following autumn.

No trading must go on, of any type, for four days before the ceremony and to begin trading before ten days have expired [36] after the ceremony is considered vulgar. So ashes or sweepings can he removed from the house during the ceremonial period and no artificial light may appear without the house, not even a cigarette nor the flash of a gun, even tho at a distance from the village.

The songs and dances which usher in the ceremony continue for several days until the rising of the morning star, "the warrior to the sun father " announces the propitious time for the making of the New Fire. The New Fire is produced, as at Walpi, by the drill method and with cedar bark tinder, two men taking turns in twirling the sticks. The ignited fiber is lifted and waved about in order to fan it into flames. It is taboo to blow upon the Fire lest the gods be offended and the rains withheld. A fire brand is carried out to ignite the fuel on the altar. Then the whole fire making group proceeds out of the kiva, carrying fire and sprinkling corn grains

---

[40] Fewkes "Lesser New Fire" *op. cit*, p. 452.

[41] Mrs. M.C Stevenson, "The Zuni Indians" 23rd Ann. Report B.A.E, pp. 108-9, 114, 120, 130 ff.

and meal about. The group proceed to a spot some distance from Zuni where they ceremonially set fire to the grass in order to create a great cloud of smoke which will, by sympathetic magic induce rain, while prayers are being offered for the same.

After the New Fire is lit the women and children remaining in the village proceed to clean out the houses and to carry the sweepings and ashes out in the fields and deposit them there.

> To the sweepings the woman says 'I now deposit you as sweepings, but in one year you will return to me as corn', and to the ashes she says 'I now deposits you as ashes, but in one year you will return to me as meal'.[42] [37]

The time for the Summer Solstice Ceremony is also set by the priest observing the sun. At this time he is supposed to be in direct communication with the sun. The sacred fire is made by wood friction as in the winter rite but we are given no details of this ceremony beyond the fact that the grass is set fire and a vast cloud of smoke produced. Both the Summer and Winter Ceremonies occupy some days, but how many we are not told.[43]

There are two organizations connected with Fire − The Little Fire Fraternity − which is connected with the Hopi, and has four subdivisions, practices medicine, and has elaborate fire rites every four years − and the Greater Fire Fraternity with three subdivisions under the patronage of anthropic gods, possessing elaborate rites of initiation and practicing medicine.[44]

The New Fire Rites of the Zuni and Hopi are the only ones that have been really considered in any detail by observers in the Southwest. The Keresan tribes were in possession of a rather complex Fire Cultus from which it is difficult to extract evidence of a true New Fire Rite. At Cochiti on the Summer Solstice, according to Curtis.

A new fire is kindled in every house, and the old ashes are swept out.[45]

According to the same author a January purification ceremony [38] also involves kindling of a New Fire.[46] The June Ceremony also has Ritualistic Rabbit Hunts, Prayer Sticks and Prayers for rain in these details resembling the rites of the Hopi. There are Fire Shamans at Cochiti also, who among other feats extinguish fire in the mouth.[47] At Acoma, in the Fire Katsina Rite of the Corn Clan, New Fire is kindled. Initiation into the Fire Society at Acoma involves complicated fire rituals.[48] All of these rites remain undescribed at present and it would be idle to speculate as to their extent and mutual relationships.

In summarizing the New Fire Rites of the Pueblo Area it appears that the main significance attaching to them lies in their symbolism of maize fertility and plentiful rain. Altho the November Ceremony of the Hopi is not held at the time of first maize yet the connections with the maize cycle are copiously in evidence. Its position at the end of the harvest is analogous to that of the Inca New Fire Rite at *Pauca Huatay*. In the trait of using the New Fire to kindle sacrifices at the shrines the Pueblo rites resemble the Mexican. The feature of quadrennial elaboration is also reminiscent of Mexico. The strong phallic emphasis of considerable sections

---

[42] Fraser, *op. cit*, vol. 10 p. 132.

[43] Stevenson, *op. cit*, pp. 148, 157.

[44] *Ibid*, p. 549 ff; p. 485 ff.

[45] Curtis, ES, The North American Indian, vol. 16, p. 101.

[46] *Ibid*, p. 120.

[47] *Ibid*, p. 87.

[48] *Ibid*, pp. 190, 228.

of the Hopi rites introduces elements not hitherto found in New Fire ceremonies. At the time of the discovery New Fire Rites were probably observed by all of the Pueblo Peoples even the Tanoans [39] probably sharing in this feature since the Sumaicoli Rites of the Hopi were introduced at Walpi by natives from Tewa. Further investigations may point out relations between the summer solstice rites at Walpi, Zuni, and Cochiti, and the Busk New Fire of the Southeast. [40]

Karuk New Fire

In northwestern California along the Klamath River dwell the Hokan tribe of the Karok. This tribe is culturally allied with the neighboring Algonkian Yurok and also to a considerable extent with the Hupa. Common to these three tribes is a world renewal group of rites having to do with first acorn and first salmon ceremonies. (Map V, p183)

With the Karok these contain the superadded feature of new-fire making.[49]

Aside from the general ethnographical compendia of Powers and Kroeber no notice has been taken of this peculiar feature. We will follow here the account given by Kroeber since it furnishes the best general resume' of the data.

The ceremonies described are all unquestionably of 'new years' type and have calendrical association with the moon. Yet, to judge by Yurok analogy, the Karok year, or reckoning of the moons, begins at the winter solstice, when there were no public rites. The concept of a renewal or reestablishing of the world for another round of the seasons was, however, strong in all four of the ceremonies, each of which was believed to contribute an indispensable part to this end. The new fire element, which is so marked, has not yet been discovered in any part of California other than the northwest; some form of first salmon rite appears to have been common in nearly all those parts of the state in which the fish abounded.[50]

The esoteric first fruits or new years element which underlies all of the great dances of the northwestern tribes comes out clearly in these world making ceremonies. There are [41] some nine local ceremonies of this type among the three tribes.[51]

Karok	Yurok	Hupa
Inam	Weitspus	Takimitlding
Katimin	Kepel	
Amaikiara	Pekwan	
Panamenik	Rekwoi	

---

[49] A.L Kroeber, Handbook of the Indians of California, p. 867; Stephen Powers, The Tribes of California, p. 31 sqq; quoted by Fraser, The Golden Bough, vol. VIII p. 255.
[50] Kroeber, *op. cit*, p. 105.
[51] *Ibid*, p. 98 ff.

These ceremonies took place mostly in early autumn, and a few in the spring, and have reference either to the beginning of the acorn crop or of a run of salmon. They are rites designed to renew and establish the world.

Rites at Katimin (October) The old man in charge of the ceremony sleeps for ten nights in the sacred sweat house. During the days he is in the sacred living house. Each day he visits a different spot or rock in the hills and speaks to it the requisite part of his sacred verbal formula. This latter is family property transmitted only thru relatives. The old man has an assistant and also two virgins or perhaps a preadolescent girl, who gather wood for his fire in the living house and cook the light portions of acorn gruel which is all that he eats. He speaks to no one, listens to none and is addressed by none. At each visit to a sacred spot he is accompanied by a group of young men who shoot at marks and play along the way. Meanwhile visitors begin to arrive and to camp on the sand by the river.

The climax comes at the last night of the ten days at the *yuhpit*, a hillock of clean sand one foot high, near a large [42] pepper tree at the edge of the bluff. First, rubbish is cleaned out and clean sand deposited by the two maidens. They then cook some acorn gruel at the water's edge and carrying it up to the *yuhpit*, give it to the old man's assistant. In the evening the old man brings out a sacred stool or seat from the sweat-house, sets it on the sandpile and with his drill kindles New Fire before the assembled people, as the Fire rises he orders them to cover their faces until he tells them to cease. Whoever looks will be bitten by a snake during the year. For the rest of the night he sits or stands on his holy seat reciting prayers or formulas at times and the people remain about helping him to keep awake by jests and laughter. The Karok call the New World thus establisht "*Isivsanen*". The next day follows the Deerskin Dance. The priest casts angelica root into the Fire before the dancers commence. For the last day's dance they line up between the yuhpit and the pepperwood and two parties compete in the dance.

Rites at Panamenik and Inam (October and August) At Orleans (*panamenik*) the course of the ceremony is similar. Its central features, the kindling of a Fire which mortals may not see is called *wilela'o* by the Yurok. There is a sweat house, dances, etc. The Inam Ceremony is called *irahivi* and is said to have been establisht along with the two foregoing ceremonies by the same *Ikhareya* or ancient spirit, as he travelled downstream. The formulas are distinct but of a similar tenor. [43]

Rites at Amaikiara (April) The New Year's Ceremony here also centers about a Fire which mortals may not look at, but this is made during the day and there is a ritualistic eating of the First Salmon of the season. The priest or formula reciter (*fatewenan*) and his assistant have subsisted on acorn gruel for many (possibly ten) days. Early in the morning of the great day the men who have been with him in the Amaikiara sweat house emerge and shout to the people of the town and of *Ashanamkarak*, across the river, to leave. Everyone picks up his bundle of food and trudges up the hill. Here they feast and play shooting at marks but never look back for, whoever saw the sacred smoke arising would sicken before long. A woman assistant is ferried across the river to *Ashanamkarak*. Here, going up on a hill, she cuts down a small madrona tree and splits it up into kindling. She carries it to the water's edge and returns to *Amaikiara* across the river. She then fasts at the sacred house or *wenaram*. Toward noon the priest and assistant leave the sweathouse, bathe and paint themselves and cross to *Ashanamkarak*. Here, in a small cleared space among the tumbled rocks, stands an altar, a small rude cube of stone about a foot high and the only true altar in all California. This the assistant repairs and then starts a New Fire near it of the madrona wood. He then cooks and eats salmon. The priest deposits tobacco to the deities, directs by signs and thinks or mumbles his formulas. He utters no word and performs no acts. Late in the afternoon the pair return to *Amaikiara* and are [44] received by the same men who have remained in the sweat house and to the same songs as were sung when they left. Toward evening these men come out and shout to the people to return, for ten days more the fatewenan and his assistant remain seated in the *wenaram* and sleep in the sacred sweat house. The people perform the Jumping Dance at *Ashanamkarak* using long poles, painted red and black, which afterwards the young men try to take from each other and break.

The major purpose of all of these New Fire rites is to secure bountiful wild crops, abundance of salmon, and the prevention of famines, earthquakes and floods.[52]

The New Fire Rites of the Karok standing isolated in far northwestern California are an outstanding example of the difficulty of applying any theory of historic diffusion to account for the New Fire generally. The history of these Karok Rites is unknown but they certainly have existed thru the nineteenth century and possibly much further. [45]

Muskogian New Fire

The authorities whom we have followed on the New Fire rites of the Southeast are Swanton's paper on "*Creek Religion and Medicine*" and also his paper on "*Indian Tribes of the Lower Mississippi Valley*" and Speck's "*Ethnology of the Yuchi Indians.*" Gatschet's *A Migration Legend of the Creek Indians* has also proved of value.

The Green Corn Dance of the Southeastern Area was inextricably intertwined with the New Fire Rite. The First Fruits Feature looms as equally important with the New Fire Rite and both are linked with the Busk or Fast which is indeed the term usually applied to the Ceremony in the Muskogian Confederacy. Anciently, widely distributed, the Busk Ceremony with its New Fire Features still "carries on" in some score of the Creek, Cherokee, Yuchi, and other settlements in Oklahoma, according to Swanton, and also in the Seminole settlements of Florida. On the lower Mississippi the majority of the tribes of pre-Muskogian linguistic affinities also had the institution of the perpetual fire.

The Busk was the outstanding event in the social life of the tribes of the Southeastern United States. In the larger towns it occupied eight days due to reduplication of its features, in the smaller it was four days long. It was held in the public square. The New Fire was built either on the first, second, third, or fourth day, depending on the locality. Previous to the Busk no one was allowed to eat any green corn owing to [46] its association with the renewal of the maize diet at the ripening of the first new corn of late July or early August. The Busk was really the fourth of a series of stomp dances, the first of which came in April. Ceremonies continued after the Busk until October, the close of the ceremonial season. The New Fire was associated with the life of the new maize as in the Southwest.[53]

It was obligatory for every member of the tribe to be present at the Busk. Every man was notified of the event and if he failed to appear he was subject to fine of whatever the members sent by the chief could lay their hands on. It was an urgent duty for all to attend therefor.

---

[52] Kroeber *op. cit*, p. 63; also see Geo. Gibbs "Journal of the Expedition of Col. Redick M. Kee thru Northwestern California in 1861, in Schoolcraft Indian Tribes, vol. III, pp. 99-107, p. 634 (Phila. 1853).

[53] The best general discussion and analysis of the busk is in J.R Swanton's "Creek Religion and Medicine 42nd Report, B.A.E 1924-26, 1928.

Before celebrating the Busk the people collected their old clothes, furniture and utensils and cast them into a pile to be consumed with fire. They thereupon provided themselves with new clothes, new furniture and new utensils. All of the old fires were extinguisht, being polluted by long association with the affairs of men, and the ashes were swept away. The public square was swept clean in preparation for the feast.

The Busk was the great unifying element in the Creek Confederacy, all of the tribes who joined the confederacy adopting it. All crimes were forgiven at this time, except murder, which was a crime against life. All personal quarrels were adjusted. The Busk was the great peace ceremonial, "the great [47] white day." The New Year began with this event.[54]

As a preparation several days' fast was indulged in by men of particularly holy eminence, in the public square, accompanied by the use of the ceremonial emetic (*Asi* or Cassine Tea).

The sequence of events at any one Busk were different from those of every other and the vast number of descriptions corralled together by Swanton can only be logically understood in considering the relative importance of the constituent elements. Of these the New Fire, with which we are concerned here, is easily one of the outstanding single elements in all of the Busks.

The Fire was generally made by the medicine maker i.e, the priest. A typical Fire is described by Ellis Childers at the *Chiaha* Busk.

> To make the fire, four green sticks are cut from tree limbs extending toward the east.... To renew the fire they use the term *to' hsoloti'*, 'to shove them together.' Four roasting ears are placed across the back sticks .... Then kindling hay or other dry stuff is placed on top and ignited by rubbing two dry sticks lengthwise over it. All the fires in the camps have meanwhile been put out, and the new fire is taken to them. It is used for the first time in cooking the first meal after the men break their fast."[55]

or the Eufaula Busk.

> ... all the ashes of the previous fires are raked away and in the place which they occupied a quantity of new earth is deposited brought in from the outside of the grounds. On this the fire-maker kindles a new fire made of four sticks of wood pointing to the four cardinal points. One person is detailed for the sole purpose of watching and keeping up the fire [48] during the day in which the medicine is being taken ....[56]

The new fire at Eufaula is now lighted with a match but earlier flint and steel and before that two sticks of wood were used.[57] This indicates that at least among these groups the Eire itself was sacred, not the fire sticks as among some of the Plains Tribes.

The Busk was also the occasion for much speech making on the part of the chiefs or elders of the tribe. These speeches were often formal and required a peculiar intonation. Each clan held a council.[58]

A certain group of old and revered men. the elders of the tribe, who were called "the brains of the Busk" planned all of the details of the Ceremony. These were men skilled in the

---

[54] Swanton, Creek Religion, *op. cit*, p. 548.

[55] *Ibid*, p. 555.

[56] *Ibid*, p. 581.

[57] *Ibid*, p. 609.

[58] *Ibid*, p. 122.

lore of the tribe. The elders took little or no active part themselves, since they were generally seasoned veterans too old to fight but advanced in knowledge and experience.[59]

At the Busk certain ceremonial names and titles were given to persons, towns and tribes for warlike accomplishments, hunting exploits, and the like. These descended to new aspirants after the death of the old bearer.[60]

Numerous animal imitation and other dances are characteristic of the Busk. The ceremony generally ends in a great feast on the new maize. [49]

Other Features of the Busk are the medicines or black drink in which some fourteen species of physic plants are mixed in a pot and blown into by the priest. This mixture is then drunk in great quantities as an emetic. The scarification of the males is also an important feature of the Busk.

The miko's (chief's) cabin has a cane with feathers displayed in front which seems reminiscent of the *natcis* of the pueblos.[61]

Tobacco is thrown into the fire as a sacrifice during the Busk.[62] The old people were formerly of the habit of putting a little food into the fire before eating.[63] A little of the medicinal drink was often spilt on the edge of the fire.[64] These rites seem identical with the Mexican habits of "the throwing" and "the tasting".

Passing over into the lower Mississippi valley region we find the New Fire conjoined with the Perpetual Fire and the latter maintained in temples wherein the bones of chiefs were laid. The Perpetual Fire was renewed yearly with New Fire at a special and highly dramatic ceremony among the Natchez.[65] There was a class of "buzzards" or professional bone pickers in the [50] southwest {southeast} who cleaned the flesh from the hones of the dead and then deposited them in ossuaries or temples. This trait is found in Mexico and among the Talamancas of Panama.

The Natchez New Fire appears to have had considerable resemblance to the Inca. A crier was sent out to command the people to renew their household utensils and garments; to wash their houses and to burn their old belongings in a common fire. He proclaimed an amnesty for all criminals. The next day he appeared again, commanding a three-days fast for all and the use of the medicine of purification or emetic. On the third day of the fast the crier summoned all to the Festival on the following day. Accordingly the people assembled the following morning at the Temple of the Sun, where the sacred perpetual fire of last year had just been suffered to die out. The Great Sun" or Chief was present, surrounded by his retainers in the order of their rank, but the high priest presided at the festival as in Mexico. Here they awaited the sunrise.

> The high priest, standing on the threshold of the temple kept his eyes fixed on the eastern horizon .... In his hand he held two dry pieces of wood which he kept rubbing slowly against each other muttering magic words. At his side two acolytes held two cups filled with a kind of black sherbet. All the women, their backs turned to the east, each leaning with one hand on her rude mattock and supporting her infant

---

[59] *Ibid*, p. 301.

[60] *Ibid*, p. 100.

[61] Gatschet, A Migration Legend of the Creek Indians, p. 177 ff.

[62] *Ibid*.

[63] Swanton, Creek Religion, *op. cit*, p. 517.

[64] Frazer, *op. cit*, vol. 8 p. 72 ff.

[65] Swanton, "Indian Tribes of the Lower Mississippi Valley and Adjacent Coast of the Gulf of Mexico", Bull. 43 BAE.

with the other; stood in a great semicircle at the gate of the temple. Profound silence reigned thruout the multitude while the priest watched attentively the growing light in the east. As soon as the diffused light of dawn began to be shot with beams of fire, he quickened the motion of the two pieces of wood which he held in his hands; and at the moment when the edge of the sun's disc appeared above the horizon, fire flashed from the wood and was caught in tinder. At the same instant the women outside the temple faced round and held up their infants and their mattocks to the rising sun. [51]

The great chief and his wife now drank the black liquor {black drink, herb water, {*asi* = *'leaf'*}. The priest kindled the circle of dried reeds; fire was set to the heap of oak bark on the altar, and from the sacred flame all the hearths of the village were rekindled.[66]

The first sheaves of the new maize were brought in from the fields and unleavened bread baked. At the end of the day the multitude assembled once more at the temple and presented the unleavened bread to the setting sun while the priest struck up a chant to the descending light. Music and feasting then occupied the evening.[67]

Every morning at sunrise the Natchez are said to have lit a fire before the door of the temple and also every evening at sunset. If the sacred fire in the temple went out they had to go to the Tunicas to relight it.

The temple of the Natchez had a palisade surrounding it on which were spitted the skulls of sacrificed victims.[68] This resembles the Aztec custom of spitting the skulls of the sacrificed at Tzompantli at the First Festival of the Fire God.[69]

Human Sacrifice was both an occasional and a customary feature of the Natchez Sun-Fire Cult. The deaths of Chiefs, who were all accounted descendants of the Sun, were marked by the death of many retainers by strangling. Children were occasionally sacrificed to the fire. [52]

All of the tribes surrounding the Natchez were Sun and Fire Worshipers and those noted particularly by early writers were the Taensa and the Tunicas. We seem, however, to have no record of the New Fire Rites of these tribes.

The perpetual fires of the Hatches temples were guarded by men who were put to death if they allowed the fires to go out.[70]

Passing eastward to the Cherokee country we find

....that on the occasion of the annual Green Corn Dance it was the custom in ancient times for each household to procure fresh fire from a new fire kindled in the town house.[71]

Mounds were built up over sites for town houses. Fires built on the level surface were surrounded by stones and by burials, a hollow log was placed above for a chimney,

---

[66] Chateaubriand, Voyages in Amerique, pp. 130-6; quoted by Frazer, *op. cit*, vol. 8, p. 135.

[67] *Ibid.*

[68] Swanton, "Indian Tribes", *op. cit*, p. 269.

[69] Bancroft, *op. cit*, vol. 3, p. 387.

[70] Frazer, *op. cit*, vol. II, p. 263

[71] *Ibid.*

the earth piled above this as a mound, and, on this a town house was built. This fire was in charge of a fire maker and was never allowed to go out. It served as a reservoir of fire for all the houses of the village.[72]

The Yuchi, an aberrant {!?} group of the Southeast, called themselves offspring of the sun. They are to be found today in three settlements in Oklahoma, extending between Polecat Creek and Deep Fork of the Canadian River, and here Speck working [53] in the early Twentieth Century studied their culture and especially their still surviving rite of New Fire, which is here, as elsewhere in the Southeastern Area, connected with the Green Corn Dance.[73]

The ceremony lasts three days and New Fire kindled after sunrise of the second day is symbolic of a new period of life for the tribe. The fires of the various household hearths are not extinguish^ as among the Creeks, for the kindling of the New Fire by the Town Chief is symbolic of this and suffices for all.

The fire place had been swept clean and covered with sand. The *Yätcigi* now walked sunwise around the spot three times, then stopped, each one standing at one of the cardinal points. They deposited the four logs with their ends pointing toward the cardinal points, thus, + , then retired to the west lodge behind the town chief. He was now preparing punk and fire materials, having taken them from his bag suspended from the post near his head. He struck the fire into a tray of bark filled with dried pith, in the manner described elsewhere. When the spark had sprung into flame the *Yätcigi* took the tray, and ignited sticks between the logs and thus the New Fire for the New Year was started. They concluded by walking four times around it. During this time at intervals a few taps were given on the water drum.[74]

The constituents of the Yuchi busk were, as elsewhere, clan dances imitating totem animals to the accompaniment of music and musical instruments, fasting, sex intercourse taboo, scarification of males and blood letting, rite of the emetic by males, and, sacrifices. [54]

The Green Corn Dance had some wide diffusions and in 1832 George Catlin found it at Minatarree {Hidatsa} Village, Dakota, eight miles from the Mandan village, on the Missouri River. Here he painted a picture entitled "Sacrificing the First Kettle to the Great Spirit." Four medicine men, painted with white clay, dance about the kettle until the corn is boiled and then they burn the corn as a sacrifice to the Great Spirit. The fire is then put out and a New Fire obtained by desperately rubbing two wetted sticks together and with this the corn for their own feast is cooked. The festival lasts for a week or ten days, while the corn is green, and is accompanied by feasting, sacrifices, songs of thanksgiving and dances.[75]

Among the ancient tribes of the Eastern Woodlands, according to one, Picart, quoting from Hennepin, before a hunt the natives

---

[72] James Mooney, "Cherokee Mound Building", Amer. Anthrop, N.S vol. II, April 1889, pp. 167-171.

[73] F.G Speck, "Ethnology of the Yuchi Indians", Anthropological Publications, U of Pennsylvania, vol, no. I, Phila. 1909, pp. 114-130.

[74] Speck, *op. cit*, p. 120.

[75] Geo Catlin, *"New Fire among Mandans of Upper Missouri at Minitaree Green Corn Dance"*, pp 186-7, 189 (in Report of United States National Museum 1885, p. 315).

.... lighted up Bull's Dung dried in the Sun, and primed as it were, their Calumets with the New Fire, which they presented those Hunters who had been out upon the Scout, in order for them to smoke.[76]

The tribes of Florida, according to this same authority, in the course of their sun worship threw perfumes into a sacred [55] fire which was lit before the gate of their temples (ossuaries?).[77] We ho not know for certain, if the Busk extended anciently into Florida or not. However, it seems quite certain that New Fires of a type were kindled in connection with temple worship in the peninsula. Later, of course, with the ingress into Florida of numerous Muskogian refugees, the Seminole, the true Busk was carried into that area.

In the Texas Area the Busk or any other New Fire seems to have been totally lacking among the Caddo, Attacapa, Tonkawa, and Karankawa hunters. Thus an immense gap cleaves the Southeastern New Fire Ceremonies from those of the Pueblo and the Mexican Areas.

Of the Virginia Indians in the northeastern reaches of the Gulf Area we are told that:

After their return from War or escaping some danger, they light Fires, and make merry over them, each having his gourd bottle, or his little Bell in his Hand. They all, men, women and children, often dance in a confused manner about these Fires. One would be apt to imagine this was their chief Devotion. Some travellers pretend that they pay a Religious Worship to Fire on this Occasion ....[78]

Furthermore these same tribes had the fire rites of "the throwing" and "the tasting."

The Indians of the Virginia area also had bone houses wherein

A Priest watches Day and, Night in this Mausoleum by a lighted Fire and 'tis there that he acquits himself of some pious duties which he imagines affect the Deceased in some Measure.[79] [56]

Since the trait of the Funeral Fire is so widely distributed, being found among the Botocudos of the East Brasilian Coast, the Arawakan Goajiro of the Gulf of Venezuela, the aborigines of Porto Rico, and the Talamanca of Panama it may possibly be that the bone house or temple fires of the Southeast are a development from this trait into a perpetual fire. Building a shelter would naturally have a great effect in lengthening the life of the original funeral fire and in making it perhaps a sacred perpetual fire under the watch of a guardian. Such is the sacred fire of the Natchez-Tunica Area in essence. The Fire seems to serve as a joint symbol of the lives of all the deceased whose bones repose within the ossuary.

According to Speck's account of the *Tuskegee* Creeks after a burial:

---

[76] Hennepin, Voyage into a Country bigger than Europe in vol. V of Collection of Voyages to the North quoted by Bernan Picart in *The Ceremonies and Religious customs of the various Nations of the Known World*, p. 107.

[77] Picart, *op. cit*, p. 126.

[78] *Ibid*, p. 120.

[79] *Ibid*, p. 123.

> A small house, either of logs or of boards, is then constructed over the grave. A fire is kindled at the head of the grave and tended for four days by the relatives until the soul is believed to have reached the passage to the sky.[80]

Among the same tribe

> The fire which was always burning in the house, was allowed to go out when a death occurred so when the mortuary rites were concluded a new fire was kindled with a ceremony and song called *tu tkamodjasa ingasupid*, 'fire new its cooling'.[81]

> The grave fire was characteristic rite of the tribes belonging to the Muskogian Confederacy and this shows the fundamental underlying ceremonial matrix of perhaps all New Fire [57] Rites. At Creek burials in Oklahoma according to Swanton:

> A fire was lighted near by and kept burning for four days, because, as one ~~informant~~ explained, the ghost of a dead man stays about for that length of time.[82]

Amongst the Mikasuki *Chiaha* likewise

> A fire was formerly built at the head of the grave, and it was kept up for four days. At the end of that time the fire was put out in the house where the man had died and a new one was built.[83]

A similar ceremonial prevails among the Alabama now in Texas:

> For four days the wife or husband and the children and near relatives visited the grave every morning before breakfast and every evening before supper, and at their evening visits they lighted a fire at the head.[84]

According to MacCauley the Seminoles of Florida retain a grave fire.

> The bearers of the body made a large fire at each end of the *'To-hŏp-ki'* (grave) .... The fires at the graves were renewed at sunset by those who had made them, and after nightfall torches were waved in the air, that the 'bad birds of the night' might not get at the Indian lying in his grave. The renewal of the fires and the waving of the torches were repeated three days. The fourth day the fires were allowed to die out.[85]

---

[80] Speck, "The Creek Indians of Taskigi Town, "Memoirs of the American Anthropological Association, vol. II, p. 119, 1907-15.

[81] *Ibid*, p. 119.

[82] Swanton, "Social Organization and Social Usages of the Indians of the Creek Confederacy" in 42nd Rep't BAE, 395.

[83] *Ibid*, p. 396.

[84] *Ibid*, p. 398.

[85] MacCauley, "The Seminole Indiana of Florida " in 5th Ann. Rep't BAE, pp. 520-522.

The Tunicas were also in possession of a grave fire according to Swanton.

> For four successive nights thereafter (following burial) a fire was lighted at the head .... to keep away the bad spirits who sat in that direction for the same period.[86] [58]

From these examples of the alliance of the fire with the afterlife and with life in general it can toe seen that possibly the kindling of New Fire at the Busk was derived therefrom since the new life of a new maize crop came to signify a new year and new life for the tribe.

In summarizing the New Fire of the Southeastern Area we may note first, its common association with the renewal of the maize diet at the Busk ceremony and with the beginning of a new year. Secondly, New Fire appears to have been used to renew sacred temple fires on the lower Mississippi and perhaps also in Virginia and Florida. Thirdly, the New Fire is allied with grave ceremonies all over the Southeast. The association of the New Fire with fasts, scarifications, the emetic, ceremonial hunts, the calumet, asperging, the sun and fire gods, the sacred number four, the new maize and the new year are all allied with similar associations in the Southwest and in Mexico. [59]

Delaware New Fire

The Algonkian Tribes of New Jersey formed at the time of the discovery a strong confederacy known as the Delaware or Lenape composed of three tribes – the Unami, Munsee and Unalachtigo. A remnant of the Unami still live in Oklahoma and a section of the Munsee in Ontario. Among these M.R Harrington, working between 1907 and 1910, collected evidence of an important annual ceremony involving New Fire rites. These rites are evidently extremely ancient and are described by such early observers as William Penn, Zeisberger, and others. The Great Annual Ceremony of the Unami of Oklahoma is held when the leaves turn yellow in the fall of the year usually between the tenth and twentieth of October. There are certain individuals of proper qualification who take the responsibility of "bringing in" the meeting and acting as leaders. These are persons who have had true visions. Each totemic group has a ritual of its own so that the phratry of the leader determines the exact form of the rites to be held. In former days when one phratry had finisht another would enact its own rites and so forth.[87]

The Ceremony lasts twelve days. First the leader sends out a messenger to notify the people and invite attendance. The assembly takes place about the gray walls of the old "big [60] house" temple or *xi ngwikan* {*xing wikawn*} standing on the banks of the Little Caney River near Dewey in Northern Oklahoma. There are carvings on the posts of the inside of the house some twelve in number and these idols are called *Mising*[w] {*məsing*[w]} or "masks." The temple is used only in the Annual Ceremony.

The messenger sent to assemble the people is one of three male attendants chosen by the leader and these three men appoint three women to serve also. To these six attendants or *a'ckas* {*ashkas*} falls all of the laborious work of the meeting. It is accounted quite an honor to be selected for this office altho much menial work is involved. The *ackas* camp separately. Two

---

[86] Swanton, "Indian Tribes of the Lower Mississippi Valley", Bull. 43 BAE, p. 325.

[87] M.R Harrington, "Religion and Ceremonies of the Lenape", Indian notes and Monographs. New York: 1921, p. 81 ff.

singers called *Tale gunuk* {*talegak*} or "cranes" {geese} whose duty is to beat the dry deerskin drum and sing necessary songs are appointed by the leader and also a chief hunter who is delegated to supply venison for the feast.

In preparation mud mortar is used to rebuild the walls of the temple. Two sapling poles are cut and set upright and a long pole laid across. From this a huge twenty gallon kettle is hung in which to cook hominy. A cord of wood is gathered. Then the first night a New Fire is made with a Pump Drill resembling the Ceremonial Fire Drills of the Iroquois.

This Fire and this only, may be used in the temple, and no one is permitted to take it outside for any purpose.[88]

The temple is swept and with the two fires burning the people assemble. The chief makes a speech. Then the dreamer or [61] leader shakes a rattle of box tortoise shell and recites his vision in a high monotone word for word. The drummer soon learns the words of the recital and sings them to a dance tune while beating the drum in slower time. The leader conducts a dance about the fire. Then follows the recital of more visions by others. During intermissions tobacco is smoked or hominy eaten. And this is repeated for three nights. On the fourth morning the hunters are sent out to hunt, after tobacco sacrifices have been made to the fire and prayers for success. They return, at least by the third day, with their deer or other kill. The usual program runs on every night until the ninth.

On this night a new fire is kindled with the sacred pump-drill called *tu^{n}dai wahe^{n}ji manitowuk* or 'Fire maker of the Manittos', and the ashes of the old are carried out thru the west door of the Big House, which is used only for this purpose (among the Unami), and is usually kept closed. The new fire seems to symbolize a fresh start in all the affairs of life.[89]

On the twelfth night the women recite their visions, amidst the anointing with grease and paint of all present including the idols and other ceremonial apparatus. On the next morning there is ritualistic dancing around a pole, more prayer words are uttered and wampum payment is made to all who took part. The meeting then breaks up.

A slightly different ceremony lasts eight days and involves the stuffing of the slain deer and its installation in the center of the temple, the building of a sweat house and [62] indulgence in sweet bath by visionaries. This way have been an Unalachtigo variant.[90]

William Penn in 1683 wrote an account of these rites,[91] as did Zeisberger in 1779[92] and Adams in 1890.[93]

---

[88] Harrington, *op. cit*, p. 87.

[89] *Ibid*, p. 101.

[90] Harrington, *op. cit*, pp. 122-6.

[91] Wm Penn, A Letter from William Penn, Proprietary and Governour of Pennsylvania in America to the Committee of the Free Society of traders of that Province, Residing in London p. 6, London 1683. Quoted by Harrington, *op. cit*, p. 115.

[92] David Zeisberger's "History of the Northern American Indians," Ed. by A.B Hulbert & N. Schwarze, Ohio Archeological and Historical Quarterly, vol. XIX nos. 1 & 2, p. 128 Columbus 1910, cited by Harrington, *op. cit*, p. 116 ff.

Among the Minsi of Ontario a similar Ceremony is held in which New Fire figures.

The fire was made with a fire-drill by a group of old men for use in the Big House but, as among the Unami, none of it could be taken outside during the ceremony.[94]

Possibly the New Fire of these Dream Ceremonies lapped over into southern New England hut available evidence is lacking. On the other hand we have not been able to determine whether the Algonkians around Chesapeake Bay had the Busk or the Dream New Fire. Among the Saponi, Tutelo, Ocaneechi and other Eastern Siouan tribes around Fort Christanna in Virginia:

On the occasion of any religious ceremony new fire was always made for the purpose from two sticks which had never before been used, as it was deemed sacrilege to use the fire already kindled.[95] [63]

The Delaware New Fire is imbedded in the ancient Dream Ceremony. In this matrix it is connected with vision recital, tobacco sacrifice to fire, the sweat house rite, temples and idols, hominy feasts, ceremonial hunts, dancing around a pole and the like. Evidently this ceremonial context is vastly different from that of the Muskogian New Fire. Fire is called "grandfather" and is thought to be a manitu or spirit power. The New Fire symbolizes for the Lenape a new start in life, a new revelation of tutelary guidance and perhaps a new year. It is held at a time appropriate for maize harvest ceremonies but the connections, if any, that it has with the maize cycle are not evident. On the other hand the Delaware New Fire does link up in ritualistic significance with the New Fire of the Iroquois Dream Ceremonies. [64]

Iroquois New Fire

The New Fire Rites of the Iroquois are mentioned by several writers of note and we have largely followed Hewitt. Good descriptions of the ceremonial context, the Dream Ceremony or, as it is later called "The White Dog Sacrifice" are furnished by W.M Beauchamp, L.H Morgan, Horatio Hale, A.C. Parker, and J.V.H Clark.
The Iroquois Feast of the White Dog in January was the occasion of the kindling of a New Fire and the commencement of a New Year. There exist numerous accounts of this ceremony which is now confined mainly to the Ontario Reservations. Beauchamp's resume of the rite in 1885 gives the best general perspective.[96]
The White Dog Sacrifice seems to have come from the west at a recent time and was first adopted by the Senecas, and then by the Onondaga and later extending partially to those further eaBt. It was superimposed upon the ancient Dream Feast of New Years, a kind of Saturnalia or period of license and general madness. The New Fire was a feature of the more ancient rite.

---

[93] R.C Adams, "Notes on Delaware Indians " in Report on Indians Taxed & Indians not Taxed, U.S Census 1890 p. 299, cited by Harrington, *op. cit*, p. 118 ff.
[94] Harrington, *op. cit*, pp. 132-3. At Munceytown and Grand River Reserve.
[95] James Mooney, "The Siouxan Tribes of the East", Bull. 22 BAE, Wash. 1894.
[96] W.M Beauchamp, "The Iroquois White Dog Feast", American Antiquarian and Oriental Journal VII pp. 235-9 1885.

According to Pere Jaques two bears were offered in 1642-3 by the Mohawks. Dablon and Chaumonat among the Onondagas in 1655-6 mention no dogs. In the dream festival recounted by Charlevoix in 1721 a dog sacrifice is noted among the Miamis. [65]

Late in the eighteenth century Rev. Kirkland mentions a seven days' feast among the Senecas wherein two white dogs were sacrificed. During the Revolution a Mrs. Campbell saw the sacrifice at the Seneca Capital, Canadesaga (Geneva), and Mary Jemison saw it at Jamestown also. In 1813 the White Dog feast was held at Rochester. J.V.H Clark's account in 1841 has some detail.[97] On the first day all of the fires were extinguisht and ashes scattered, and a New Fire kindled with flint and steel. On this day also, the managers went around gathering the sins of the people and danced off the witches in the evening. On the second day gifts for the festival were gathered and games were played. On the third day the white dog was sacrificed amid processions, shooting, yelling, singing, prayers, and tobacco sacrifice. L.H Morgan attended a seven day feast among the Seneca in the middle of the nineteenth century. Here, the white dog was sacrificed on the fifth day but before that the people had confessed their sins. On the first day the two dogs were strangled. On the second day the hearths were cleansed but there is no record of extinguishing and rekindling the fire. There were processions on the fifth day and the last two days were spent in feasting and the peachstone game.[98] In a ceremony recorded in 1882 the New York [66] Onondaga celebrated with but one dog. This dog hung over the shoulder of a tall Indian and was laid later on a platform. It was burned as usual. Hale's account of the 1884**5 sacrifices is on the Ontario tribes.[99] A.C Parker,[100] also, has published an account of the New Year's festival held at Newtown, Cattaraugus Reservation, in January 1905.

The New Fire element seems to have been a rather minor feature of almost all of the Iroquois New Years feasts recorded and most of the emphasis on this element has come from secondary sources such as Daniel Wilson,[101] H.R Schoolcraft,[102] and J.G Frazer.[103] J.N Hewitt, in addition, mentions a New Fire or rather a "need fire" which was kindled in time of plague for pyrotherapy.[104]

The general Season for the White Dog festival was late in January or early in February. It is a time at which nature has reached its lowest ebb, insofar as Life is concerned and the Festival becomes a sort of combination World Renewal and [67] Scapegoat Rite. The god, *Teharonhiawakon*, who is the Life God or "Master of Life" hae dreamed of the renewal of life which is to take place shortly and the imminent victory over *Tawiskaron*, God of Winter. The object of the ceremony is then to recruit the vigor of the Life God and so help fulfil his dream.[105]

In the preparations two fire rites are performed which consume three days. One is for the purpose of rekindling the fires after removing the ashes of the old from all of the cabins of the

---

[97] J.V.H Clark, Onondaga, Vol. I pp. 55-62.

[98] L.H Morgan, The League of the Iroquois, New York 1922 pp. 199-213.

[99] Horatio Hale, "The Iroquois Sacrifice of the White Dog", Amer. Antiq. and Oriental Journal VII, pp. 7-14 (1885).

[100] A.C Parker "Code of Handsome Lake, The Seneca Prophet", NY St. Mus. Bull. 163, Albany 1913, pp. 81-5.

[101] Sir Daniel Wilson, Prehistoric Man, p. 146.

[102] H.R Schoolcraft, Notes on the Iroquois, p. 137.

[103] J.G Fraser, *op. cit*, vol. 10, p. 299; Vol. X, p. 134; Vol. IX, p. 209.

[104] J.N.B Hewitt, "New Fire Among the Iroquois." American Anthropologist II, p. 319 (1889).

[105] L.H Gray, Article "Iroquois " in Hastings Encyclopedia of Religion and Ethics. Also Hewitt in F.W Hodge, Handbook of the American Indians, Bull. 30 BAE Wash, 1911, Article "White Dog Sacrifice."

community. The directors of the four ceremonies appoint two persons, one from each phratry, to do this. These must have special costume and the rank of federal chiefs.

The duty of the Deer Herald in every lodge is, while rekindling the fire to deliver a thanksgiving address with the announcement of the beginning of the *Gano 'hwai-wi,* or New Year's Ceremony, and to urge the inmates to abandon their labors and amusements to attend in person at the Long House or tribal assembly hall; the duty of the Wolf; Herald is continuously to chant on the way and in the lodge the *Gano hwi-wi* , or the Death Chant of <u>*Teharonhiawagon.*</u>[106]*

On their return these heralds recount how they have rekindled the fires in behalf of the Life God with their paddles and that in the ensueing fire rite that they will pass thru the fire in his behalf. Then follows a long speech by a person receiving the report. The *Aoutaenhrohi* "To asperge with ashes" [68] is the Huron equivalent of the second fire rite. The two fire rites combined serve to cleanse and disinfect from sicknesses and fevers with the aid of the Fire God. Barefoot walking over the ashes was formerly common hut now the ashes are merely lifted up.

The Dream Festival proper which follows, lasts three days and is for the purpose of rejuvenating old tutelaries by magic charms and the acquirement of new tutelaries by the children. The four ceremonies are: first, the Great Feather Dance (150 songs with dances); second, the Drum Dance (with a like number of songs); third, the Clan Personal Chant (with 100 songs); fourth, the Great Wager or Bet (Ceremonial Game of Plum-Pits).

The white dog sacrifice centers around the scape-goat or expiation idea rather than the New Fire.[107]

The dog is marked with red dots and white, blue, red, and green ribbons are tied about his neck, body, tail, and legs. His feet are fastened with ribbons and in such a manner that the legs remain at right angles to the body, a headdress of feathers is placed on the head and around the neck a string of wampum. The strangled creature is then placed with its head facing west in the assembly to represent the God of Life. He is offered, together with bow and arrows and tobacco, to the [69] Life God and is accepted along with the tobacco. Whereupon he is cast into the fire.[108]

The Iroquois also had the Green Corn Feast but the New Fire does not appear in this context.[109]

The New Fire among the later Iroquois seems to have especially centered about the veneration of the pumpdrill as a peculiarly Indian institution much as the later Ghost Dance and Sun Dance Ceremonies of the West venerated the Fire Drill as a means of making fire rather than the fire itself.[110]

---

[106] Hewitt in Handbook of Amer. Ind, *op. cit*, pp. 942 ff.

[107] Hewitt in Handbook, *op. cit*; Fraser, *op. cit*, vol. 7, pp. 127, 209; Morris Wolf, Iroquois Religion and its Relation to their Morale, NY 1910 pp. 69-70; W.M Beauchamp, "Onondaga Customs" Jour. Amer. Folk-lore I, pp. 195-203 1888.

[108] Hewitt in Handbook, *op. cit.*

[109] SH Stites, Economics of the Iroquois, p. 138 footnote says "The Green Corn Festival of the Iroquois was the less developed form of the great feast of the Busk observed by the Gulf States Indians."

[110] Hough, "Fire Making Apparatus in the United States National Museum" p. 546 Report of U.S Nat Museum 1881 pp. 531-587.

In sum, then, the Iroquois New Fire was symbolic of the renewal of all life which begins in mid winter and heralds the coming spring. It is in a sense, a prayer to the god of life to call him back that he may conquer the forces of cold, death, and famine. It is allied with tobacco sacrifice, dream recital, white dog sacrifice, feather and drum dances, ceremonial wagers, aeperging rites, masked society rites, new life, and new year significance. The ancient tutelary divining function of the Hite was later eclipsed by the sacrificial element, the white dog feast. The later emphasis came to lie in cleansing from sin and disease and in the new start in life resulting therefrom. [70]

New World Fire Myth And Ritual

Having concluded the empirical survey of the known New Fire Rites of America we will now turn to a brief consideration of the Fire Cultus which serves as a background for the New Fire. A consideration of the psychological attitudes toward fire developed by the various tribes of the New World, brief tho it may be, will possibly help to explain some elements in the New Fire Rites which we have just finisht reviewing. (Map VI, p184)

Fire is easily one of the most important single elements in the mind of the average Indian amongst the majority of the New World tribes. From this importance issues, at a later date, in the advanced agricultural groups, a peculiar emphasis on the sun cult in such forms as heliogonic legends Sun temples with perpetual fires, and virgins of the sun. Fire is also inextricably linked with the color, red, with blood and with all animal and vegetable life.

According to Brinton, among the Natches, Kolosch {Tlingit}, TeSuque and the Arawak the word for sun is derived from that for fire and the sun is often referred to as "the great fire " thus assigning to fire the priority in importance. The Nahuas, according to one observer, regarded, not the Sun but Fire as the father and mother of all things and as the author of nature. Fire was the Life Giver, the source of animate existence and the basis of the heliolatry observed so often in America. Fire and Light are likewise identified.[111] [71]

Among the Eskimos, according to C.F Hall, at New Year's two men went from house to house (in the village wherein he resided at the time) and blew out all of the lights in the houses. An Eskimo woman on being asked the meaning of this replied that the new sun meant that a new light must be lit, thus implying that the sun was at that time renewed for the year.[112] Among the Eskimos of Igulik when the sun first appears above the horizon after the long winter night the children run into the houses and blow out the lamps, receiving presents of pieces of wick for so doing. This practice of the Nagamiut (on the plateau between Cumberland Sound and Frobisher Bay) is paralleled by one of the Akudnirniut of Cumberland Sound who also blow out all the fires."[113]

Among the Algonkian Speaking Tribes the cult mythology clusters largely around the concepts of light and the fire, for which, according to Brinton, the very names are identical.

'Know that the life in your body and the fire in your hearth are one and the same thing, and that both proceed from the same source'; said a Shawnee prophet. Such an

---

[111] D.G Brinton, Myths of the New World, p. 163.

[112] C.F Hall, Life with the Esquimaux II, 323 quoted by Fraser pp. cit, vol. 10 p. 134.

[113] Franz Boas, "The Eskimo of Baffin Land and Hudson Bay" Bull. Amer. Mus. Nat. Hist. XV, Part I (NY 1901), p. 151 quoted by Fraser as in (1); also see Boas, "The Central Eskimo" p. 607 Ann Report. BAE vol. 6 1884-5.

expression was wholly in the spirit of his race. The greatest feast of Delawares was to their 'Grandfather the Fire.' 'Their fire burns forever' was the Algonkian figure of speech to express the immortality of the gods.[114]

The Iroquois are credited with having a God of Fire. [72]

Passing to the South, the Fire cult grows in strength. The Chickasaw supreme deity was *Loak-lshto-hoolo-Aba* "the Great Holy Fire Above" and who was connected with the Sun, the sole author of warmth, light, and animal and vegetable life.[115] The *viva' shił* or "Big Fire" was the Natches word for the Sun, their highest object of worship. According to Adair, among the Chickasaw

> .... the divine omnipresent Spirit of fire and light resides on the earth, in their annual sacred fire while it is unpolluted[116]; *

> .... the giver of virtue to nature resided on earth in the unpolluted holy fire, and likewise above the clouds and the sun, in the shape of a fine fiery substance ....[117]

The Muskogee call the fire their grandfather ....[118]

Fire is called "grandfather" to the present day.[119]

The Muskogians are afraid to extinguish even culinary fire with water.

> .... an actual connection was supposed to exist between the sun and the busk fire and thus between the celestial deity behind the sun and this fire .... and that the renewal of the fire was an actual renewed presence of the deity among them, the old fire having polluted by long separation from its source.[120]

> On going to war they (the Choctaw) call for aid on both sun and fire; 'but except as fire, they do not address the sun, nor does that body stand in any relation to their religious thought other than as fire.'[121] [73]

Turning to the Great Plains region we find the Sun Dance is the greatest and most important ritual. This is an annual affair occupying about eight days and is undertaken often in consequence of a vow made in gratitude for some favor bestowed by the gods, sometimes in

---

[114] Brinton, op cit, p. 169.

[115] Swanton "Creek Religion, *op. cit*, p. 482.

[116] Adair History of the American Indians, p. 35 quoted by Swanton, "Creek Religion " *op. cit*, p. 483.

[117] *Ibid*, pp. 92-3 quoted by Swanton, p. 483 ff.

[118] *Ibid*, p. 116 quoted by Swanton, p. 483 ff.

[119] Bartram in Transactions of American Ethnological Society vol. III, p. 26 quoted by Swanton p. 483 ff, *op. cit.*

[120] Adair, pp. 105, 107 (not a quotation).

[121] Brinton, *op. cit*, p. 165 quoting from Byington, A Grammar of the Choctaw Language, p. 43.

order to obtain the charm of success in an imminent undertaking, and on other occasions such as the result of a woman's promise to the Sun God for the recovery of the sick. The ceremonies consist of processions, symbolic dances, the telling and enacting of deeds of valor, and the fulfilment of vows made during the year.[122]

Altho the Sun figured highly in Plains Mythology, Fire took a more subordinate place. Possibly the New Fire was incipient among the rather atypical Eastern Plains Tribes along the Missouri who were influenced by the Fire Cultus of the lower Mississippi. Such were the Arikara, Hidatsa, Mandan, Santee-Dakota, Yankton, Ponca, Omaha, Iowa, Pawnee, Oto, Osage, Missouri, Kansas, Wichita, Quapaw, Caddo, Kichai, Waco, Tonkawa, Karankawa, and so forth. These tribes possessed a whole yearly cycle of ceremonies centering around the cultivation of maize and had the ceremonial emetic, scarification and even incipient human sacrifice (Pawnee).[123] [74]

According to Wissler

> the conception of renewing the fire was found in most agricultural tribes, often associated with planting and general seasonal rejuvenation. In modern times, the fire is still kindled with the fire drill or other primitive appliances. In the north, the ceremony appears even among the Pawnee, where, as elsewhere, the fire was kindled by a particular shaman or priest.[124]

Speck sees considerable unity in the ceremonialism of the Plains, the Southeast, and the Pueblos and kinship of all with Mexico.[125] In the central Algonkian Area, South and West of the Great Lakes the esoteric Midé ritual[126] took the place of maize ceremonies and there seems to be no record of true New Fire Rites. It is extremely doubtful if any of the Plains tribes had a New Fire Hite in any of their rituals. In the promulgation of the relatively synthetic movement in modern times, called the Ghost Dance Religion:

> they must have done with the white man's flint and steel, and cook their food over a fire made by rubbing together two sticks, and this fire must always be kept burning in their lodges, as it was a symbol of eternal life, and their care for it was an evidence of their heed to the divine command.[127]

---

[122] Alexander, North American Mythology, p. 89; also see A.L Kroeber, The Arapaho, Bulletin of the American Museum of Natural History vol. 18 1902-7.

[123] Acc. to J.O Dorsey, "A Study of Siouxan Cults " 11th Annual Report BAE Wash, 1891, the fire cultus is allied with 4 sticks among the Kansa (p. 535) and the Osages had 4 mystic fire-places connected with fire ritual (p. 380).

[124] Clark Wissler, The American Indian NY 1922, p. 213.

[125] Speck, *op. cit*, p. 13.

[126] W.J Hoffman, "The Midewiwin or 'Grand Medicine Society' of the Ojibway" 7th Report BAE 1885-6.

[127] James Mooney, "Ghost Dance Religion" 14th Ann. Rept. BAE Part II, 1896, p. 675 quoted by Walter Hough in "Fire as an Agent in Human Culture" Bull. 139 Smithsonian institution p. 144.

In California the most outstanding single rite is perhaps the annual ceremony in behalf of the dead known as the " burning " or the "cry " or the "dance of the dead." This is [75] an autumnal and largely nocturnal ceremony in which to the dancing and wailing of the celebrants all kinds of property are burnt to supply the spirits of the deceased after which period of mourning succeeds a feast of good cheer. The typical death customs include the burning of the house in which death has occurred.[128] Cremation was the sure path to glory in California.

In the Southwest the Navahos are much given to picturesque fire rites especially at the Night Chant and are also in possession of an extensive Fire Mythology clustering around *Hastseaini*, the Fire God.[129]

Further to the south the Hopi, Zuni, Keresans, and Tanoans possess a complex Fire Cultus of considerable antiquity. At Walpi, *Masauu* was God of Fire and ruler of the dead. At Zuni the Fire God was Shulawitsi.

As the Hopi regard fire as life there is naturally in their fire ceremonies a connection between the creation of life and the procreation of life. Hence it is impossible to adequately understand the new fire rite without considering the symbols of fertilisation and ceremonies connected with the propagation of life.[130]

Accompanying fire worship, or more accurately speaking, the worship of the magical powers of life as exemplified in fire, is its curative power, claimed by those who maintain that, since they are able to create fire they can likewise control it.[131] [76]

Still further south, in the western escarpments of the great Mexican Plateau, dwell the Huichol Indians whose *tatevali* or "grandfather fire" is the deity of life and health and also of shamans and prophesying. Great Grandfather Deer-Tail is also a fire god and a singing shaman; he is the son of Grandfather Fire and yet his elder because Great Grandfather Deer-Tail is the spark produced in striking flint while Grandfather Fire is the flame fed by wood. Father Sun is another important deity.[132]

Among the Coras of the same region a like mythology prevails. Where the light comes from other than from the Sun is not clear but there is an explanation in the somewhat uncertain power, the fire, and this is mainly represented as a certain personality or fire god. This fire is among the Cora the origin of all heavenly fire, the sun as well as the stars of the night and the day sky.[133]

In ancient Mexico Fire was

'The ancient God, the Father and Mother of all Gods, says an Aztec prayer, 'is the God of the Fire which is in the center of the court with four walls, and which is

---

[128] Alexander, *op. cit*, p. 215.

[129] Washington Matthews "The Mountain Chant" 5th Ann. Rept. BAE 1887, pp. 379-465.

[130] J.W Fewkes "Fire Worship of the Hopi Indians" Ann. Report Smithsonian Institution, 1920. p. 389; also "The Sun Worship of the Hopi Indians " Ann. Rept Smith. Inst, 1918.

[131] Fewkes, "Fire Worship of Hopi, *op. cit*, p. 389.

[132] Alexander, *op. cit*, p. 121.

[133] T Preuss, Die Religion der Cora Indianer, Erster Band-Die Nayarit Expedition, Leipsig 1912 (Transl. paraphrase of unpublisht note, of E.M Horner).

covered with gleaming feathers like unto wings'; dark sayings of the priests, referring to the glittering lightning fire borne from the sides of the earth. In their rituals fire was named *Tota*, 'Our Father' and *Huehueteotl*, 'oldest of Gods'; the infant passed thru a baptism of fire on the fourth day of its life, up to which time a fire is lighted at its birth was kept alive in order to nourish its life.[134] [77]

In Mexico Fire Worship often partook of phallic relationships as in the Hopi Rites since the reproductive principle which generated life was identified with fire.[135]

It is possible that the bloody sacrifices of the Mexican Aztecs arose not from a desire to obtain thru sympathetic magic an amount of rainfall equal to sacrificial bloodshed, as Seler supposes, but rather from the far more ancient association of blood with fire and of both with sacrifice. The life of the Gods was kept up by the blood of the sacrifices and was symbolized by the duration of the perpetual fires. The blood sacrifice appears as scarification in the Antilles, the Southeast, the Plains and the Pueblo Areas in the north, in the Gueso Sacrifice of the Chibchas and in the festivals of Peru and of the Araucanians.

Fire worship was well developed in Yucatan. The Ancient Mayas had the rite of walking barefoot over fire.[136] 2 Another fire rite consisted in putting out a large bonfire with water in order to insure rain. This rite was called *Tupp-k'a'k* and took place at the vernal equinox (*Mac*) just before the rains.[137] Among the modern Maya maladies of many kinds are cured by virtue of the properties contained in a fire kindled by two sticks. New [78] Fire kindled in this way is called by the name of the goddess of virgin fire Suhuiqaq and has a special glyph character in the inscriptions. A stone heated in this fire Imbues water with a magical power to cure calenture.[138]

Among the Araucanians of Southern Chile the Chief of the Gods was Pillan, the Fire-God and the "Lord of Thunder". In the forest Regions of Brazil the Fire and Thunder Deity was Tupan.[139] The Botocudos of East Brazil attribute all the blessings of life to the "dayfire" or Sun and all evil to the "nightfire" or moon. At the graves of the dead they kept fires burning on two sides for some days to keep away the evil spirits.[140] The Goajiros of Venezuela kept fires burning on graves and surrounded by cactus hedges for long periods after death to keep off evil spirits.[141]

When the Spaniards arrived in Colombia the Chibchas set out to greet the "Children of the Sun" kindling fire and burning incense to recompense for past sins against the God, and it is said, were accustomed to cast gold, emeralds, and other valued things into the fire, as sacrifice to the Sun.[142] [79]

Among the Tupi it is Mhoitata, the fire snake, who is the great protector of the country against lightning and destroying fires.[143] Fire, being connected with the Sun, was an object of

---

[134] Brinton, *op. cit*, p. 169.

[135] Brinton. *op. cit*, p. 171 ff.

[136] Frazer, The Golden Bough, X, 35 quoting from Landa, pp. 231-232.

[137] Seler, article "Central America " in Hastings Encyclopedia of Religion and Ethics basing on Landa.

[138] Tozzer, A Comparative Study of the Mayas and the Lacandones, p. 164.

[139] Alexander, *op. cit*, Latin American Mythology, p. 325.

[140] Article "Botocudos" Encyclopedia Britannica, 1923 edition; Prince of Wied-Neuwied, Reise nach Brasilien, II 57.

[141] W Sievers, Reise in der Sierra Nevada de Santa Maria, p. 258.

[142] V Restrepo, Los Chibchas antes de la Conquista Espanola, p. 76.

[143] Seler, Article "Brasil" in Hasting's Encyclopedia of Rel & Ethics.

profound veneration in Peru. Stones, especially, were symbols of Fire since it could be made to issue forth from them with a sharp blow.[144]

Funeral rites in Porto Rico were, as in South America and the Southeastern United States connected with fires built over graves. Quoting from Fewkes

> After a death they make fire, rubbing two sticks together, the act being connected in an esoteric way with the perpetuation of the life of the deceased.[145]

Likewise Picart, speaking of grave rites among the "Caribees" Says:

> They first lay the corpse into the Pit then light a Fire just by, when everyone squats himself round by it.[146]

From these examples it can be seen that the position of fire was outstanding in the focal areas of America. To explain this position requires an analysis of each particular phase of the fire cult. This we are attempting to do in the case of the New Fire. Before proceeding to a theoretical consideration of the New Fire as such it may be well to glance at the views of Tylor, Fraser, and others who have attempted to explain the position of Fire in the Religious and Folklore complexes in both the Old and the New World. [80]

Tylor notices the extremely important nature of fire worship as an Anthropological phenomenon and, true to his general habit, finds two stages in its development, first, fire as a fetish in which individual fires are regarded as sacred and, second, fire as a god in which the general element is categorically placed in the sphere of a particular deity.

> .... it must be borne in mind that rites performed with fire are the often, yet by no means necessarily, due to worship of the fire itself. Authors who have indiscriminately mixt up such rites as the new fire, the perpetual fire, the passing thru the fire, classing them as acts of fire-worship, without proper evidence of their meaning in any particular case, have added to the perplexity of a subject not too easy to deal with, even under strict precautions.[147]

Two especial sources of confusion must be borne in mind. First, fire is often a mode of sacrifice to any deity, hence the fire is secondary in a case of this sort as a general thing; Second, Fire-worship becomes a celestial or sun cult in many agricultural regions and the primary emphasis shifts.

Frazer notes two somewhat contrasting theories of Fireworship among modern students. On the one hand he finds Mannhardt advocating the principle of imitative magic in relation to the sun, because in kindling fires at the necessary seasons the needed supply of sunshine is secured for the crops and for life. On the other side he finds Vestermarck and Mogk advocating the idea that fire is employed for purificatory purposes to burn up and destroy all harmful influences such as witches, demons, monsters, and disease corruptions of all kinds. [81]

---

[144] A Reville, Hibbert Lectures on Religions of Mexico & Peru, p. 195.
[145] J.W Fewkes, The Aborigines of Porto Rico and the neighboring islands, p. 69.
[146] Picart, *op. cit*, p. 141.
[147] E.B Tylor, Primitive Culture, Vol. II p. 277.

On the one view, the fire, like sunshine in our latitude, is a genial creative power which fosters the growth of plants and the development of all that makes for health and happiness; on the other view, the fire is a fierce destructive power which blasts and consumes all the noxious elements, whether spiritual or material, that menace the life of men, of animals, and of plants. According to the one theory the fire is a stimulant, according to the other, it is a disinfectant; on the one hand the virtue is positive, on the other it is negative.[148]

In summing up the position of Fire in the New World it may be said that Fire has numerous connections with the sun, with the dawn, with light in general and with lightning. Fire is regarded generally as a helpful influence, altho evil devouring fire is also recognised. As a life principle we find it used as a constant remedy in numerous magical rites concerning disease and death. A fire built on a grave is an ancient association. Host feasts involve fires for cooking maize and other purposes. Various animals, notably the hare, coyote and raven are regarded as having aided man in securing fire, and often thru theft. Lightning and fire are connected, on the one hand with the tapir and on the other with the snake. Fire is connected with the color red, with blood and with war. Fire [82] gods arise easily and become deities of eminent importance, connected with fair-skinned, dawn gods or culture heroes. Sun gods arise from fire gods. Perpetual fires are maintained in temples for the gods and for the dead. A fire seems necessary on many special occasions and so must he kindled afresh, whereupon a New Fire Ceremony arises. The general position of fire is important in the same areas wherein the New Fire is found and also considerably beyond. New Fire arises particularly in connection with first maize or maize harvests. In general chronological sequence, the funeral fires seem to be the oldest, on top of these are the maize cycle fires, and still later arises the perpetual temple fire. [83]

The Theory of New Fire Ceremonialism

The survey of the New Fire Rites and their cultural matrix has so far resulted only in a disjointed series of observations. The problem which now arises is: Can these apparently separate and distinct groups of phenomena be linked together in any sort of a systematic theory or explanatory hypothesis? This we will attempt to answer by a consideration of the current ethnological theories which are employed to explain cultural phenomena and the possible applications that these theories may have in this case. (Map VII, p183)

The New Fire, it can be readily seen, is coincidental in the main with the areas of maize cultivation in North America.[149] Its apparent absence from the maize area south and west of the Great Lakes is to some degree explained by the fact that this region is ritualistically quite different from the more easterly Algonkian, Delaware, and the Muskogean tribes which partially

---

[148] Fraser, Vol. 10, p.329 *op. cit*, cites the work of Wilhelm Mannhardt, Der Baumcultus der Germanen und ihrer nachbarstämine, Berlin,1875, pp 521 sqq. and E Westermarck, "Midsummer Customs in Morocco" Folklore XVI, 1905 pp. 44 sqq; *Ibid*, Ceremonies and Beliefs connected with Agriculture, Certain Dates of the Solar Year, and the Weather in Morocco, Helsingfors 1913, pp. 93-103 and E Mogk, "Sitten u. Gebrauche im Kreislauf des Jahre" in R Wuttke's Sachsische Volkekunde, Dresden 1901, p. 310 sqq.

[149] Wissler, The American Indian, cf. map on p. 20 of Maize Areas.

surround it. The Central Algonkian ritual is not concerned with the maize cycle at all but rather with the esoteric dream fraternities of the Midé type.[150] Then again the New Fire is present among the maizeless Karok of California; this offering a second discrepancy. In South America where, so far as our records go, the New Fire is confined to Peru, there is little if any direct coincidence of maize cultivation with the New Fire. [84]

Being allied with the maize cultures the New fire is consequently a concomitant of the higher civilizations of America and is found especially in those regions such as Mexico and Yucatan where the leisure allowed by agriculture releases a considerable portion of the population to devote their energies to elaboration of the ceremonial life of the community. In fact the only advanced area in which the New Fire seems to have been lacking was the Chibcha, and this in spite of the fact that the Muysca possessed a rather full-blown Fire-Sun-Blood Sacrifice Cultus. The Aztecs had some four or five occasions on which the New Fire was kindled and the Pueblo tribes seem to have had at least two and possibly more, while the more peripheral Muskogians, Delaware, and Iroquois had to content themselves with but one or two such ceremonies, each, of this type.

Apparently the militaristically inclined nations had a proclivity for fire rites in general, for the Iroquois, Creeks, Aztecs and Incas were among the most warlike tribes on the continent. The Plains tribes connected the color red with fire and with war and bedecked themselves with red paint when on the warpath.

The New Fire distribution north of the Rio Grande corresponds remarkably with the area of matrilinear sibs, the Iroquois, Central Atlantic Algonkians, Muskogians, and Pueblo Indians all having the clan. Here again the Central Algonkians south of the Great Lakes offer a divergence, having the gens. [85] The only other sections possessing the clanship were some scattering Plains tribes and the Northwest Coast, which areas did not have the New Fire.[151]

Sun Worship is important in Peru, Colombia, Yucatan, Mexico, the Southwest and the Southeast, all of which except the second, possessed the New Fire. In Peru the Sun Cult existed as a political element, a part of the official policy of psychological and social uniformity thruout the Empire. In Colombia the Sun Worship seems allied to the ancient Sky and Lake Cults. In Yucatan, Mexico, the Southwest and the Southeast the Sun Worship appears to spring directly from the Fire Cultus, the Sun being accounted a heavenly fire which ripened crops and warmed the earth. Heliogony is also allied with the Sun Cult. The Incas of Peru were the direct "Children of the Sun" as were the Sun Clan of the Natchez. The Yuchi derived themselves from the sun and from menstrual blood. A Vestal Order of Virgins was present among the Incas, Mayas, and Mexicans, who tended a Perpetual Fire renewed yearly with the New Fire. Violation of duty or neglect of the Fire by the vestals was punishable by death in all three areas and there were other remarkable uniformities. Among the Natchez there was a perpetual fire tended by male servitors who were likewise slain on neglect of duty. [86]

Since the New Fire was concerned with the generation of life, it has several connections with phallic references. Thus among the Yaya priests of Walpi the notched stick is called "female" and the unnotched drill, "male." Thus the process of drilling fire takes on the character of the sexual act. This reinforces the idea of sympathetic magic in its role of renewing life in general. The phallic character of these fertility rites finds further elaboration in the obscene acts, gestures and remarks of the *Wüwütcimtû* priests at the Greater New Fire Ceremony at Walpi.

---

[150] *Ibid*, p. 195.
[151] Wissler, *op. cit*, p. 164 map of distribution of sibs.

These priests carry imitation vulvas made out of watermelon rinds and smear the women of certain societies, ritualistically prescribed, with filth and dirt. Among the Lacandones the nodules of copal offered up as incense at the *brasero* renewal are divided into "male" and "female" nodules. Abstaining from their wives was a common feature preceding the New Fire rites in Peru, Yucatan, and the Southeast. The continence demanded of the "Virgins of the Sun" was connected with their sexual devotion to the Sun God.

The custom of cleaning the flesh from the bones of the dead and then depositing these bones in certain houses or ossuaries is a trait running thru the Southeast, Mexico, and Central America down to the Talamancas. In fact, the perpetual fires of the lower Mississippi Tribes are kept in the bone houses or temples.

Geographically considered, the New Fire Rites seems to cluster around Mexico. The New Fire of the Iroquois and Delaware [87] borders on that of the Southeast which latter however is separated from the Pueblo and the Mexican by the wide gap of the Texas Plains. The Pueblo Rites may, in the early days, have been continuous with the Fire Rites of the aborigines of Northern Mexico such as the Cora-Huichol and here continuity extends almost unbroken into and past Yucatan down to the Isthmus of Panama. Then in Colombia and Ecuador comes a gap and we meet the last New Fire in Cusco.

There are some four or five methods of accounting for the New Fire Rites as we find them, namely – Diffusion, Parallelism, Convergence, Survivalism, and, possibly, European Influences. We shall review the evidence for each in turn and then, with a consideration of the time perspectives involved, try to arrive at a general formulation in conclusion.

First as to the evidence for *diffusion*. The New Fire is remarkably similar wherever it occurs in its general psychological significance. The kindling of a New Fire means the start of a New Year and New Life and is the signal for general renovation of all household goods, the adjustment of quarrels, the pardoning of criminals and a universal starting anew in all of the ceremonies except the Bribri funeral feast, where of course the rites have no public significance. The time for the New Fire Ceremonies is set generally either by crop ripening or harvest as among the Lacandones, Creek and Delaware or by the position of the Sun as among the Incas, Mayas, Aztecs, Hopi, Zuni, Keresans, and Iroquois. Among the Karok the time is [88] determined by the beginning of an acorn crop or of a run of salmon. Extreme solemnity and sacrednees marks all New Fire rites wherever they occur. Geographically, there are no hard barriers against diffusion. The grosser material elements in the New Fire Rites, such as the technique of firemaking by drill, are virtually the same everywhere save that the Incas had in addition the peculiar metal reflector kindling technique (reminiscent of Chinese New Fire).

The coincidence of the New Fire with maize cycle ceremonies and the clanship in North America suggests common diffusion of all of these elements from the south, probably from Mexico at some identical period in the past. In fact, there has been actual diffusion of New Fire Rites within historic times in the Southeast with the expansion of the Creek Confederacy from the nuclear Muskogians to the Cherokees, Yuchi, Shawnee, Chickasaw, Caddo suns and others. In the Southwest also, there is evidence that the Hopi Rites were brought in from the Gila Valley and from the Rio Grande region. And certainly the rapid diffusion of the fire rites of the Ghost Dance shows the possibility of such movements in prehistoric times.

The extreme complexity of the psychological position of New Fire in the Maya Calendrical Cult suggests an ancient center of origin for the whole New Fire Cultus in Yucatan. There was even a special goddess of New or Virgin Fire among the Mayas and a special glyph or hieroglyphic symbol for the idea of New Fire. Besides, the New Fire had numerous esoteric connections [89] with the number four, the sacredness of which crops out all over America, and also with an involved directions, time and space calculating symbolism. The use of four sticks in the Southeast and of four lines of meal in the Southwest in kindling New Fire is too suggestive of four burners of the Maya original to be overlooked. The *natcis* or feather sticks, found in both the Southeast and the Southwest New Fire Rites, suggest a common origin as does the ceremonial emetic, the ceremonial hunt, as do the fasts, scarifications and the animal dances common to both. Certainly the connections of Pueblo and Mexican New Fire Rites are too patent to be denied by anyone. The same anxiety about the Pleiades at New Fire Ceremonies is a striking case in point. The "throwing" and the "tasting" are found in Mexico, the Southwest, the Southeast, and even in Virginia. The fire is called "grandfather" among the Delawares, Muskogians, Pueblos, Huichols, and Mexicans.

Another factor to be considered in looking for the center for ceremony diffusions is in the length of the rites. These last the longest, as might have been expected, among the Lacandones, (thirty days or more), while the Mexican Toxilmopilia consumed some eighteen days, the Peruvian Rites nine days, the Pueblo Rites some five or nine days, the Muskogian some four or eight, the Delaware eight or twelve and the Iroquois about seven.

The immense importance of the fifty-two year world renewal New Fire in Mexico is but a heightened form of the miniature rites of the Karok and the other less civilised tribes. [90] The Fire Gods of the Mayas, Aztecs and pueblos are but elaborations of the Delaware Fire Manitu or the Tupi Tata, "divine fire." The perpetual fire is a later supplement to the New fire and diffuses more slowly from the original centers of both in Central America. In fact the importance of the New Fire element with reference to its ceremonial matrix decreases as we proceed outward from Mexico. Thus, while it is the main feature of the Toxilmolpilia and looms as perhaps the most important single element of the Pueblo Walpi November Rites, among the Muskogians it is only one of the main features of the Busk, and among the Karok, Delaware, and Iroquois it occupies an entirely subordinate ritualistic role. Among the Incas it was but one of the preparatory acts for the great Sun Festival. This is just as we might suppose on the hypothesis that the New Fire has been adopted by the less civilized tribes from the higher centers.

Nevertheless we may well ask; If diffusion is the whole statement of the case, how did New Fire come to be imbedded in such extremely different ceremonial matrices? A sun festival in Peru, a funeral rite in Panama, a series of calendrical rites to the gods in Yucatan and Mexico, a rain making and maize fertility cat in the Southwest, a first maize fast and stomp dance rite in the Southeast, a harvest and dream festival among the Delaware and a winter dream and scape goat festival in the Iroquois Area certainly do not tie together in any harmonious whole with evidences of a common origin. The Dream New [91] Fire of the Iroquois and the Delaware offers few resemblances to the Busk of the Southeast and the later does not fit in particularly well with the Southwest of Mexico. Likewise the gaps between the Central American and the Peruvian Areas are too great to be bridged by a theory of simple diffusion and how can diffusion account for the Karok New Fire isolated in far northwestern California? What missionary brought the good news of New Fire to them and from whence? It is quite apparent that the theory of central diffusion is open to serious question therefore on the basis of, first, immense gaps in the distribution of the New Fire and second, in the thoroly imbedded position which the rites have in extremely different ceremonial matrices does not suggest borrowing.

Therefore we turn to *parallelism.* Obviously the task is greatly increased because each rite must now be traced separately to a possibly hypothetical origin within its own area. We have national imperial celebrations in Peru and Mexico; town ceremonies among the Mayas, Pueblos, and Muskogians; village festivals among the Lacandones, Delaware, Iroquois and Karok; and finally private family funeral rites among the Bribri. And moreover these rites are held at almost every conceivable time of the year and the New Fire is kindled at any one of the twenty-four hours of the day. Where is there any unity here?

According to parallelistic theory, a fire would be necessary at any important festival and being allied with a religious event the fire kindled at this time becomes invested [92] with a superstitious sanctity of its own and the process of making the New Fire becomes ritualistic to the highest degree. Chants and prayers become necessary accompaniments of the process of fire drilling and the sacredness of the event requires that the spectators avert their faces during the procedure. Acts of this kind eventually become convenient points at which to mark the beginning of a seasonal cycle or year and secondary rationalization ensues, identifying New Fire with New Life, so that the habit gradually arises of casting off old goods and utensils and renewing everything for the new life cycle. This process becomes extended to the adjustment of quarrels and the pardoning of criminals in order that all may begin a new life.

According to this view that which we term the New Fire is in reality a series of entirely different phenomena arising thru conditioned parallelism from the inevitable elaboration of categorical groups of culture elements in communities achieving complete ceremonial cycles. Parallelism emphasizes the psychological unity of the Indian mind, its ignocentric twist, if we may use such a word, which unity arises from a common stock of traits of material culture and of somatologic constituents. Fire was the all important element in the life of the American Indian, as befitted a being scarcely emerged from the bitter blasts of Behring Straits. And, in fact, why should not parallelism explain the development of the varying types of New Fire as we see them in the different American culture areas as well as between American New Fire as a whole and the New Fire of the [93] agricultural areas of the Old World?

New Fire Ceremonies then, may he considered for the moment as a unity in name only and as arising from a common psychological emphasis on a phase which is common to many important rites, namely, the simple act of kindling a fire with a drill. Now if it can he shown that this emphasis arises from various sources and for a variety of reasons then the case for parallelism may he regarded as established.

In Peru the emphasis on New Fire lay in having the sun light the New Fire with his own hand, that is by igniting cotton tinder thru its rays being reflected from a burnished metal mirror. Only in case cloudiness shut off the sun's rays was the drill method used. Here it appears as tho the New Fire was sacred and worthy to be used to renew the Perpetual Temple Fire only because it had been lighted by the Sun, the chief God of the Incas.

The Fire of the Bribri Funeral Feast shows some degree of similarity to the grave fires kindled by the aborigines of Porto Rico, the Goajiros, Muskogians, and the Botocudos, which arose as an adjunct of the funeral feast and which were also used to keep wild beasts away from the freshly buried corpse. Secondarily, the fire becomes a symbol of the presence of the soul of the deceased and the ritualistic kindling and extinguishment change into magic rites thru which the soul's activities are controlled. Extinguishing the fire sends the soul off on its final journey to Sibu. [94]

The Maya New Fire arose simply from the incense ritual in which the sanctity attaching to divine services to the gods attaches itself to the fire with which the copal and rubber is burnt. It must be kindled and extinguished in a prescribed manner at regular intervals as becomes a holy fire.

The Mexicans developed the holy fire idea still further, probably borrowing originally from the Toltecs and mayhap, even the Mayas. Holy fire must be kindled at the solemn event of the birth of a child and b u m for four days at the end of which it was extinguisht. So also for the undertaking of a military campaign the kindling of a new sacrificial fire to the gods was sure to bring success. The sacred flame, kindled at the feasts of Camaxtli, and Motlaxquiantota, was a charm from which pure luck followed to anyone who put out his old fire and partook of the New. In the case of that extraordinary event, called the Toxilmolpilia, we have a still further elaboration of the superstitions and fears clustering about the holy New Fire. These ideas were probably encouraged as a political policy by the rulers in order that a national patriotic feeling might be engendered by the occasion of everyone partaking in the great fifty-two year achievement of renewing the world.

Amongst the Hopi the November Rites are a prayer for maize and rain. The New Fire idea may have been borrowed from Mexico at an early time, altho it might as well have been originated on the spot thru a development of the fertility idea from the phallic symbolism of the drill process. In the same manner [95] the rites of the Zuni and the Keres tribes express over and over again the fertility idea of the gemination of the maize.

Passing to the Karok, we see almost before our eyes, how first salmon and first acorn rites, in which the first new food of the season is cooked by a priest, become sacred fires. The fire is so charged with luck and with potency for good or evil that the people forbear to look at it and it must be kindled in a prescribed manner. Surely, here if anywhere, we have an entirely independent development of a New Fire Ceremony. The Karok are over 800 miles from the nearest New Fire using tribe, the Hopi, and are culturally so simple that it is difficult to imagine the New Fire surviving among them even had it been diffused to them from some higher tribe. The Karok appears to be an aberrant New Fire Rite and from all available evidence, a true case of parallelism.

The Creek Busk New Fire probably arose from the ancient fire usages of the Tunica tribes of the lower Mississippi Valley and was a life renewing event, purely. It could easily have arisen from the importance attaching to the fire used to cook the first green maize, which importance becomes great enough to demark the beginning of a new year and serve as a signal to cast off old goods and renew all household belongings.

Amongst the Delaware the New Fire used in the Dream Ceremony may have had its importance enhanced by suggestions from the Southeast. The importance of the ceremony and its ancient character shows that the fire for cooking the hominy at such a [96] feast must naturally be pure and undefiled and hence a Few Fire rite arises. At least this is what a parallelietic explanation would offer as an etiology. The Iroquois Dream Feast, which also became a rite of expiation, attaches New Fire as a purificatory agent. The asperging with ashes later becomes overshadowed by the white dog sacrifice and the Few Fire, never very prominent, almost disappears from view. Both the Iroquois and Delaware rites have many features in common and the Few Fire in these Dream Rites is quite obviously of different origin from that of the Busk.

Thruout the Eastern parts of the plains Area and also among some of the Central Algonkians, the importance attached to the fires kindled at the various rituals approaches at times strikingly near to the category of the New Fire. Such are some of the Bundle Ceremonies of the Pawnee, and even some of the Midé initiations of the Wisconsin tribes. Thruout these areas, however, the sacredness tends to get shunted off on the fire drills themselves and the importance of the medicine man handling them is emphasized.[152]

---

[152] Hough, Fire as an Agent, *op. cit*, mentions on page 88 the collection by Starr of a Sacred Bow drill of the Sac and Fox.

Such, then, is the case for parallelism. Admittedly naïve, it must be supplemented by much further work before it can serve as a satisfactory working hypothesis. Altho similarities are psychologically easier to perceive than differences, it may well be argued that Parallelism as an explanation runs counter to this tendency and often makes added work by calling [97] for lengthy explanations where simple observations will suffice. On the presentation of actual identities Parallelism merges over into *Convergence*. To this we next turn.

The later fire rites which European observers have encountered among the Indians may have been foreshadowed by a common prototype of a fire cultus in the remote past. Toward this, convergences would naturally arise later and explain apparent similarities such as the New Fire. Thus for example, the Aztecs had traditions of a sacred bundle in which they carried holy fire drills inherited from a legendary age.[153] This looks quite like the cult of sacred drills among many of the Plains tribes such as the Pawnee. Perhaps we may find in the hypothetical homeland of the American tribes in Asia traces of the possible original fire cultus and examples of convergences of a like nature.

Among the Chukchi-Koryak of Northeast Siberia, the nearest Asiatic congeners of our American Tribes, the implements for making fire (a wooden fireboard shaped roughly like a man, drills, a headpiece of stone or bone, and a bow) are reverenced and worshiped as family deities and guardians of the home and at sacrifices are smeared with the blood and fat of slaughtered reindeer; the charcoal produced in fire making is always collected and saved.[154] So also in Japan the ancient [98] sacred fire drill is used only in the Shintoistic Fire Festival of Kyoto.[155] The Taiyal of Formosa employ the drill for making Fire to he used in ceremony. The chief retires to a private room to perform the rite which comes at New Years, the beginning of the harvest.[156] These examples, together with the fire reverence of the Ainu and the New Fire Rites of the Chinese,[157] indicate a common substratum from which may have been drawn all of the New Fire Rites of the New World. Many of these Asiatic Rites converge strikingly toward the American ceremonies.

The development of agriculture and the spread of maize cultivation led to the formation of similar cults which revered the sun as the sky fire and the force which gave life to the crops and this caused, among the Yuchi, Natchez, and Incas, mythical derivation of a whole or part of the population from the sun as an ancestor.

The need of a constant fire on the chief's hearth led to the formation of a vestal order composed in Peru of the Inca's female relatives, in Yucatan and Mexico of elected women, and in Natchez of certain selected men. (Maps, p184)

Human sacrifice became necessary in Peru, Yucatan, Mexico, and Natchez since blood was identified with fire, life [99] and the sun and must he given to achieve merit. This act culminates in the heart sacrifice ritual, at which the Mexicans were so adept, and which was an achievement of the highest sublimity in the native opinion.

---

[153] Wissler, The American Indian, p. 190.

[154] Hough, Fire as an Agent, *op. cit*, p. 97 quoting from M.A Czaplicka, Aboriginal Siberia, pp. 265-6.

[155] Hough, Fire as an Agent, *op. cit*, pp. 89-90 quoting from Lafcadio Hearn, "The Most Ancient Shrine in Japan" *Atlantic Monthly*. Dec. 1891 footnote p. 792; Frazer, *op. cit*, vol. 10 p. 137 sqq.

[156] Hough, Fire as an Agent, p. 90.

[157] Frazer, The Golden Bough *op. cit*, vol. 9, p. 359, and 10, p. 136 sqq.

However probable this speculation as to the separate development of New Fire ceremonies out of a common substratum and their later convergence may appear, there is no basis for assuming a general tendency or orthogenesis toward the production of New Fire as psychologically satisfying to the Indian soul. The case for convergence is, in fact, the weakest of those yet considered. We turn to Hough's suggestions which can be termed, *"Survivalism."*[158] This postulates that the New Fire is a survival of an ancient universal rite or stage in human evolution.

It is of course apparent at once, even after a casual survey, that any map of the World or of American New Fire Ceremonies will show that the distribution of this rite is not peripheral, as we would expect in the case of a survival, but rather central and confined to the agricultural regions in both Hemispheres. New Fire is a late development arising only in communities wherein leisure allowed for an extensive ritualistic elaboration. (Excepting the aberrant Karok again)[159] We do not expect hunting and nomadic groups, hard pressed for sustenance, to develop New Fire. [100]

It is interesting, however, to note that in a sense the American Indian New Fire Ceremonies are a survival from the standpoint of European Civilization, since they serve as rallying points of the old Indian Religious Cults against European influences and as native values of the old culture wherein emphasis is especially placed on kindling fire by the drill as against the white man's matches. Thus, looked at from the European view Indian New Fire is a mass of discordant, survivals, ceremonies, various in origin, peripheral to the culture centers of today at New York and Buenos Aires. Still, for the Indian, the New Fire rites can become a unifying element, by the survival of which his path may be lit to such cultural independence as still appertains to him. In this case we might anticipate some future convergence of the surviving New Fire Rites as a common system of rallying points. Even now there are movements afoot to revive the ancient rites of Mexico.[160]

For the Indian the New Fire is probably one of his most sacred and significant ceremonial achievements. Who indeed would not be awed who once partook of the Midnight Renewal of the World on Mt Huixachtla in Mexico or of the impressive sunrise New Fire of the Natchez? These are indeed among the really great dramatic achievements of mankind if we are to believe the descriptions handed down to us. [101]

The possibilities of European influences affecting the New Fire Cults must need be considered since they are probably important. In the first place the observation of the early European observers may not have been of the keenest, and their reports on the New Fire so garbled as to exaggerate or minimise the facts. Garcilasso has been suspected of loquacious mendacity in particular. The general Iroquois descriptions were never particularly lucid and Landa's Account of the Mayas cryptic and synoptic is the pitiful documentary all of a whole civilisation. Granted these interpolations we can only check one observer against another. The Peruvian account remains open to question. There is no check on Gabb's account of the Bribri New Fire. The position of the New Fire element among the Iroquois is still largely unknown. However, for Mexico we have so many accounts that the grosser facts of the New Fire stand out

---

[158] Hough, Fire as agent in Human Culture, *op. cit.*

[159] The possibility of the Karok being a survival of an ancient stream of New Fire Rites formerly extending down the west coast is a rather wild speculation but admissible. However, we might expect to find other traces of New Fire besides this solitary one or the Karok ought to show some tendencies of a former wider distribution.

[160] See John Cornyn, Article in Chicago Tribune, Feb. 24 1930 on Revival of Ancient Mexican Rites.

quite clearly. The Lacandone, Pueblo, Karok, Muskogian, and Lenape accounts are by reliable anthropologists and should be fairly accurate.

Another channel of European influence on the New Fire would be thru the direct diffusion of ideas and customs, after the discovery, from the whites to the Indians and adopted by the latter into their ceremonies. This can of course be ruled out as a factor in the case of the Inca, Maya and Mexican Rites, but for the others it is quite possible that Christian and especially. Roman Catholic Rites have had some influence. At the Easter Rites of Modern Mexico the candles are simultaneously lit in a strikingly typical New Fire Ceremony. It is [102] possible that the Iroquois Need Fire is of European origin.

However, considering the obstinate nature of the majority of the Indian tribes in matters religious, it does not appear plausible that some of their most sacred and venerable rites should be of European borrowing or even hybridization. But we cannot be sure. The matter can only be settled by further investigation. The Talamanca Rites, especially, could bear further research since Gabb's work was done as far back as 1874. The Fire Societies of the Southwest could be further investigated, as well as the Fire Deities of Mexico.

One other aspect remains to be considered, namely, the time perspectives involved in the New Fire Rites. The Maya New Fire is undoubtedly the oldest, reaching back toward the foundation of agriculture in the New World, perhaps to 4000 BC, Considerably later the Mexican Ceremonies must have developed, possibly about 500 AD, the era of Totonac and Zapotec dominance, and certainly by the time of the Toltec at 700 AD, The Inca New Fire, probably the next oldest, reaches back toward 1000 AD, the period of the founding of the Inca State. The Pueblo New Fire Rites probably date back to somewhere between 1100 and 1500 AD, and perhaps the Tunica-Muskogi New Fire reaches back to the same period, the latter receiving later impetus with the spread in historic times of the power of the Creek Confederacy. The Delaware and Iroquois Rites reach back at least to 1500 AD, and in all probability to a couple of centuries beyond that. For the Karok and Talamanca we have absolutely no time perspective whatsoever. [103]

All of these New Fire Rites have their roots in commonplace events to which ritualistic and sacred significance gradually attach themselves, so that the real beginnings of a sacred New Fire are difficult to set. Perhaps the Delaware and Iroquois forms did not become sacred until the struggle against acculturisation by the white civilization surrounding them made them so. Certainly this was the mechanism operating in the case of Fire Making among some of the later Plains Ceremonies and especially in the Ghost Dance.

In considerations of time perspectives we may notice here a remark of Hough's that New Fire must be posterior to Perpetual Fire since the former presupposes a method of kindling while the latter does not. This reasoning, altho plausible and even supported by the relative position of New versus Perpetual Fire in Japan does not coincide with the facts of distribution in America, since the New Fire is far more widespread than the Perpetual Fire and is, as a rule, a far easier ritual than the perpetual maintaining of a sacred fire thruout the year. In fact the American Perpetual Fires are renewed exclusively by the New Fire Rite and are extinguished yearly prior to it. This then, makes it appear that the perpetual fire arises as a later development from the New Fire.

In conclusion we may sum up the theoretical consideration of New Fire by saying that diffusion is the most plausible working explanation of this element. Parallelism must be adduced, however, in order to explain such aberrant developments as the Karok New Fire and possibly, the Inca. There still [104] remains such a residuum of doubt that more evidence should be awaited before any comprehensive theory of diffusion is applied to these Rites. The New Fire Ceremony is a symbol of life generation or regeneration, and is used in connection with maize fertility or the fertility of animal and vegetable life in general, especially of that life on which the tribe depends for subsistence. Again, the New Fire may be used as a symbol of the renewal of the life of the tribe itself or of the life of the gods, which takes place with a new year. The life significance of newly kindled fire is very old and reaches back to the fires which are kindled on graves over wide areas of America. [105]

Appendix I

References in Fraser's Golden Bough to the New Fire

I. <u>Muskogian Area in America</u>
     among the Indians of Alabama, VIII, 72, n. 2
     among the Creek Indians, VIII, 74
     among the Natchez Indians, VIII, 134-135, 138
     made at festivals of New Fruits, VIII, 65, 74, 75, 78
II. <u>Miscellaneous American Cultures</u>
     among the Zuni Indians, X, 132 sqq.
     among the Iroquois, X, 132 sqq.
     among the Esquimaux, X, 134
     made at midsummer in Peru, II, 234; X, 132
     among the Karok, VIII, 255
III. <u>Classical Areas</u>
     sent from Delos and Delphi, X, 132 sqq., 138 (Lemnos)
     made at the beginning of a king's reign (Persia, Rome etc.), II, 262, 267
     made by friction of sticks at Rome, II, 207, 227 at Rome, X, 138
     among the Celts of Ireland, X, 139
IV. <u>Euro-American Civilization</u>
     kindled on Easter Saturday, X, 121 sqq.
     at Candlemas on 2nd Feb., X, 131, near Moscow, X, 139
made by friction of wood at Xmas, X, 264, 140 (Carpathians) [106]
V. <u>East African Cattle Area</u>
     at eating new fruits among the Caffres, VIII, 65
     made by friction as raincharm (Caffre), I, 290
     among the Swahili, X, 135
     in Benemetapa, X, 135
     among some tribes of British Central Africa, X, 135; 111, 286
     made by friction of two sticks at the rebuilding of a village (Herero), II, 217-222
     in Wadai, X, 134 sqq.
     made by friction of wood after a birth, II, 239 (Basuto)
VI. <u>India and Indo-China</u>
     at taking possession of a Bew House (Kachins of Burma), II, 237 sqq.
     among the Todas, X, 136
     among the Eagas, X, 136
     at Karma in Burma, X, 136
VII. *Chinese, Japanese*
     in Japan, X, 137 Bqq.
     Chinese Festival of the New FireE, IX, 359; X, 136 sqq.
VIII. Volume 10 Ch. IV, The Fire Festivals of Europe, pp. 106-32?
Ch. V, The Interpretation of the Fire Festivals, pp. 328-346 [110]

Bibliography

Acosta, Jose de Historia natural y moral de las Indias. Madrid, 1608, transl, for the Hakluyt Society as The Natural and Moral History of the Indies by E. Grimeton, London, 1880, v. 61.

Adair, James The History of the American Indians. London, 1775.

Adams, R.C "Notes on the Delaware Indians" in Report on Indians Taxed and Indians not Taxed. United States Census. 1890.

Alexander, H.B "North American Mythology," The Mythology of all Races, vol. 10, Boston, 1916.

"Latin America," The Mythology of all Races. vol. 11, Boston, 1920.

Bancroft, H.H The Native Races of the pacific States of North America. San Francisco, 1890. 6 volumes.

Bartram, W "Observations on the Creek and Cherokee Indians," 1789. With prefatory and supplementary notes by E.G Squier, Transactions of the American ethnological Society, vol. Ill, Part 1, New York. 1853.

Travels through North and South Carolina, Georgia. East and West Florida, the Cherokee Country, the extensive territories of the Muscogulges or Creek Confederacy, and the country of the Choctaws. London, 1792.

Beauchamp, W.M "The Iroquois White Dog Feast," American Antiquarian and Oriental Journal. VII, 1885, pp. 235-9.

"Onondaga Customs," Journal of American Folklore I, 1888, pp. 195-203.

Biart, Lucien The Aztecs. Transl. by J.L Garner, Chicago, 1892.

Boas, Franz "The Eskimo of Baffin Land and Hudson Bay," Bulletin American Museum of Natural History, vol. XV, Part I, New York, 1907.

"The Central Eskimo," Annual Report of the Bureau of American Ethnology, vol. 6, 1884-5.

Bossu, H Nouveaux Voyages aux Indes Occidentales. vole. I-II, Paris, 1768. [111]

Boturini, B.L Idea de una nueva Historia General de la America Septemtrionale. Madrid, 1746.

Bourbourg, l'Abbe Brasseur de Histoire des nations civilisees du Mexique et de l'Amerique central et Quatre lettrea sur le Mexique. 4 vols. Paris, 1857-9.

Bowditch, C.P The Numeration, Calendar Systems and Astronomical Knowledge of the Maya. Cambridge, 1910.

Brinton, D.C Myths of the New World. Philadelphia, 1896.

"The Folklore of Yucatan," Folklore Journal. I, 1883. p. 247 ff.

Brühl, Gustav Die Cultur-volker Alt-Amerikas. New York, Cincinnati, St. Louis, 1875-87.

Brush, E.H Iroquois Past and Present. Publisht for the Pan American Exposition. No date.

Byington, Cyrus A Grammar of the Choctaw Language. 1865? Ms. in Library of the Bureau of Ethnology. {BAE B }

Catlin, Geo "New Fire among the Mandans of the Upper Missouri at Minataree Green Corn Dance," in Report of the United States National Museum. 1885, p. 315.

Letters and Notes on the Manners, Customs and Condition of the North American Indians. 4th Ed., London, 1844.

Charlevoix, P.FX de Histoire de la Nouvelle France. VI, p. 172 sqq., Paris, 1744.

History and General Description of New France, transl. by J.G Shea. 6 vols. New York, 1900.

Voyage dans l'meriques septentrionale. transl. as Journal of a Voyage to N. America by L. P. Kelley, 2 vols. Chicago, 1923.

Chateaubriand, FAB de Voyages en Amerique. Paris, 1870.

Chavero, Alfredo Anales del Museo Nacional de Mexico. II, 483, notes 3 & 4.

Clark, J.V.H Onondaga. 2 vols. Syracuse, 1849.

Clavigero, Abbe D.F.S The History of Mexico. Transl, from Italian by Charles Cullen in 3 vols. Richmond, Va., 1806. [112]

Curtis, Ed. S The North American Indians. 20 vols. New York.

The Tiwa and the Keres. vol. 16, New York, 1926.

Csaplicka, M.A Aboriginal Siberia. Oxford, 1914.

Dorsey, J.O A Study of Siouxan Cults," 11th Annual Report Wash., 1891.

Du Pratz, Le Page, Antoine S Histoire de la Louisiane. Tomes I-III, Paris, 1758. Same in English transl., London, 1763 and 1774.

Dwight, Timothy Travels in New England and New York. London, 1823.

Encyclopedia Britannica Article "Botocudos," 11th ed, 1912.

Fewkes, J.W "New Fire Ceremony at Walpi," 1898. American Anthropologist N.S vol. 2. 1900, p. 80 ff.

The Lesser New Fire Ceremony at Walpi," American Anthropologist N.S, vol. 3, 1901. p. 446 ff.

"The Tusayan New Fire Ceremony," Proceedings of the Boston Society of Natural History. XXVI, 1895. pp. 422.

"Naacnaiya," Journal of American Folklore, 1892.

"Wuwutcimti," Proceedings of the Boston Society of Natural History, 1894.

"Fire Worship of the Hopi Indians," Annual Report of the Smithsonian. 1920-3. pp. 589-610.

"Sun Worship of the Hopi Indians," Annual Report of the Smithsonian, 1918.

"The Group of Tusayan Ceremonies called Katcinas," 15th Annual Report of the Bureau of American Ethnology. Washington, 1897. p. 263.

"Hopi Katcinas," 21st Annual Report Bureau of Ethnology. Wash, 1903. p. 24.

"The Aborigines of Porto Rico and Neighboring Islands," Annual Report of the Bureau of Ethnology No. 25, 1903-4.

Fraser, Sir J.G The Golden Bough. 12 vols. London, 1922-5. 3rd ed. (especially vols. 2, 8, 9 and 10).

Gabb, W.M "Of the American Tribes and Languages of Costa Rica," in Proceedings of the American Philosophical Society. 1874. vol. XIV, No. 92. [113]

Gama, Leon y, D.A Descripcion histories y cronologica de las dos Piedras. II ed. Mexico, 1832.

Garcillaso de la Vega. Royal Commentaries of Peru, in 2 parte, tranel. by Sir Paul Ricaut. London, 1685.

Gatechet, A.S A Migration Legend of the Creek Indiana, vol. I, Phila., 1884 In Brinton's Library of Aboriginal American Literature No. 4, vol. II. St. Louis. 1888. (Transactions of the Academy of Science of St. Louis, vol. V, nos. I & II).

Gibbs, George "Journal of the Expedition of Col. Redick M. Kee through Northwestern California in 1851," in Schoolcraft, Indian Tribes, vol. Ill, pp. 99-107, 634. Phila., 1853.

Gilbert, William Harlan 1947 *New Fire Ceremonialism in America.* Revista del Instituto de Antropología de la Universiddad Nacional de Tucuman, República Argentina.

Gomara, F. Lopez de "Primera y Segunda parte de la Historia general de las Indias," in Vedia, Hiatoriadores primitivos de Indias. tom. I. Antwerp, 1554.

Goodman, J.T The Archaic Maya Inscriptions. (Archeology Appendix to Biologia Centrali-Americana).London, 1897.

Gray, L.H "Iroquois," Article in Hasting's Encyclopedia of Religion and Ethics.

Grinnell, G.B "The Northern Cheyenne Ghost Dance," in Journal of American Folklore, vol. V, and also 19th Annual Report of the Bureau of Ethnology. Part II. 1900. p. 925.

Hale, Horatio "The Iroquois Sacrifice of the White Dog," American Antiquarian and Oriental Journal. VII, 7-14. 1885.

Hall, C.P Life with the Esquimaux. 2 vols. London, 1864.

Harrington, M.R "Religion and Ceremonies of the Lenape," Indian Notes and Monographs Series. New York, 1921.

Hawkins, Benj A Sketch of the Creek Country in 1798 and 1799. Georgia Historical Society Collections, vol. III. Savannah, 1848.

Hearn, Lafcadio "The Most Ancient Shrine in Japan," Atlantic Monthly. Dec. 1891, footnote p. 792.

Hennepin, L Description de la Louisiane. Paris, 1663.

Herrera, A. de Historia general de los Hechoe de los Castellanos en las Islas y Tierra Firme. Madrid. 1726. transl. by J. Stevens as General History of the Vast Continent and Islands called America. London, 1725-6.

Hewitt, J.N.B "White Dog Ceremony," Article in vol. II of the Handbook of the American Indians, 2 vols. P. W. Hodge, editor. Bull. 30 of the Bureau of American Ethnology. Wash. 1907-10. [114]

"New Fire among the Iroquois," American Anthropologist. II, 1889. p. 319.

Hitchcock, Gen. F.A Mss Notes on Busk in possession of Mrs. W. H. Croffut, Wash., D.C.

Hodgson, Adam Remarks during a journey through North America in the Years 1819. 1820 and 21. New York, 1823.

Hoffman, W.J "The Midewiwin or Grand Medicine Society of the Ojibway," 7th Annual Report of the Bureau of Ethnology.

Hough, Walter The Hopi Indians. Cedar Rapids, Iowa, 1915.

"Fire as an Agent in Human Culture," Bulletin 139. Smithsonian, p. 144.

"Fire making apparatus in the United States National Museum." Rep't of U.S Nat. Museum. 1881. pp. 531-587.

article "Fire making," in Handbook of the American Indian, Vol. I. Bull. 30. BAE Wash., 1907-10.

Ixtilxochitl, "Historia Chichimeca & Relaciones" in Lord Kingsborough's Mexican Antiquities. vol. IX.

Jones, C.C History of Savannah. Georgia, from its settlement to the close of the 18th Century. Syracuse, New York, 1890.

Joyce, Thos. A Central American & West Indian Archeology. London, 1916.

Kingsborough, Lord Antiquities of Mexico. 9 vols. London, 1831-48.

Kroeber, A.L Handbook of the Indians of California. Bulletin 78 of the Bureau of Ethnology. Wash, DC, 1929.

"The Arapaho," Bulletin of the American Museum of natural History, vol. 18. 1902-7. New York.

Native Culture of the Southwest," University of California Publications in Archeology and Ethnology. vol. 23, no. 9, 1928.

Lafitau, J.F Moeurs des sauvages Ameriquains. Paris, 1724. I, 367-9.

Landa, Diego de Relacion de las Cosas de Yucatan transl. by l'Abbee Brasseur de Bourbourg into French as Relation des Choses de Yucatan. Paris, 1884. Also transl. par Jean Genet into French in a 2 vol. ed. at Paris, 1928. [115]

Leon, P. de Cieza de Travels. transl. by C.R Markham for Hakluyt Soc'y, London, 1854 in Works Issued by the Hakluyt Society. vol. 48.

Second part of the Chronicle of Peru, also' transl. by C.R Markham for Hakluyt. London, 1883, in Works Issued by the Hakluyt Society, vol. 88.

Lettrea edifiantes et curieuaes. Rouvelle ed. VII, Paris, 1781, pp. 7-16. Reprinted in Recueil de voyages au nord IX. Amsterdam, 1787, pp. 3-13.

Long, R.C.E "The Burner Period of the Mayas," Man 108. Nov. 1923.

Lowie, R.H Ceremonialism in North America from Anthropology in N. America. New York, 1915.

MacCauley, Clay "The Seminole Indians of Florida," 5th Annual Report Bureau of Ethnology. Wash., 1887. pp. 469-531.

Mannhardt, Wilhelm Der Baumkultus der Germanen und ihrer nachbarstämme. Frster Teil in Wald u.Feldkulte. Berlin, 1875.

Markham, C.R A History of Peru. Chicago, 1892.

Matthews, Washington "The Mountain Chant," 5th Annual Report Bureau of American Ethnology. Wash. 186.7. pp. 379-465.

Mendieta, Fray Geronimo Historia eccleslastica Indiansa. La publica Joaqu. Garcia Icazbalceta. Mexico, 1870.

Milfort, (LeClerc) Memoire ou coup-d'eil rapide sur mes differens voyages et mon sejour dans la nation Creek. Paris, 1802.

Mogk, E "Bitten u. Gebrauche im Kreislauf der Jahre," in R. Wuttke's Sachsische Volkekunde. Dresden, 1901. p. 310 sqq.

Mooney, James "Cherokee Mound Building," American Anthropologist. vol. II. April 1884. pp. 167-171.

"Ghost Dance Religion ....," 14th Ann. Report of the Bureau of Ethnology. Part II. 1898. Wash. p. 675.

"The Siouxan Tribes of the East," Bull. 22 BAE Wash. 1894.

Morgan, L.H The League of the Iroquois. New York, 1922. [116]

Muller, Baron J.W von Reisen in den Vereinten Staaten, Canada, u. Mexico. 3 vols. Leipeig, 1864.

Muller, J.G Geschichte der Amerikanischen Urreligionen. Bâle, 1887. pp. 559-61; 519-20.

Parker, A.C "Code of Handsome Lake, the Seneca Prophet," New York State Museum Bulletin 163. Albany, 1913.

Payne, E.J History of the New World called America. vols. I & II. Oxford, 1892.

Penn, Wm A Letter from Wm. Penn. Proprietary and Governour of Pennsylvania in America to the Committee of the Free Society of Traders of that Province, Residing in London, p. 6. London, 1863.

Picart, Bernan The Ceremonies & Religious Customs of the various Nations of the Known World together with Historical Annotations and several curious Discourses equally instructive & entertaining. 6 vols. London, MDCCXXXIV.

Pope, John Tour through the northern and Western Territories of the United States. Richmond, 1792.

Powers, Stephen The Tribes of California. Washington, DC, 1877.

Prescott, W.H History of the Conquest of Peru. 2 vols. New York, 1909.

History of the Conquest of Mexico. 3 vols. Phila. 1874.

Preuss, K "Die Religion der Cora Indianer." Erster Band Die Nayarit Expedition. Leipeig, 1912.

"Die Feuergotter als Ausgangspunkt zum Verstandnis der Mexikanischen Religion," Mittelungen der Anthropologischen Gesellschaft in Wien XXXIII. 1903.

Relation de la Louisianne in Receuille de au Nord V,de Tonti Amsterdam 1734, p. 23 sqq. & p. 122; also see Relation des Natches by Le Petit Ibid. IX, p. 13 sqq.

Reville, A Native Religions of Mexico and Peru in Hibbert Lectures. London, 1884,

Restrepo, Vicente Los Chibchas antes de la Conquista Espanola. Bogota, 1895.

Romans, Bernard A Concise Natural History of East and West Florida, vol. I. Sew York, 1775.

Sagard, F.G Le Grand Voyage au pays des Hurons. Paris, 1865. [117]

Sahagun, B. de Historia General de las Co sag de Nueva Espana. 3 vols. Mexico, 1829. C.H deBustamente, 2d. transl. into French by D. Jourdanet et R. Simeon, Paris, 1880, as Histoire generale des choses de la Nouvelle Espagne.

Schoolcraft, H.R Historical and statistical information respecting the history, condition and prospects of the Indian Tribes of the United States. Phila. 1851-7. 6 vols.

Notes on the Iroquois. New York, 1846.

Sievers, W Reise in der Sierra Nevada de Santa Maria. Leipsig, 1887.

Southey, R Madoc. Boston, 1806.

Speck, F.G Ethnology of the Yuchi Indians. Anthropological Publications of the Museum. University of Pennsylvania, vol. I. Phils., 1909.

"The Creek Indians of Taskigi Town," Memoirs of the American Anthropological Association, vol. II, Part 2. Lancaster, Pa. 1907.

Spence, Lewis Mythologies of Mexico and Peru. Chicago. No date.

"Brazil." Article in Hasting's Encyclopedia of Religion and Ethics.

The Gods of Mexico. London, 1923.

Stevenson, M.C "The Zuni Indians," 23rd Annual Report Bureau of Ethnology. Wash., 1904.

Stiggin, Geo A historical narrative of the genealogy, tradiditions {!}, and downfall of the Ispocoga or Creek tribe of Indians writ by one of the tribe. Ms. in the possession of the Wisconsin Historical Society.

Stites, S.H "Economics of the Iroquois." Bryn Mawr Dissertation, 1904.

Swan, Caleb "Position and state of manners and arts in the Creek, or Muskogee Ration in 1791," in Schoolcraft, Indian Tribes, vol. V, pp. 251-283. Phila., 1855.

Swanton, J.R Indian Tribes of the lower Mississippi Valley and adjacent coast of the Gulf of Mexico. Bulletin of Bureau of Ethnology Vol. 43. Wash., 1911.

Religious Beliefs and Medicinal Practices of the Creek Indians. 42nd Annual Report of the Bureau of Ethnology. Wash., 1924-5. 110.

Torquemada, F. Juan de Los Veynte y un libros Rituales y Monarquia Yndiana. Madrid, 1723.

Toy, C.H Introduction to the History of Religion. New York. 1913.

Tozzer, A.M A Comparative Study of the Mayas and the Lacandones. New York, 1907.

Tylor, E.B Primitive Culture. 2 vols. 2nd ed. London, 1873.

Velasco, Juan de   "Histoire du Royaume de Quito in H. Ternaux-Compano's Voyages, Relatione, et Memolrea originaux pour servir a 1'Histoire de la Decouverte de L'Amerique XVIII. Paris, 1840.

Veytia, Mariano Historia antigua de Mejico. ed. by C.F Ortega. 3 vols. Mexico, 1836.

Waitz, Theodore Anthropologie der Naturvolker. vols. 3 & 4, "Die Amerikaner" Leipsig, 1862-4.

Wied-Neuwied, Maximilian, Prinz au Reise nach Brasilien in den Jahrew 1815-17. 2 vols. Frank-a-M., 1820-1. **

Westermarck, Edward "Midsummer Customs in Morocco," Folklore XVI. 1905.

 Ceremonies & Beliefs Connected with Agriculture, Certain Dates of the Solar Year, and the Weather in Morocco. Helsingfors, 1913.

Wilson, Sir Daniel Prehistoric Man. London, 1876.

Wissler, Clark The American Indian. New York, 1922.

Wolf, Morris   "Iroquois Religion and its Relation to their Morals," Columbia University Dissertation, 1919.

Zeisberger, David   "History of the Northern American Indians," ed. by A.B Hulbert & N Schwarse, Ohio Archeological and Historical Quarterly, vol. XIX. nos. I & II, p. 128. Columbus, 1910.

See 1947 printed maps, pp. 182-6

4 hand- drawn maps, hand- scrawl lettering:

108a Distribution of New Fire Ceremonialism in America
108b Religions of Native America
 NoAm > Sea goddess cult (arctic), sky raven cult (NWC), season cult, death & creation cult (Calif), sun coyote cult (Plateau), rain god cult (SW), manitu hare dream cult (Great Lakes), sun busk cult (SE)
 SoAm > war god & calendric cult (Mex), Zemi earth goddess cult (Caribean), creation sun lake cult (Andes), spirit dualism (Amazon) huaca creator & sun cult (Chile), creator fire & season (cone)

109a Distribution of Perpetual Fires (Incas) & Funeral Fires (Botocudo)
109b Distribution of Fire Gods, etc Fire, Sun Light, Heliogonic Myths

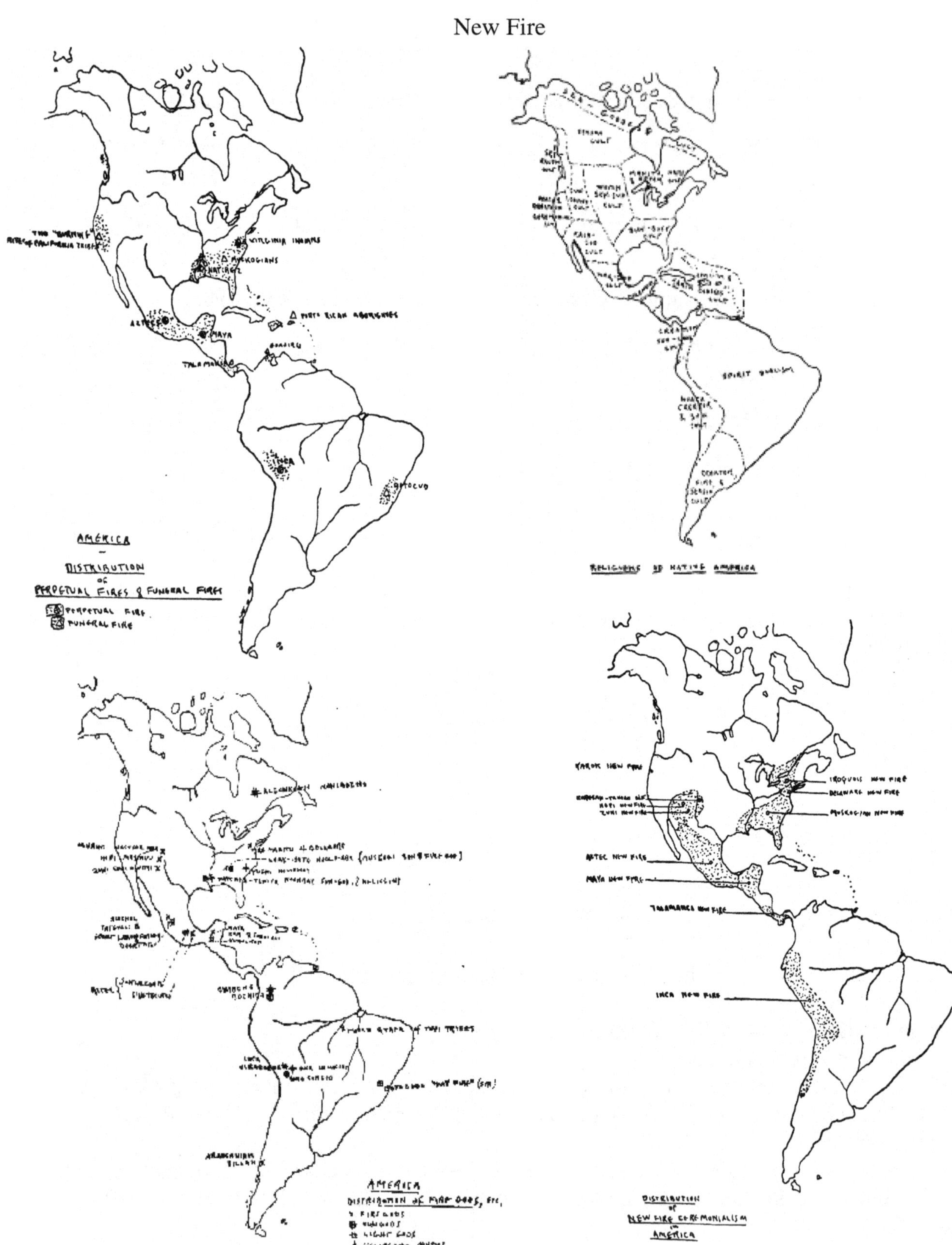

Appendix II

Tabular Survey of New Fire & Allied Rites ~

[107]

	Inca	Tlmca	Maya	Aztec	Pueblo	Karuk	Mskgi	Dlwr	Iroq
Calendric postion	Fall Harvest March		New Maize winter	winter	Harvest Equinox solstice	1st fruits April August October	1st corn July	Harvest October	winter
Fire technique	Metal Reflector drill	drill	drill	drill	drill	drill	Drill, matches	Pump drill	Pump drill
Chant?		X	X		X				
Time of day	day	day	day	Mid night	day	day	dwn sunset		day
Matrix	harvest nw year	funeral	1st maiz nw year	World renewal	Rain magic nw year	1st acorns & salmon	Green corn nw year	Dreams nw year	Dreams white dog nw year
importance	major	major	major	major	major	minor	major	minor	minor
Perpetual	X		X	X			X		
Fire god			X	X	X		X	X	X
Sun god	X		X	X	X		X	X	X
Heliogony	X						X		
Asperging			X	X	X		X		X
Cremation				X		X	X		
Pyrotherapy			X		X				X
Ordeal			X	X	X				X
Calumet					X		X	X	X
Scarification			X	X	X		X		
Emetic					X		X		
# of Days	9 days	9	30	18	9	10	4 or 8	8 or 12	7 days

Tlmca = Talamanca   Mskgi = Muskogee   dlwr = Delaware   iroq = Iroquois

1904-1988

New Corn

Renew Ritual Return

OCCASIONAL CONTRIBUTIONS FROM
THE MUSEUM OF ANTHROPOLOGY OF THE
UNIVERSITY OF MICHIGAN
NO. 13

GREEN CORN CEREMONIALISM IN THE EASTERN WOODLANDS

BY

JOHN WITTHOFT

ANN ARBOR
UNIVERSITY OF MICHIGAN PRESS

1949

CONTENTS

Introduction[161]

FOR some centuries prior to the appearance of Europeans on the North American continent, the aboriginal peoples of the Eastern Woodlands and of the eastern plains shared an economic cultural complex that depended largely upon agriculture and chiefly upon one plant, *Zea mays* L, for its staple. The colonists quickly adopted this agricultural complex, and today we still use techniques of agriculture that are native American in origin (the hilling of corn, for

---

[161] This study is revised from a master's thesis in anthropology presented to the University of Pennsylvania in June, 1946. I wish to thank Dr. Frank G. Speck, Dr. William N. Fenton, Mr. Merle Deardorff, and Mr. Volney Jones for their helpful suggestions and criticism.

example, and the planting of pumpkins, squash, and beans in corn hills), whereas in Europe, American plants were broadcast or planted in rows, the traditional methods of European grain culture. It is interesting to note that some of the American Indians first planted rice in hills, rather than in rows or broadcast in fields.[162] Along with traditional and complex techniques for the cultivation of these crops, however, the aborigines also possessed a large body of folk-belief and ritual which was an integral part of their maize complex. It was precisely this phase of Indian agriculture which the white colonists did not adopt; in fact, they seem to have been only slightly aware of its existence and never seem to have noticed it as an American equivalent of the European complex of agricultural beliefs, festivals, and magical practices with which they were familiar. One still notes, in the folklore of white American communities, survivals of European practices of planting by the moon, of European festivals having agricultural significance, in addition to many similar vestiges of an extinct folk agricultural complex, grafted on the part of their agricultural economy that is largely of American origin.

At the time of the colonization of America, many parts of Europe still preserved an integrated cycle of festivals, popular observances, and supernaturalistic practices directly concerned [2] with the agricultural year, a complex which had survived until very recent times, but which now exists almost entirely as a cherished memory of the folklorist. This religio-magical complex is certainly as worthy of study by the ethnologist as any comparable systems from other parts of the world and presents a basic pattern not too unlike corresponding agricultural complexes of other cultures. James Frazer, in *The Golden Bough,* attempted a reconstruction from the European and Mediterranean material of this sort, which he has used to interpret similar complexes in Asia, Africa, and the Americas and in turn reinterpreted European data in terms of conclusions drawn from the other continents. Earlier observers of the American Indian had fallen into the same pattern of fanciful treatment and had frequently looked to Hebrew, Tartar, or Middle American parallels for the origin of the Indian festivals they observed, In no case did an observer conclude that he had seen one item of a comparable and nonrelated system which would present a very different picture if he had collected more data. Later ethnological investigators did not commit such gross errors of judgment, but they rarely attempted to gather enough information to justify more objective conclusions.

Actually, today there is not enough data on the nonmaterial aspects of the agriculture of most of the eastern tribes to attempt a synthetic picture of the maize complex of any particular people. We do have indications that information which is now available existed as part of an integrated system of belief and practice, a pattern perhaps comparable in complexity, elaboration, and interest to the well-described European system which has been mentioned. It seems hopeless, however, to attempt to fit these fragments together into an understandable whole. The processes of acculturation are bringing the same destruction to Indian cultures that they have brought to older European folk-belief, yet even modern ethnographies dealing with the eastern areas do not emphasize the survivals and modified units of these agricultural complexes that still remain. Students of this area have also failed to elucidate the maize complex, in both its material and nonmaterial aspects, as a set of related phenomena possessing some unity in each culture. [3]

A very interesting and difficult historical problem is suggested by these ideas. It is known from the archaeology of the eastern United Spates that maize agriculture is of no great antiquity in this area. Most authorities date the introduction of maize into the Eastern Woodlands as not earlier than 500 {now 800} A.D.[163] The area of maize cultivation in eastern

---

[162] Bartram, 1853, p. 48; Hawkins, 1848, p. 66.
[163] Webb and Snow, 1945, p. 312; Ritchie, 1944, p. 323.

North America is geographically separated from the nearest occurrence, in the Southwest, by a nonagricultural area. Within this eastern area are uniformly distributed specific material traits concerned with maize cultivation which are not characteristic of areas farther south and west in the Americas. These include the hoe, replaced in other areas by the digging stick and the foot plow[164] (spade); the corn mortar and pestle (present in some Mexican areas); the use of mats of braided corn husks (the ears are braided together to hang for drying and storage; later the corn is removed for use, and the braids are utilized); the use of corn as hominy (shell leached from the kernels with potash from wood ashes); corn bread wrapped in corn leaves and baked in ashes; and use of a wooden dish of special shape for mixing corn-bread dough, a utensil which may possibly be descended from a pre-agricultural type of soapstone bowl of the same shape found archaeologically throughout most of this area. Irrigation was not practical in this area. Botanical study of the maize varieties of the eastern United States also supports this conclusion, as noted especially in the studies of Carter,[165] who finds a concentric distribution of corn varieties in this area, with the oldest varieties in the North, correlated with the stratigraphic position of similar varieties in the Southwest. Carter's conclusions about the ultimate origins of maize cultivation are not of concern here, except that they support the theory of the uniform diffusion of maize agriculture throughout eastern North America from a single direction.

It seems probable that the diffusion of maize within this eastern province would not have represented merely the borrowing of seed corn by the neighbors of agricultural peoples and [4] their handing on of seed to their neighbors. In actuality a real maize complex would have been diffused, including specific techniques for the growing and utilization of maize, knowledge of its botanical peculiarities (such as its inability to reproduce itself by self-sowing, and its tendency to grow extra "prop-roots" when dirt is hilled around the base of the plant), a set of magical and ritual precepts and traditions directly concerned with the cultivation and utilization of maize, and mythological and folktale material concerning the origin, nature, history, and use of maize. Such a nonmaterial culture complex would no doubt be distorted and modified in the transmission. It might be adjusted to, and combined with, existing institutions and come to present a somewhat differing entity in each cultural setting. It might later be modified or even replaced by the diffusion of other systems of belief or come to fulfill a differing function in each cultural group and so start a specific evolution of its own. The impetus given to an already existing culture by a new and more productive economy might also result in the evolution of a new ceremonial pattern from preagricultural systems of ritual, Later developments and modifications within small ethnic groups might come to influence the culture of large sections of the area.

Since the technology centered about maize shows a rather similar basic pattern throughout the eastern United States and a somewhat different pattern from that of other areas, a comparative study of nonmaterial aspects of maize agriculture might be justifiable. Unfortunately, as I have previously indicated, material for such a study is rather sparse In comparison to the information on many other phases of the cultures of this area. Perhaps future ethnographic study may contribute enough data to make such a survey more feasible, but the amount of survival of aboriginal traits of this sort may be very small. For this reason I intend to restrict this study to one particular ritual, the one about which most Is known and which seems to have been of major significance.

---

[164] Linton, 1924; Wissler, 1922, pp. 19-23.
[165] Carter, 1945, pp. 39-55.

There are enough data from most parts of the eastern United States to indicate that three major festivals were immediately [5] concerned with the cultivation of corn, but in few areas is there further information. Two of these ceremonies, the planting ceremony and the harvest festival, seem to have been of secondary importance and did not attract much attention among observers. The so-called green corn dance, however, seems to have been the most significant to the aborigines, and much fuller accounts of it from several areas exist. Recent ethnographic studies of this ceremony from several tribes have also been made, and there is a sense of its homogeneity throughout fairly large geographic areas. It was a ceremony held when the green corn was first edible, and, at least in some areas, marked a major division of the year. The time of its occurrence would make historical connection between the same rite in different areas more likely, for the coincidence of such rites as planting and harvest festivals as parallel developments in different cultures would be more expected. It is surprising that neither of these rituals was selected for the place of first importance and for elaboration by the aboriginal maize farmers.

The problem in this particular ceremony is severalfold. First, I intend to indicate the distribution of this rite, and then, by comparative study, to point out similarities and differences between different areas, and point to some evidence of historical connection. The second problem is to note special modifications and differences in function of this ritual as found in the different ethnic groups. These two lines of inquiry, however, would be difficult to separate and will be pursued together. Finally, as a sort of philosophic background for the ceremony, I should like to introduce a distributional study of the Corn Mother myths and point to some possible relationships between these tales and the ceremony with which I am chiefly concerned.

The ideal method for the study of green corn ceremonialism would no doubt be to chart and plot the distribution of all traits associated with the green corn ceremonies and then to analyze these trait distributions. In view of the limited amount of data for most areas, however, such a study could include only a small part of the traits actually characteristic of each locality's ritual. The data are generally too sparse to permit the necessary [6] evaluation of such traits as might be considered diagnostic. This study does not presume to offer a final trait-distribution study. The object has been to interpret the data available as carefully as possible in terms of two hypotheses: first, the green corn ceremonies of the various peoples in the Eastern Woodlands are historically connected phenomena; second, these rituals have been subjected to considerable elaboration and specialization in different locales- Some attention is also given to the possible place of origin of green corn rituals.

The Algonkian Peoples of
New England and New York

THE data for the area of Algonkian peoples are sparse. For New England, especially, there is very little information on agricultural ceremonies. In northern New England maize cultivation seems to have been an irregular and speculative venture, but according to John Gyles's *Captivity* the Malectte were growing maize in the St. Johns Valley about 1686; he described some of the ceremonial life of the people among whom he was a captive, but mentioned nothing comparable to the corn ceremonialism.[166] It seems probable that such festival observances as the green corn ceremony were lacking in the cultures of this area, on the margin of practical maize cultivation. Chamberlain mentioned a Malecite (?) tradition of a green corn

---

[166] Gyles, 1851, p. 83.

dance from the Penobscot of Indian Island, Maine, but it seems probable that the tradition was handed down from a non-Malecite (Iroquois?) source.[167] This is the same area from which the mortar and pestle and other ethnological traits of the maize complex are missing.[168]

The earliest reference to what would appear to be a green corn festival in New England is the Narraganset account of Roger Williams:

> But their chiefest Idoll of all for sport and game, is (if their land be at peace) toward Harvest when they set up a long house called *Qurmekamuck* which signifies *Longhouse,* sometimes a hundred, sometimes two hundred feet long upon a plaine near the Court (which they [7] call *Kittsickanick*) where many thousands, men and women meet, where he that goes in danceth in the sight of all the rest; and is prepared with money, coasts, small breeches, knives, or what he is able to reach to, and gives these things away to the poor, who yet must particularly beg and say, *Cowegustummous*, that is, I beseech you: which word (although there is not one common beggar amongst them) yet they all often use when their richest amongst them would obtain ought by gift.[169]

The other reference to this Narraganset festival reveals little except the date for its observance. In July, 1689 (these dates are old-style), an Indian war was feared in this part of New England, and it was believed that *Ninegrat*, a Narraganset chief, was laying plans for warfare at a series of Indian festivals. In a Hartford, Connecticut, manuscript is a reference to one of these ceremonies:

> Relation of Goodwife Osborn that the war had been planned at the dance at Robin's Town and would be concluded at the great dance at Ninecrafts, which would be held when 'greene Indian corn was high anufe to make their bread of.[170]

The chief was questioned, and the following bit of testimony seems to relate to this festival, indicating the use of a bark-covered structure:

> Hee says hee sent for two Indians named *Cajanottore*, a Narragansett Indian, that now lives at Pocasset, and *Nattawhahore*, formerly a Cononicut Indian, now at Pocasset, because hee knew they were formerly his Indians, and had skill to bark cedar trees and to make bark houses, which he men had not good skill in, and that they had gott the barks, but being disturbed by these troubles had not used them.[171]

In the succeeding testimony are references to the major ceremony at which the English feared the materialization of [8] this plot:

> Hee, being demanded what was the reason for this great dance, replied; it is known to you it is noe unusual thing for us soe to doe; but that it is often used from the time after

---

[167] Chamberlain, 1904, p. 285.
[168] Speck, 1940, pp. 93-94.
[169] Williams, 1827, pp. 146-47.
[170] MS "Indian Papers," I: 17; quotation kindly supplied by Mrs. Eva Butler.
[171] Rhode Island Historical Society Collection, l (1829): 272.

the weeding of our come till such time as wee doe eat of it; and farther said it was a kind of invocation used among them, that they might have a plentiful harvest.[172]

And as to his present making a great dance, hee answered it was knowne to us, that it was noe unusual practice; it being their manner of Invocation in the time of the growing of their corne, until it was neere riped, that they might receive a plentiful harvest.... [173]

It seems probable that similar green corn festivals were known among most tribes of southern New England, but references are scant. We have one older mention of a green corn festival among the Mohegan of eastern Connecticut, and a recent description of a broken-down survival of this ritual. Ezra Stiles {president of Yale} recorded one mention of the Mohegan green corn festival:

Aged Mr. Waterman, born 1708, in 1790 tells me that aet. ten he was present at an Indian Powwaw at Mohegan – and also at New Corn Feast at which last they danced all night – no Sacrifice of Animals.[174]

The Mohegan still preserved some remnant of this ceremony in the first decade of the twentieth century. Frank G. Speck participated in a number of these meetings and has recorded a brief description of the procedure:

There is no doubt, however, that the Mohegan, like most of the Atlantic coast sedentary tribes, had a ceremony to signalize the season of the corn harvest. This ceremony, known widely among other tribes as the Green Corn Dance, has a degraded survival in a modern September festival. The festival is now simply a sort of fair for the benefit of the Indian Church. A suitable time is appointed, and the men proceed to erect a large wigwam as a shelter. An area adjoining the church at least sixty feet square, is covered by this arbor. Crotched chestnut posts are erected in the ground about ten feet apart, and, [9] from one to the other of these, crosspieces are laid, a construction previously described (p. 188). Quantities of green white birch saplings have been cut and are then strewn over the roof quite thickly. The sides are filled and woven in with these also, in such a manner as to make a fairly weather tight enclosure. A portion of the wigwam's side is visible in the background of plate XXXI. For some days before the festival, several men are kept busy pounding up quantities of corn for *yokeg* which the women and children have roasted. Several large mortars are kept exclusively for this purpose, and are the common property of the tribe. The days of the festival are merely the occasion for a general informal gathering of the Indians from far and near, and the sale, for the benefit of the church treasury, of such things as they are able to make. Many articles of Indian manufacture already described are displayed on benches in this wigwam, for sale as souvenirs and articles of utility; while various dishes of food, ancient and modern are made and sold on the grounds. Some other kind of amusement is usually introduced from outside for the three days and an admission price is charged. They also have someone appear in full Indian costume as an added

---

[172] *Ibid,* p. 173.
[173] *Ibid,* p. 277
[174] Stiles, 1916, p. 409.

attraction. The Mohegan make this annual gathering a sort of national holiday. The fact it takes place at the height of the corn season, and that corn products, particularly *yokeg* and *suktac*, play such an important part in it, are clear indications of the early nature of this festival.[175]

Speck has elsewhere published a photograph of the "wigwam" built in 1909 for this occasion[17616] and has personally supplied additional data concerning the structure. It was rectangular, flat-roofed, at least sixty feet long, and built against the church, so that the front wall and one side wall of the church formed parts of two sides of the "wigwam," the whole church being enclosed in the rectangle. The back door of the church opened into this structure, and the other door, on the opposite side of the bower, was overlapped like the entrance to a New England Indian stockade. This building, really a bower longhouse, may be typical of certain ceremonial structures in southern New England, and may have been associated with the green corn festival in some localities.

The proper name for the festival was "wigwam." The women [10] decided when the corn was ripe enough for the "wigwam" to be held. Proceeds from the festival and from the articles sold went to the church, suggesting a transference of the gift association noted by Roger Williams.

One early New York reference, recorded by Daniel Denton in 1670, is from Long Island, an area most closely related ethnically to southern New England. His description is probably from his own observations, but the details are quite vague, and the account shows small understanding:

For their worship which is diabolical, it is performed usually but once or twice a year, unless upon some extraordinary occasion, as upon making war or the like; their usual time is about *Michaelmas,* when their corn is first ripe, the day being appointed by their chief Priest or *pawwaw*; most of them go a hunting for venison: when they are all congregated, their priest tells them if he wants money, their God will accept of no other offering, which the people believing, everyone gives money according to their ability. The priest takes the money, and putting it into some dishes, sets them upon the top of their low flat-roofed houses, and falls to invocating their God to come and receive it, which with a many loud hallows and outcries, knocking the ground with sticks, and beating themselves, is performed by the priest, and seconded by the people.

After they have thus a while wearied themselves, the priest by his conjuration brings in a devil amongst them, in the shape sometimes of a fowl, sometimes of a beast, and sometimes of a man, at which the people being amazed, not daring to stir, he improves the opportunity, steps out, and makes sure of the money, and then returns to lay the spirit, who in the meantime is sometimes gone, and takes some of the company along with him: but if any *English* at such times do come among them, it puts a period to their succeeding, and they will desire their absence, telling them their God will not come whilst they are there.[177]

Earlier students seem to have agreed that the Algonkian tribes of the Hudson River observed a green corn festival. Ruttenber said merely: "The Harvest moon, or the new moon in

---

[175] Speck, 1909a, pp. 194-95.
[176] Speck, 1928, p. 158 (Plate 36).
[177] Denton, 1937, pp. 8-9.

August, they also honored with a feast, in acknowledgement [11] of the product of their fields and their success in the chase.[178]   Alanson Skinner remarked:

> The religion of the Indians was marked by periodic ceremonies, one of which has come down to the present day among the modern remnants of the Shinnecock of Long Island and the Mohegan of Connecticut. This is the June Meeting, which was formerly a ceremony held for the green corn. The Delaware in Oklahoma and Canada still perform a number of other annual ceremonies.[179]

The "June meeting" was held on Long Island, but not in Connecticut.

Nevertheless, there is but slight evidence of such rituals among the tribes of the upper and lower Hudson. Wassenaer, writing about 1624, gave some notes on the Indians of New Netherlands and a brief account of their ceremonialism, apparently including all of the tribes of the Hudson in his description. Especially, he noted the midwinter and green corn festivals: "They allow the succeeding moons to appear without any feasting (that is, since the winter festival); but they celebrate the new August moon by another festival, as their harvest then approaches".[180]

The Delaware and Southeastern Algonkians

THE various dispersed bands of Delaware in Canada, Oklahoma, and other localities have carried on their green corn festivals almost to the present day, but recent accounts are not as thorough as might be desired and are difficult to correlate with earlier historical data. It is often considered that Delaware ceremonialism has been deeply affected by Iroquois influence; yet a better knowledge of the rituals and traditions of both the Lenape and of the peoples of southern New England might demonstrate closer relations between these two areas than between the peoples of either area and the Iroquois. It is believed that available data on green corn ceremonies of the [12] various eastern Algonkian peoples may show such basic similarities. Comparison of the older Lenape data with the recent ethnological data from various Delaware communities may throw light on older practices and also help to explain-some of our New England material.

William Penn, in the summer of 1683, witnessed what was apparently a Lenape festival in Pennsylvania and recorded some details in a published "letter." The whole account is worth quoting:

> Their worship consists of two parts, sacrifice and cantico. Their sacrifice is their first fruits. The first and fattest buck they kill, goeth to the fire, where he is all burnt, with a mournful ditty of him who performeth the ceremony, but with such marvellous fervency and labor of body, that he will even sweat to a foam. The other part is their cantico, performed by round dances, sometimes words, sometimes songs, then shouts; two being in the middle who begin, and by singing and drumming on a board, direct the chorus. Their postures in the dance are very antic and differing, but all keep measure. This is done with equal earnestness and labor, but great appearance of joy. In the fall, when the corn cometh in, they begin to feast one another. There have been two great feastivals already, to which all come that will. I was at one myself. Their entertainment was a great seat by a spring under some shady trees, and twenty bucks, with hot cakes of new

---

[178] Ruttenber, 1872, pp. 28-29.
[179] Skinner, 1915*a*, p. 10.
[180] Wassenaer, 1850, p. 29.

corn, both wheat and beans, which they make up in a square form, in the leaves of the stem, and bake them in the ashes, and after that they fall to dance. But they who go must carry a small present in their money; it may be sixpence, which is made of the bone of a {shell}fish; the black with them is as gold; the white silver; they call it wampum.[181]

Gabriel Thomas, in 1608, said of the Delaware:

They observe new moons, they offer their' first fruits to a Maneto, or suppos'd Deity, whereof they have two, one as they fansie, above (good) another below (bad).[182]

John Brickell, who was carried to Ohio in 1791 by the Delaware and who stayed with them near Sandusky until 1795, [13] indicated that a green corn ceremony preceded the first seasonal use of the new corn:

They have their regular feasts, such as the first corn that is fit to use is made a feast offering; and when they start on a hunting expedition, the first game that is taken they skin and dress whole, breaking not a bone, leaving on the head, ears and hoofs.[183]

John Wampum (Chief Waubuno), writing in the latter part of the nineteenth century, remarked: "They keep annual feasts.. A feast of the first fruits which they do not permit themselves to taste until they have made an offering of them to the *manitu oo al*, or gods.... "[184]

In the major early Delaware sources, usable material on Delaware ritual is surprisingly sparse. Loskiel gave only the most generalized account,[185] and Heckwelder only added some notes to Loskiel's account without clarifying any of it.[186] Zeisberger gave a general account of what would appear to be an artificial synthesis in which he has mixed elements of a number of different rituals, and said: "There are four or five kinds of feasts, the ceremonies of which differ much from one another".[187] His account was incorporated into Loskiel's description of Delaware ritualism.

Loskiel described several types of rituals, only a few of which are tentatively identifiable and spoke in very general terms of feasts, by which he seems to mean nonperiodic feasts given by private households for special purposes. He differentiated sacrifices, which apparently are parts of various rituals, and overlooked the seasonal periodicity of certain rites, the green corn festival and the big house ceremony included, confusing them in his account with other rituals which are nondistinctive. It is well to remember, however, that Loskiel had no direct contact with the Indians he described and had all of his data at second hand, from the accounts of other Moravian missionaries [14] in America. One remark may apply to a corn ceremonial: "To Indian corn they sacrifice bears' flesh, but to deer and bears, Indian corn. "[188]

Heckwelder, despite his many years of residence among these Indians, did not attempt to improve on Loskiel. In view of the confusion in all three of these Moravians' works, it is

---

[181] Penn, 1862, pp. 233-34.
[182] Thomas, 1900, 5:7.
[183] Brickell, 1844, p. 49.
[184] Waubuno, p. 27.
[185] Loskiel, 1794, pp. 33-47.
[186] Heckwelder, 1876, pp. 208-14.
[187] Zeisberger, 1910, p. 137.
[188] Loskiel, 1794, p. 40.

questionable whether they had any but the most superficial knowledge of their Indian parishioners, despite their knowledge of the Delaware language. It is known from early and contemporary sources that the Delaware actually clung to their native religion with the utmost tenacity and that these rituals survived the Moravian missionaries, yet these historians have certainly left a meager record of Delaware ceremonialism. Mrs. Jameson, who visited the Moravian Delaware at Thames, Ontario, Canada (the present Moravian town), about 1835, gave a surprising insight into the actual extent of Christianizatton of these people:

> The Moravian missionary admitted that only a small portion of the tribe under his care and tuition could be called Christians. There were about two hundred and thirty baptized out of seven hundred, principally women and children, and yet the mission had been established and supported for more than a century. Their only chance, he said was with the children; and on my putting the question to him in a direct form, he replied decidedly, that he considered the civilization and conversion of the Indian, *to any great extent,* a hopeless task.[189]

F.G. Speck, in his recent studies of Oklahoma Delaware religion,[190] discovered that the green corn festival (*xaskwi'•mi•' la^akeyɔ'k'an*, "corn ceremony") had not been performed in the lifetime of his informants. Traditional accounts, derived from their parents who had witnessed this observance, make it possible to venture some statements about this ritual. The rite was announced in advance by two masked messengers wearing corn-husk clothing, who rode about demanding a trifling contribution from each person that they met. If refused, [15] they smeared excrement upon the person as a punishment, this preliminary rite being called we 'muiha'lɔwe^es 'excrement daubing"). These messengers were also the dance leaders at the festival which was held a week or so later and at which they used at least two special masks.

The feast itself was opened with an address by a speaker chosen for the occasion and a series of traditional dances for the earlier part of the day. Men's dances led by the masked messengers alternated with women's dances, the leaders of which were not masked. A feast, with corn bread and hominy, followed, and an all-night series of social (mixed) dances concluded the observance.

The use of corn foods, with prayers for the propitiation of the Corn Mother, was emphasized. The dance had to continue until morning. It is said that this ceremony originated in a time when the corn had been offended and had left the people, the green corn ceremony beginning as a device to plead with the Corn Mother for the return of the maize to the people. This ceremony was addressed to the Creator and the Corn Mother, the dances were accompanied by rattles and drums, and the ceremony was held outdoors on a prepared piece of ground.[191]

Alanson Skinner has carelessly equated such rituals as the green corn festival with the big house ritual. After giving a brief outline of the Oklahoma Delaware big house ritual, he said:

> Such are the old-time ceremonies as they are tenaciously preserved by the survivors of the old New York Delawares. Even the degenerate remnant of the Mohegan in Connecticut have a pathetic survival of the olden times in their "Green Corn Dance,"

---

[189] Jameson, 1839, 2: 40.
[190] Speck, 1937, pp. 79-90.
[191] *Ibid,* p. 26 (chart).

which has now become a sort of church fair. The Shinnecocks and the Montauks of Long Island still hold a "June Meeting," which is but a pitiful memory of some ancient ceremony that was no doubt like the annual ceremony of the Delawares.[192]

M.R Harrington, in his extensive study of Oklahoma [16] Delaware ritual, apparently found little evidence of green corn ceremonialism, for he has included no data pertaining to such a festival in his published accounts. According to the protagonist of his book, *Dickon Among the Lenape*:

Green corn time was always a happy time in Lenape land, with much feasting; yet I never saw a public dance to celebrate the occasion, as I hear is the custom among many other tribes. Of each kind of First Fruits, however, a little was offered to the *man-it-to-wuk*, or unseen powers.[193]

Speck, in his recent study of the Munsee-Mahican big house which functioned at Smoothtown, Six Nations Reserve, Ontario, Canada, until about 1850, included a good account of the green corn festival as known from the tradition of his oldest informants. This ceremony was held in the big house and included many of the features noted for the winter big house ceremony. It was held in September, *Xwathkwi•' mkan ki' coX* ("corn beginning to ripen month"):

In the September phase of the new moon, usually late in the period, the Green Corn Ceremony was performed. Lasting for seven days and nights, It was a harvest ceremony in a broad sense with reference to the maturing of beans and other crops as well as corn. Terminating the agricultural activities of the year and being therefore considered as the ritual only second in importance to the Bear Sacrifice Ceremony occurring about six months later, it introduced the hunting season. Its rites included about the same repertoire as the Bear Sacrifice Ceremony, but were distinguished by a substitution of corn-husk false face dancers for the wooden false face dancers of the other. The ceremony, opening with a prayer and sermon by the chief on the afternoon of the first day, began with the dance of the corn-husk mask company. Three men wearing corn-husk masks and naked except for breech-cloth, led by another man without mask but with a long staff, entered each door of the Big House. They converged upon the center-post in crawling motions which "swept" the floor of the sanctuary and purged it from evil influences, especially disease. Each standing in his own place, not circling around, they performed a dance at the center-post. [17]
The second event on the program was another sermon by the chief. Then followed the Men's Dance, the dancers being either naked or in full costume. The mixed dance followed this, then the Woman's Dance. In succession the Nighthawk Dance, the Robin Dance, and the Raccoon Dance followed these. The night's celebration was terminated with a sermon by the chief.
The same order of performance was the rule for seven days and nights. On the last night of the ceremony just before sunrise the women performed a procession around the center-post and left the Big House by the west door. They passed around the south side of the building toward the east door. Here the men are waiting. As they passed the men, they held aloft a cake which was grabbed for by the men until the supply was

---

[192] Skinner, 1915*b*, p. 55.
[193] Harrington, 1938, p. 55.

exhausted. Then all of those who took part entered the Big House through the east door and took their places. The chief of the band gave another sermon, terminating the ceremony.[194]

Several features in this account are worthy of note. The nighthawk dance is probably the equivalent of the widely performed eagle dance, but in no other instance is the eagle dance a part of the green corn ceremony. This is also the only modern account in which the center post is mentioned as utilized in this ritual, but there are parallels in older Creek, Cherokee, and Natchez accounts which will be discussed later. The all-night duration of the dancing and the morning greeting of the sunrise are significant and widely distributed traits which will be discussed later.

The Algonkian tribes of the Virginia area observed some sort of festival when the green corn was mature enough for eating, but there is almost no information about the content or function of such a ritual. John Smith, in 1624, made vague reference to harvest observances:

From September until the midst of November are the chief feasts and sacrifice. Then have they plentie of fruits as well planted as natural, as corne, greene and ripe, fish, fowle, and wilde beastes exceeding fat.[195]

It could not be perceived that they keepe any day as more holy [18] than another: But only in some great distress of want, feare of enemies, trains of triumph and gathering together their fruits, the whole company of men, women, and children come together to solemnities.[196]

Thomas Grover referred to a similar ritualism:

They offer the First fruits of all things; the first *Deer* they kill after they are in season, they lay privately on the head of a Tree near the place where they killed it, and they say, no good luck will befall them that year if they do not offer the first of everything.[197]

Robert Beverley gave a more complete but rather fanciful account of a first fruits ceremony:

They use many Divinations and Enchantments, and frequently offer Burnt Sacrifices to the Evil Spirit. The people annually present their first Fruits of every Season and Kind, namely, of Birds, Beasts, Fish, Fruits, Plants, Roots, and of all other things, which they esteem either of Profit or Pleasure to Themselves. They repeat their Offerings as frequently as they have great success in their Wars, or their Fishing, Fowling or Hunting.[198]

I never could learn that they had any certain time or set days for their Solemnities: but they have appointed Feasts that happen according to the several seasons. They solemnize a day for the plentiful coming of their Wild Fowl, such as Geese, Ducks, Teal, etc. for the returns of their Hunting Seasons, and for the ripening of certain Fruits: but the greatest Annual Feast they have, is at the time of the corn gathering, at which they revel several days together. To these they universally contribute, as they do to the

---

[194] Speck, 1945, p. 31
[195] Smith, 1907 I: 58.
[196] *Ibid*, p. 74.
[197] Grover, 1904, p. 24.
[198] Beverley, 1705, 3: 34.

gathering in the Corn. On this occasion they have their greatest variety of Pastimes, and more especially of their War-Dances, and Heroick Songs; in which they boast that their Corn being now gathered, they have store enough for their Women and Children; and have nothing to do, but to go to War, Travel, and to seek out for New Adventures.[199]

Beverley seems to have been the last observer to record so much as a note on these ceremonies, and thus there is but a mere suggestion of the significance of a green corn festival. FG [19] Speck, in a general account of the culture of the Powhatan tribes, drew some conclusions from the data then available:

In the North Carolina sub-group we have strong indications, from the Illustrations of White, of what is evidently Muskogian influence in the ceremony of the corn harvest (the "busk" of the Creek) with its ceremonial adjuncts, the emetic of "black drink," the scratching rite, and other details. Except that in White's pictures the people of Secotan are seated in a circle instead of in the "square" ground of the southeastern tribes, we might imagine the procedure to be a Muskogean one.[200]

A.H Keane had previously equated White's dance scenes with the Iroquois green corn festival.[201] Unfortunately, there are no features indicated in White's drawings which are diagnostic of any particular ceremony or indicative of any special direction of influence, in the light of present data, and it would seem impossible to decide which, if any, of White's drawings might refer to a green corn ceremony.[202]

Certain traits in the green corn ceremonies of the Algonkian speaking peoples seem significant. First of these is the sacrifice element. In Roger Williams' Narraganset account, presents. of all sorts are given away to the participants; in Denton's Long Island account, wampum is collected and presented, apparently to some deity; in Speck's account of the modern Mohegan meeting, the proceeds from the sale of handicrafts are given to the church; in Penn's Lenape account, wampum is brought as a present to the festival; in Speck's Oklahoma Delaware account, the masked messengers who notify the people demand presents. Nothing is known of the method of disposal of these presents at the green corn festivals, but their use for the ceremonial payment of major participants in the big house ceremony of various Delaware communities has been noted. This sacrifice element is reminiscent of the Iroquois collection of food for the longhouse feasts, of tobacco for the sacrifices, and of wampum and ribbons for the decoration of [20] the sacrificed white dog in the midwinter ceremony, and especially of the wagers for the great bowl game. The ideal of sacrifice is especially noteworthy in the Iroquois bowl game, which is closely associated with the Iroquois green corn festival, but the Algonkian peoples do not seem to have used the dice game in any similar ceremonial association. This sacrifice motif is not recorded for the southeastern Algonkians.

The bark-covered longhouse, best known as an Iroquois ceremonial structure associated with the green corn as well as other festivals, is specifically associated with the Narraganset

---

[199] *Ibid*, p. 43.

[200] Speck, 1924, p. 193.

[201] Keane, in preface to Frobenius, 1909, p. viii.

[202] Three variant sets of these plates were consulted, as follows: Beverley, 1705; White, n.d; and Hariot, 1895.

green corn festival in the accounts both of Roger Williams and of Ninegrat. The survival of the Mohegan ceremonial structure was a longhouse-like bower, perhaps similar to structures associated with various summer ceremonies in other parts of southern New England. The Smoothtown band of Munsee-Mahican held their green corn festival in the big house, but according to Penn's account and Speck's Oklahoma Delaware account the ceremony was held outdoors on a prepared ground. Other writers are silent on this point. Only in Speck's Smoothtown account is there any mention of a centerpost and its function in the Delaware ceremony. The rectangular longhouse seems to be replaced by a rectangular square ground as one goes south, a matter of some significance in the comparison of southeastern ceremonial grounds with the structures of the Northeast. The Shawnee ceremonial structure is described as a rectangular, pine-bark covered structure,[203] but there are no data on green corn ceremonies.

The Iroquois and Delaware ceremonial structures are replete with direction and world symbolism, but no data on this point are extant from New England. The Narraganset longhouse seems to have been specific for the green corn festival and may have carried similar interpretations. It is possible that the Narraganset preserved an older order of things and that the Iroquois and Delaware longhouses originally associated with the green corn festival were later transferred to additional associations. The Delaware structure survived to serve generally [21] for winter ceremonies, and the southeastern square ground may have originally been a house structure.

The Iroquois

AMONG the existing Iroquois groups which preserve a pattern of aboriginal ceremonialism, two rituals are most prominent. The midwinter festival, generally held in late January, marks the beginning of the Iroquois ceremonial and economic year, and the green corn festival, in August, is held when the new corn is first abundantly available. The great significance of these two ceremonies is indicated by the precept of Handsome Lake that all children must be formally given names before the green corn and midwinter festivals, although most of the lone-houses bestow names during these functions. At Allegany Reservation the day before the beginning of the ceremonies is set aside for naming children.[204]

A basic concept of Iroquois ceremonialism is the thanksgiving function of ritual; each ceremonial observance is intended to thank the Creator and his agents for certain phases of the world structure from which all the benefits of man are derived, as a result of his position in this structure and his relationship to all the other members and parts of it. As a secondary objective each ceremony is intended to honor and propitiate both the Creator and specific features of the world which he has set up, thus making more probable the continuation of man's benefit from the proper functioning of the various members and agents of this universe. The midwinter festival marks the beginning of the new Iroquois year. It is a period of meditation and thanksgiving for all the benefits of the previous year, and of prayer for similar blessings in the new year. In this ritual man's essential relationship to the rest of the universe is defined and proclaimed, and whatever strains this relationship has been subjected to in the past year are patched and healed. It is probably due to this concept that such features as the dream guessing and the procedures of medicine societies have become important in this special ceremonial association. [22]

---

[203] Hawkins, 1848, p. 41; 1916, p. 63.
[204] Fenton, 1936, p. 10.

The universality of the midwinter festival is sufficient cause for its position as the most important Iroquois ritual. Flannery's suggestion as to the recency of the great importance of this ceremony is certainly highly conjectural: Apparently the Festival of Dream Fulfillment '(Midwinter Festival)' was so emphasized among the Huron-Iroquois, at the beginning of the 17th century, that the corn festival had faded into the background."[205]

The green corn festival, the culmination of a series of rituals directly concerned with the planting and growth of cultivated crops, is held when the unripe corn is available as food and is primarily concerned with returning thanks for the gifts of agriculture and with prayer and propitiation that this good fortune may extend into the future and that winter will not arrive until crops are in. There seem to be no references to a green corn ceremony prior to the early nineteenth century, unless Lalemant's statements concerning the Huron of the seventeenth century may have been occasioned by such a festival.[206]

Lewis Morgan witnessed this ritual in 1846 and published a good description of it in 1851.[20747] He gave the wrong name for the ceremony, but noted the occurrence of the four sacred ceremonies in the content and discussed the ideological background of the ceremony, noting the significance of the "Three Sisters" (corn, beans, and squash). In the century following Morgan's publication, one finds abundant references to the Iroquois green corn festival but no thorough study of the ceremony until the past decade, when Arthur C. Parker, J.N.B Hewitt, F.G Speck, and William N. Fenton began to study the ceremonial cycles of various Iroquois communities.

Fenton[20848] seems to have first discovered the structural unity of the green corn festival as a recurring part of the midwinter festival and the reappearance of the procedures of a single day of the green corn festival in yet other festivals:

> The Green Corn Festival marks the middle of the year. When [23] the corn is ready to eat, late m August or early September, the Faith-keepers gather the community to the Longhouse to name children born since the Seneca New Year. The festival lasts four mornings until noon, including the preliminary day to name the children. The women's song (*towi'sas*) occurs on the fourth afternoon, after the Bowl Game. Identical in form with the later three days of the midwinter ritual, which are devoted to the Four Sacred Ceremonies, the Green Corn Festival may extend beyond the minimal number of days, before one moiety defeats the other in the bowl game. Then a social dance must be held every evening before the game until it is finished. The Green Corn Festival returns thanks to all the spirit-forces. It is especially for the vegetables and fruits which have ripened during the season. The Creator and his Appointed ones are thanked that the crops planted in spring have reached fruition, and he is remembered for life, health, and sustenance during the past six months. It is hoped that the winter will not be too severe, and will not approach until they have gathered in their crops and have gone hunting.[209]
>
> The Seventh day (of the Midwinter Festival) marks the celebration of the Great Feather Dance, which is the first of four ceremonies left by the Creator for the people to

---

[205] Flannery, 1939, p. 134.

[206] Lalemant, 1898*a*, p. 53; 1898*b*, p. 81.

[207] Morgan, 1851, pp. 196-205.

[208] Fenton, 1936.

[209] *Ibid*, p. 9.

enjoy, and later confirmed by Handsome Lake. Since the ceremonies performed on this day comprise the external form of the Planting, Strawberry, second day of the Green Corn (i.e, first day of the ritual proper, after naming of children), and the Harvest Festivals, I will describe them below in some detail. In brief, they consist of a first Feather Dance for the Faith-keepers, the Women's Dance, an intermission for changing adult names, installing new Faith-keepers, or appointing their moiety reciprocates, which occurs only at the New Year and Green Corn, and the final Great Feather Dance.

The eighth day is identical in form with the third day of the Green Corn. It consists of: a tobacco burning invocation to the Creator, which was once used over the white dog; a rite of personal thanksgiving and singing a Personal Chant (*adõ•wɛ'*), which is the second of the four ceremonies, for chiefs, headmen, Faith-keepers and common gentry, ending with Handsome Lake's version; and the performance of the Thanksgiving Dance, the third ceremony, in which a priest, holding a miniature bow, intersperses the songs with fourteen prayers of thanks to the Creator for the things he prayed for in the tobacco invocation. Coldspring alone celebrates the Personal Chant and [24] Thanksgiving Dance on the same day. The evening is devoted to a social dance, which opens and closes with a brief Feather Dance.... The moieties separate for the bowl game.

The ninth day should terminate the festival if one moiety wins all 102 beans (in the Bowl Game) from its cousins before noon. One moiety is previously selected to represent the Creator, and the game of bowl and counters, which is the fourth ceremony, epitomizes the struggle of the good brother over his evil twin for the control of the earth, as described in the origin legend. The women celebrate their rite (*tõwi'sas*) in the afternoon, giving thanks for the crops and begging for their return in the spring. It corresponds to *adõ•wɛ'* for the men. If the bowl game is not finished on the first morning, as is frequently the case, a social dance is held every evening until someone wins the game on a following morning. That ends the festival. Then all are freed of their responsibilities and sent back to their daily tasks.[210]

Fenton has kindly made available his notes on the green corn festival at Coldspring longhouse, Allegany Reservation, New York, and I give here a synopsis of this ceremony, as performed in 1933 and 1934. The preliminary wampum confession rite is held a week or ten days before the green corn festival, this being the purifying ritual of the Handsome Lake religion. A second wampum confession ritual occurs several days later. At this meeting the date for the green corn festival is announced,[211] and the speakers and officials for the festival are appointed:

The confession rite, which should precede all festivals addressed to the Creator, is an opportunity for the community to prepare itself for the coming celebration and has some claim to antiquity.[212]

The first day of the green corn festival at Allegany is not properly a part of the festival, but is a preliminary day set aside for the naming of children. A general thanksgiving to all the

---

[210] *Ibid*, p. 13.
[211] Fenton, MS*a*.
[212] Fenton, 1936, p. 16.

spirit forces (*ganõ•nyŏk*), a great feather dance for the faithkeepers, the naming of children, the regular great feather dance (*'ostówä'go•wa•*), and a feast are the chief events of this day. [25]

The second day (September 5, 1933; August 28, 1934) is the first day of the green corn festival proper, the first day of the *hẹnondekwe•s* ("gathering the crops"). On this day the preliminary announcements to the people are followed by the announcement of the good health of the settlement, a thanksgiving address (*ganõ'nyŏk*), and the first part of the feather dance for the faithkeepers (similar to that of the first day). This is followed by the women's dance, dedicated to the agricultural plants, the *'ɛskänye'gainõgayõka•'* ("women's dance, old time song"), in which the women carry ears of corn. After this follows the ritual for changing adult names, then the first of the four sacred ceremonies, the great feather dance (*'ostowɛ' go•wa ganonyowáneh*) in costume, and the final announcements, thanks to participants, assignment of the next day's duties, and the feast,[213] concluding about noon:

> The program on this day recurs five times; the seventh day of the Midwinter Festival, the Planting Festival, the Strawberry Festival, the second day of the Green Corn, and the Harvest Festivals. This day exhibits the ritual pattern which underlies all of the Seneca Ceremonies.[214]
>
> The Traditional Women's Dance (*'ɛgsägnye'•gainõgayoka•'*) returns thanks only to the (three) sisters, Our-life-supporters (*dowɛ•'nondɛnonde djõhéhgo*) – the corn, the beans, and the squash – which are on the earth.[215]

The third day begins with the collection of tobacco and food from the various households and with the usual chores at the cookhouse and longhouse. The usual announcements and thanksgivings follow, and the tobacco burning invocation, as described previously, is conducted. Then the men's *adõ•wɛ'* are sung, this being the second sacred ceremony, followed by the thanksgiving dance, *ganeõwo*, the third sacred ceremony. This is followed by the usual thanksgivings and a feast, which is concluded a little after noon. This day's ritual corresponds to that of the eighth day of the midwinter festival.[216] [26]

The personal chant is composed of individual thanksgiving for one's wife, one's family, or the life of a friend, and the singing of one of many songs which are to some extent the property of one family and possibly of the clan. It is the last song sung by a warrior[217] before death:

> The tobacco invocation, formerly over the white dog, is addressed to the Creator. It contains the most elaborate references to the duties of the appointed-ones to the people. It is performed twice a year, but less elaborately in the summer.[218]
>
> The Thanksgiving or Harvest Dance is a costumed dance for men and women, which is interspersed by fourteen thanksgiving chants by a priest, who addresses the several groups of spirit-forces.[219]

---

[213] Fenton, MS*a*.

[214] Fenton, 1936, p. 14.

[215] *Ibid*, p. 17.

[216] Fenton, MS*a*.

[217] Fenton, 1936, p. 16.

[218] *Ibid*, p. 16.

[219] *Ibid*, p. 16.

The ninth day is dedicated to two separate ceremonial observances. The great bowl game is held in the morning, preceded by collection of wagers and must be finished at noon, to be resumed on the following morning[220] if necessary:

> The Great Bowl Game or wager, symbolizes the struggle of the good brother, the Creator, with his evil twin brother for the control of the earth. The town divides spatially into moieties which exchange the role of playing for the Creator from Green Corn to New Year.[221]

In the afternoon the women meet in the longhouse to hold their thanksgiving rite (*tõwi'sas*), which returns thanks to the life supporters (vegetable crops) and is the equivalent of the men's *adõ•wɛ'*. First, the women's songs are sung to the sound of rattles and of broom handles struck on the floor (like pestles). The men interrupt these songs with their *adõ•wɛ'* and then join them in the round dance, now singing for the corn. This day's ritual corresponds exactly with that of the ninth day of the midwinter festival at Allegany.[222] The *tõwi'sas* rite seems to correspond to the linking arms dance, a social dance, and its relationships are discussed later:

The women's song corresponds to the Personal Chant for men, and [27] embraces all the Appointed-ones from food on earth through the middle pantheon to the Creator.[223]

The afternoon of the women's thanksgiving rite is followed by a series of social dances in the evening:

> The Creator's evil brother is credited with social dances, which he intended as his Sacred Ceremonies. Devil Dance (his Feather Dance), Grinding-an-arrow (Harvest Dance), and the Linking-arms Dance, sometimes called Bean (Traditional Women's Dance), were frowned upon by Handsome Lake. The latter was the only dance permitting physical contact between sexes. It is now frequently performed in single file, sometimes using the ancient songs which ridicule a youth's devotion to an older woman with bumps on her forehead.[224]

The social dance equivalents may reflect a more ancient ceremonial usage of the features which Handsome Lake condemned. In particular, the linking-arms dance and the women's thanksgiving rite suggest a Cherokee parallel, the so-called green corn dance, *ani'tikwɔlɛluhuska'hi* ("they have bumps on their foreheads"), which will be discussed elsewhere in this study. The *towi'sas*, according to an origin tale collected by Jeremiah Curtin, was introduced by captives who escaped from the Cherokee.[225]

The green corn ceremony as described for Allegany Reservation may be representative of this Iroquois ceremony, but variations occur in each locality:

---

[220] Fenton, MS*a*.

[221] Fenton, 1936, p. 16.

[222] Fenton, MS*a*.

[223] Fenton, 1936, p. 16.

[224] *Ibid*, p. 18.

[225] Mooney, 1900, pp. 16.

All of the Iroquois longhouses share the Four Sacred Ceremonies. They are: Feather Dance, Personal Chant, the Harvest or Thanksgiving Dance, and the Bowl Game. Nevertheless, the sequence of performances differs from group to group. At Coldspring for the last three days of both the Midwinter and Green Corn Festivals, the order is Feather Dance, Personal Chant, and Harvest Dance on the same day, with the Bowl Game last. Coldspring is alone in celebrating the second and third of the ceremonies on the same day. At Newtown and Plank Road the Feather Dance and Harvest or Thanksgiving Dance come on the same day, at Tonawanda the Personal Chant and the [28] Bowl Game come together on the last day of the New Year Festival, but separately on the third and fourth days of the Green Corn.[226]

The modern Green Corn Dance at Tonawanda longhouse has undergone a change since Morgan's observation (circa 1850). Now, the festival lasts two mornings, and a third night is dedicated to Our-life-supporters since they grow only at night. The Bowl Game and Personal Chant occur on the second morning.[227]

At Newtown longhouse the bowl game occurs on the third day, but the women's thanksgiving rite is held on the afternoon of the following day, with the social dances on the evening of the fourth day.[228]

Despite these local differences, some of which are still evolving, the same major outline seems to underlie the green corn festival and the last three days of the midwinter festival at all of the longhouses for which there is adequate data.[229] The underlying concepts of thanksgiving are dominant everywhere, and the major significance of the green corn festival in the ceremonial cycle of each Iroquois community is apparent. It seems probable that either the green corn festival procedure was incorporated into the midwinter festival and that changes in both have been kept parallel by conscious efforts of the Iroquois, or that the present duplication is the result of a revamping of Iroquois ceremonialism at some time in the past. The green corn festival is a major and integral part of the yearly cycle of ritual observances, and can hardly be considered a recent development. The revelation of Handsome Lake, the Seneca prophet, occurring before 1800, pushed many specific features of less importance out of the ceremonies proper into the associated groups of social dances; this revelation sharply denned ceremonial observances. The influence of the Handsome Lake religion has not been sufficient to suppress entirely the features it condemned, and it seems to have only strengthened the place of the major and central ceremonial features which Handsome Lake respected and upheld. The [29] structural pattern of Iroquois ceremonialism seems to be older than Handsome Lake's influence and is probably a principle which Handsome Lake understood and recommended. It represents an existing functional pattern which he tried to perpetuate, to judge by his precepts regarding the four sacred ceremonies and the various ritual sequences.[230]

The sparsity of material relating to green corn ceremonies from the various Algonkian areas has already been noted, especially in the older and standard historical sources, yet there are sufficient data from those areas to indicate the existence of such rituals. The Iroquois are the

---

[226] Fenton, 1936, p. 21.

[227] *Ibid*, p. 21 (footnote).

[228] Fenton, MS*b*.

[229] Fenton, 1936, 1941, and MSc; Morgan, 1851; Witthoft, 1946a; Parker, 1912; Speck, MS*b*.

[230] Parker, 1913, pp. 40-42; Morgan, 1851, pp. 242-44.

only group in the Northeast for which there is any body of modern ethnological data pertaining to green corn ceremonialism, yet there seems to be nothing In the extensive early literature which refers to such a ceremony. The ethnologist, proceeding only from his data, might conclude that such a ceremony is Iroquoian, and that any remnants of such ritualism among modern Algonkian peoples would be due to Iroquoian influence. The historian might conclude that the Algonkian peoples could have had minor ceremonies devoted to the green corn, but that such rituals were unknown among the Iroquois; if familiar with modern ethnographic material, he would possibly conclude that most of it was a modern fabrication on the part of the Iroquois. It would seem probable that peoples of both stocks had a major ritual concerned with the availability of the new corn and that each group may have evolved specializations in the function and content of this ritual.

Probably not much more will ever be known about it, because the ethnological sources in most of the area are destroyed. A continued study of the whole of Iroquois ceremonialism may sometime permit a more thorough knowledge of one part of this large territory, but progress even in that area will come to a halt with the end of the various Iroquoian communities. From the historian's data one can hope for little knowledge of the actual life of the people; every reference is a mere puzzle to be explained or discarded through observation of the existing [30] ethnic reality. The accounts of early observers, who overlooked what is now known to be the most significant objective aspects of Indian religion, certainly can give no useable picture of aboriginal life; they furnish only footnotes and occasional documentation on the more spectacular incidents which may have attracted their attention. Such material, however, is considered a final check on the field data of the ethnologist; the value of an account is believed to increase with its age; history is considered necessary to give credibility to modern objective accounts. One can gain abundant footnotes from the early accounts, and one can even synthesize them into a sizable description of what appears to be a sketch of a culture, but attempts to study one particular feature as it is noted in the older sources, rather than to collect a hodgepodge of assorted curious details, may soon come to an end because of inadequate data.

An ethnological investigator among any of the existing eastern tribes finds that the clergy, storekeepers, agents, and other white people who are in close contact with Indians actually know and care very little about Indian culture, unless, as rarely occurs, they have also become students of this subject. He prefers to put no faith in their accounts, but classes them as another ethnic factor interesting because of their functions, not because of their knowledge. The so-called "White Cherokee," white people who live with the Eastern Cherokee, who have been raised on a reservation and who often speak Cherokee, are conspicuous examples of persons ignorant of almost everything Indian. The ethnologist, however, is expected to pay lip service to the written accounts of earlier representatives of the whites who stood in similar relationship to Indian cultures, on the general assumption that proximity results in knowledge and culture transference, a misconception to which white neighbors of Indians have always adhered. Anyone who has attempted to understand Iroquoian institutions in terms of both the ethnological picture and the early accounts is probably conscious of the huge gap in understanding and observation between Indian and European cultures. In [31] order to interpret the *Jesuit Relations* properly, one might have to study not only the existing Iroquois communities but also existing Jesuit communities. Then he could accurately weigh and evaluate these authors' knowledge and understanding of the peoples with whom they were acquainted, provided that he also considered the public for whom they wrote, and the distortions and selectivity that were introduced into their writings by the demands of their market. Both historical accounts and ethnographic data should be utilized with some consideration of the shortcomings which may be found in both bodies of information, and with some attention to acculturation and recent culture history.

The Cherokee

THE Cherokee, perhaps more than any other Indian group in the eastern United States, responded to the efforts of the missionary and teacher with a strong desire to become responsible and enlightened participants in the culture of their white neighbors. This hope was frustrated by their forcible removal to the West in 1838, although this incident did not result in a reaction against acculturation. Only the Cherokee who lived farthest from white communities, the so-called "Mountain Indians" seem to have resisted the impact of European culture at all effectively. James Mooney, earliest student of Cherokee ethnology, formed some definite opinions about the destruction of Cherokee culture:

> For many years the hunter and warrior had given place to the farmer and mechanic, and the forced expatriation made the change complete and final. Torn from their native streams and mountains, their council house fires extinguished and their townhouses burned behind them, and transported bodily to a far distant country where everything was new and strange, they were obliged perforce to forego the old life and adjust themselves to changed surroundings. The ball play was neglected and the green-corn dance proscribed, while the heroic tradition of former days became a fading memory or a tale to amuse a child.[231] [32]

Only the "ignorant mountain people" (as they were described by Armstrong, an agent in Indian Territory about 1842)[232] seem to have been able to conserve much of their aboriginal culture, and even these remnants seem to be on the same road their less marginal neighbors had previously chosen. One group, the Cherokee of Qualla Reservation, still remain in their original habitat and constitute the best field for Cherokee ethnography; another, the group noted by Armstrong in Indian Territory, form a conservative group in Oklahoma today. It is not surprising that almost all data on green corn ceremonialism come from the Qualla Reservation, and that data from all available sources vary considerably and give evidence of drastic change in the past two centuries.

Charles Hicks, a mixed blood Cherokee chief of the early nineteenth century, has left a brief notice concerning the Cherokee green corn festival and related observances, written for the Reverend Hoyt of the American Board of Missions in 1817-18 and published in the Raleigh *Register*:

> Before eating the green corn when in the milk, the people collect in the different towns and villages at night, when the – (not understood in Mr. Hicks' original) comes, the conjuror takes some of the grains of seven ears of corn and feeds the fire, i.e. burns them. After this each family is allowed to cook and eat their roasting-ears, but not before they drink a tea of wild horehound. In like manner they observe the same custom before eating the bean when it fills in the hull.
>
> The green corn dance, so called, has been highly esteemed formerly. This is held when the corn is getting hard, and lasts four days, and when the national council sits – a quantity of venison being procured to supply the dance. It is said that a person was formerly chosen to speak to the people on each day in a language that is partly lost – at least

---

[231] Mooney, 1900, p. 146.
[232] Schoolcraft, 1858, 6: 531.

there is very little of it known now. At such times as the above, a piece of land is laid off and persons appointed to occupy it – no others being allowed to use it while the feast continues.[233]

A paraphrase of this account is included in an 1833 mission tract: [33]

Cornelia. Indian conjurers are generally called *medicine men,* and rank next to the chiefs. They are consulted with great ceremony, by all descriptions of persons, and are accounted to be very powerful; formerly, there were annual festivals, in which the conjurers bore a very conspicuous part.

Delia. Please to describe some of their festivals.

Cornelia. They used to have one when the corn was in the milk, before they tasted it; on these occasions, there was a general meeting of all the inhabitants of the district or village, and, after all were assembled, the conjuror took the kernels from seven ears of corn, and after burning them in the fire, with many foolish ceremonies, the whole company were allowed to feast upon *roasted corn,* and eat it in their cabins, after they went home. Before eating the green bean, they go over the same ceremony. When the corn gets hard, they have another frolic called the *green corn dance,* which lasts several days. In March, they used to have a yearly frolic called making *new fire.*[234]

George Foster, Sequoyah's early biographer, has succinctly characterized the green corn festival as known to his Oklahoma Cherokee informants in the 1880's:

The Green Corn Dance was the annual festival, the origin of which is not now known. At this the conjurer prepared a sort of medicine, on a day appointed by the old people, and seven families were appointed to furnish corn for the feast. Every one was obliged to take a portion of the medicine, and a portion was offered, by throwing corn into the fire before any one could eat. Before the feast it was unlawful to eat of the new corn of the season, and no person was ever known to transgress. After that all might eat freely.[235]

James Mooney was present at the last green corn festival to be held on the Qualla Reservation in 1887. He has left a brief notice of this ritual as well as of a surviving part of the rite which he observed in 1913 and 1914 and which is still observed by some families. Unfortunately, he published very little of his data on this ceremony, and his notes relating to this function have not been found among his papers in the archives of the Bureau of American Ethnology: [34]

By special permission of some of the Indian priests Mr. Mooney was able to be present for the second time at the family ceremony of invoking the blessing upon the new corn and on those about to partake of it for the first time. This ceremony, probably never witnessed by another white man, is still strictly observed in private at their homes by most of the full-blood families before tasting the new corn of the season, the priests who conduct the rite going, while yet fasting, from house to house through the settlement for that purpose. The so-called Green Corn Dance, the great tribal

---

[233] Hicks, 1818.

[234] Tuttle, 1833, pp. 147-48.

[235] Froste, 1885, pp. 57-58.

celebration of thanksgiving for the new corn, was last performed in 1887, on which occasion Mr. Mooney was also present.[236]

Opportunity was also afforded for special studies and observations, particularly of the ceremonial "going to water," and augury with the beads to forecast the health prospect and lifespan of each member of the family, before partaking of the first corn of the new crop.[237]

Swimmer, one of Mooney's chief ~~informants~~, wrote out the words of at least some of the songs and of one speech for the green corn festival in 1887. This manuscript is still preserved, but not transcribed and translated, in the archives of the Bureau of American Ethnology.[238] Part of the content of this ritual is doubtless missing. An attempt to interpret the manuscript with Cherokee informants failed, as these forms of the songs were unknown to them, and they felt that this lack of knowledge reflected on their dependability; however, the general contents of the manuscripts were outlined with the help of Will West Long, of the Big Cove. The sequence, is as follows:

I. An address of a chief to the people at a preliminary feast seven days before the green corn festival, setting the date and admonishing the people not to be drunk, to behave themselves, and not to interfere with others at the festival.

II. A series of sixteen songs called *ani'tikwɔlɛluhuska'hi* ("they have bulging foreheads"). [35]

III. A series of five *wili'sa* songs. This is the men's dance.

IV. A series of eight *i•tsq* ("meal") songs. This is the women's dance.

V. A series of *gana'hiya'a'* along the trail") songs. According to Will West Long, guns are fired in this dance.

VI. A series of social and animal dances, as follows: friendship dance (*ayɛ•lulehi'* and *dilsti'*), buffalo dance, raccoon dance, pheasant dance, hog dance, corn dance, and running dance. Two bear dance songs and a medicine dance song are also included, but they doubtless pertain to other rituals, as may some of the other animal dances.

Will West Long, of Big Cove, dance leader and authority on Cherokee tradition, was familiar with the current green corn feast, and he functioned as a leader on occasions when its performance was required. He had not seen the periodic green corn festival. Drawing on information which he received from his mother, and from his older brother, however, he was able to supply some information about this extinct ceremony.

Will West Long's information revealed that this green corn festival was held the day and night before the first corn was to be eaten. A medicine was first prepared, and an emetic was drunk by everyone present, followed by "going to water."[239] Then the medicine was administered to all who were present at the ceremony. A formula may have accompanied the

---

[236] Explorations, Smithsonian Institution, 1914, pp. 72-73.

[237] *Ibid.,* 1913, p. 64.

[238] Mooney, MS*b*.

[239] The "going to water" ordeal is an important item in Cherokee ritual. The purifying nature of the river was resorted to as a cleansing and protective symbol at almost any crisis in the life of the Cherokee individual or community. This formalized ceremonial bathing in the water of the river became an integral part of many ceremonial and curative procedures.

going to water,[240] but no formula was required as an accompaniment to the medicine that followed.[241] Then a series of animal and [36] social dances lasted all night. This dance series seems to have been the same as that in the modern green corn feast used for curative purposes, described by Speck and discussed hereinafter.

In the morning the conjuror who served as dance leader took all the people "to water" again and then examined each person with the beads and cloth to see whether they would live until the next year's green corn festival. In this form of divination the conjuror places two beads (glass beads were used in recent time, but these were said to have replaced seeds of *Lithospermum*, uni•sko "–" heads"), one black and one red or white, on a piece of white cloth, the red (or white) bead to the conjuror's right. The cloth is provided by the person being examined and is given to the conjuror as a token payment. The conjuror then speaks to the beads after a fixed formula, asking first the red bead if the person is to live until the next year, and then asking the black bead the same question. If the red bead moves by itself, the person is expected to survive the year, and if the black bead moves, the patient will not live the year out.[242]

In case the divination indicated that someone would not live that long, a similar green corn feast was held at night. Dances [37] were held and no person was allowed to sleep. The proper formulas were recited by the conjuror, and further divination by the beads was tried until it was found that the person would live. Then that person's life was believed to be secure until the next year.

Will West Long's brother, who died in 1904, was a leader at those ceremonies. According to Will, he once examined a girl with the beads under such circumstances, and he found that she would not live until the following summer. He attempted to arrange the feast which would prolong her life until the next year, but her family would not co-operate by providing a feast and helping with the ceremony. Therefore, it could not be held, and the girl died the following winter.

It is probably this secondary phase of the ceremony that has survived as a curative feature in association with certain forms of diagnoses and therapy. When one considers that among the central features of the green corn festivals of the Cherokee and Creek, as recorded by the earlier

---

[240] Mooney and Olbrechts (1932, pp. 232-34) gave a formula like that used in this connection and (pp. 289-91) a formula used when "going to water" on the following morning.

[241] Cherokee medicinal practice and certain phases of Cherokee ritual depended in part on traditional spoken charms, called prayers and formulas by the Cherokee. These are memorized, must be spoken very exactly, and are the property of a semiprofessional "conjurer" class. These formulas have been [36] written in the syllabary invented by Sequoyah (also spelled Sequoya) about 1820, and some are no longer understandable because of the archaic forms preserved in them. It is probably the ritual language of these formulas to which Hicks refers as a forgotten language in the account previously quoted.
For a thorough study of Cherokee formulas and their function, see Mooney and Olbrechts, 1932.

[242] Divination seems to have been an important feature in Cherokee culture; it may even once have constituted a distinct profession. The observation of the motion of suspended magical stones and, more important, of beads laid on cloth or held between thumb and forefinger was resorted to in the foretelling of death, the diagnosis of disease, the finding of lost and stolen objects, and the discovery of the identity of a witch or conjuror responsible for magically caused disease, to mention but a few of the more important uses of these divination devices. Different formalized procedures were resorted to for different purposes, and in some cases even bits of roots or twigs were employed instead of beads.

observers, the expiation of crime and the beginning anew of all phases of tribal life attracted much attention, the curative features of these ceremonies may also have been of great significance In aboriginal times.[243]

Some published notes of Mooney's contain traditions that relate to a period prior to the festival he observed:

> Just before the Green-corn dance, in the old times, every fire in the settlement was extinguished and all the people came and got new fire from the townhouse. This was called *atsi'la galûnkw'ti'yu,* "the honored or sacred fire."[244]

> Some say this everlasting fire was only in the larger mounds at Nikwasi, Kitn'hwa, and a few other towns, and that when the new fire was thus drawn up for the Green-corn dance, It was distributed from them to the other settlements.[245]

> From conversation with old Cherokee it seems probable that In cases where no satisfaction was made by the relatives of the [38] man-slayer, he continued to reside close within the limits of the town until the next recurrence of the annual Green-corn dance, when a general amnesty was proclaimed.[246] (Mooney here describes Chota as a peace and refuge town.)

> At daybreak the whole party went down to the running stream, where the pupils or hearers of the myths stripped themselves, and were scratched upon their naked skin with a bone-tooth comb in the hands of the priest, after which they waded out, facing the rising sun, and dipped seven times under the water, while the priest recited prayers upon the bank. This purificatory rite, observed more than a century ago by Adair, is also a part of the ceremonial of the ballplay, the Green-corn dance, and in fact, every important ritual performance.[247]

Frank G. Speck, during the course of his extensive study of surviving Cherokee dances, observed and described a modern green corn ceremony still in existence in the Big Cove community of Qualla Reservation.[248] This ceremony, however, is not held at any fixed time and seems to have lost all connection with the cycle of the agricultural year. It is performed for curative purposes and for spiritual benefit at whatever time in the summer it may be needed by persons desiring spiritual help. The performance is accompanied by a feast provided by the patients or sponsors and their families. Apparently, one sequence of the old agricultural festival has continued its existence after the passing of the green corn festival, and has come into new associations, perhaps long before the major, fixed ceremony had been discontinued.

This ritual, as described by Speck from the account of several Big Cove informants, lasted a day and the following night. It is sponsored by some individual who feels a need for giving it in order to achieve some spiritual benefit and to avert or remedy poor health. Its additional functions are the prevention of illness resulting from eating green corn and the stimulation of the growth and bearing of the corn crop; it is allegorical of the men's and women's

---

[243] Witthoft, 1946*b*, p. 115.

[244] Mooney, 1906, p. 396.

[245] *Ibid.*

[246] *Ibid*, p. 207.

[247] *Ibid*, p. 230.

[248] Speck, MS*a*.

roles in Cherokee culture. The [39] benefits of the ritual accrue to all who participate, but especially to the sponsors, and everyone around is invited to the ritual and to the feast accompanying it. There are no restrictions as to the foods which may be eaten during the ceremony.

The ceremony, consisting of both men's and women's parts which occur simultaneously and blend in certain parts of the procedure, is divided into four portions or stages. The first part, with some variations, consists of the men's dance (*uli'si*), which is held at a distance from the main dancing ground, and guns are fired. The women's dance (•łsy, "meal") is meantime held in the center of the main dance ground, with several different dance movements. Leg rattles are worn by the leader. The men sing responses to some of the women's songs. These two sets of dances continue simultaneously until afternoon, when the men's dance line surrounds the women's line and merges with it. The second stage is a feast provided by the women of the sponsoring group.

The third portion of the ritual occurs just before sundown. Men and women first dance separately, then, still carrying guns, the men surround the women's group and mingle with them, dancing to gourd rattles and the leg rattles of the woman leader, who is now in charge, until the sun has set (*gɑnɑ'ni'•*, "along the trail," is the name of the mixed stage of the dance).

The entire night is then spent in social and animal dances, starting with the friendship dance (in which men and women alternate), and concluding with the round dance (running dance), which, however, is preceded by the corn dance (*sɛlu ulsk'ita'*, "corn dance"). The other dances which might be performed were beaver dance, buffalo dance, pigeon dance, chicken dance, partridge ("pheasant") dance, ground hog dance, horse dance, knee-deep (small frog) dance, ant dance, raccoon dance, and gizzard (bird) dance. These animal dances are all somehow concerned with the placation of animal spirits and are said to have been learned from the mythical Stonecoat monster and culture-hero (a possible parallel to the Iroquois tradition of the origin of social dances from the Creator's [40] evil-minded twin brother, "Flint"), Stonecoats are also prominent in the Iroquois literature.

Speck's informants called the green corn dance (the surviving green corn ceremony?) *akɔhadi* (literally "big foreheads in, motion") and reported a tradition that the ceremony was named after a group of Cherokee called *di•ni•kɔhįnɑ"* ("big foreheads projecting out"), who were most devout in performing this ceremony and who practiced head deformation, hence their name.[249] Mooney, in a manuscript of the 1880's, called the green corn dance *a'năgahųskų•ĭ*.[250] If Will West Long's translations of the names of the dance songs of the 1887 manuscript are correct, a specific set of dance songs for the green corn festival bore a similar name. It was previously noted that a Seneca social dance, the bean or linking-arms dance, which is traditionally the evil twin brother's version of the Creator's traditional women's dance (*towi•'sas*), specifically dedicated to corn, beans, and squash, tells of a young man's infatuation with an older woman who has bumps on her forehead. Other curious parallels, occurring in equivalent ceremonies in both groups, are extremely puzzling. More recent field studies of Allegany Seneca ceremonies by Merle H Deardorff, of Warren, Pennsylvania, indicate that this dance (*wen ontowtsas*) and its equivalent ritual performance are considered non-Iroquois in origin by Seneca informants and may represent the vestiges of an introduced ritual which has been added to the end of the Seneca green corn festival. The movements and the interplay of men's and women's parts, as described to me by Deardorff, suggest that the green corn ceremonies of the Southeast may show close relationship to this Iroquois ritual, which the Allegany Seneca consider a distinct

---

[249] *Ibid.*
[250] Mooney, MS*b*.

rite. It is possible that this particular sequence was introduced among the Iroquois by adopted captives from the Cherokee country in the seventeenth or eighteenth century.[251] [41]

Jeremiah Curtin's Seneca origin story for the *tonwi'sas* rite tells of its introduction by two women who had been captured by the Cherokee and later escaped. They received supernatural aid during their escape and return home and received the songs in a vision while fleeing from the Cherokee.[252]

The only early account of Cherokee ceremonialism, made by John Howard Payne and David Buttrick about 1835, is preserved in the Newberry Library, Chicago,[253] but I have not yet had access to this material and must depend upon the published fragments until such time as I may be in Chicago. Unfortunately, these published fragments show very little correlation with the other Cherokee data, and in some ways suggest a Creek ceremonial cycle. Buttrick was for many years a missionary in the town of Chickamauga, which was a mixed community of Cherokee, Creek, Shawnee, and other peoples. It is possible that here the Cherokee, already losing the knowledge of their own ceremonial complex, adopted many Creek traits from their neighbors, or even that the ceremonies Buttrick described had taken on an international character.

E.G Squier had access to these manuscripts about 1860, and reprinted parts in his appendix to Bartram's observations. More recently, W.H Gilbert utilized the original manuscripts while engaged in field work among the Qualla Cherokee and published paraphrased parts of these manuscripts with some additional field notes. The parallel published extracts from the Payne manuscript follow:

2d *Sah-looh stuknee, keel-steh-steeh*; a preliminary or new green-corn feast, held when the young corn first became fit to taste.

3d *Tung-noh-kaw-hoough-ni*; mature or ripe green-corn festival, which succeeded the other in some 40 or 50 days, when the corn had become hard and perfect.[254]

2. The preliminary Green Corn Feast. – This is entitled *sah-lookstiknee keehstehsteeh* in the Payne Manuscripts and rendered *selu* [42] *tsunistigistiyi*, or "roasting ears" time, by present day ~~informants~~. It was held in August when the young corn first became fit to taste.

3. The Green Corn Feast – This is called *tungnahkawhooghn*i in the Payne Manuscripts and is rendered *donagohuni* by present day ~~informants~~. The ripe or mature Green Corn Feast succeeded the Preliminary Green Corn Feast of August in about 40 or 50 days in the middle or latter September when the corn had become hard or perfect and is still held.[255]

The name of the preliminary feast, as used by Payne and Gilbert, may possibly refer to the green corn medicine ritual which I have described and which Mooney witnessed in 1913 and 1914. (This ritual will be discussed hereinafter.) Gilbert's name for the main feast would appear to be *di•ni•kɔhɛnǫ*,"("big foreheads projecting out"), the modern corn ceremony which Speck has described and which I have previously discussed.

---

[251] I am indebted to Mr. Deardorff for the use of his notes and for many helpful suggestions concerning various phases of Iroquois ethnology.

[252] Mooney, 1900, pp. 365-67.

[253] Payne, MS.

[254] Bartram, 1853, p. 74 (footnote by E.G Squier).

[255] Gilbert, 1943, pp. 326-27.

Squier also reprinted a part of the Payne material describing the preliminary feast; this is included in Gilbert's reproduction of Payne's account, which is here presented:

> The second great festival, the Preliminary New Green Corn Feast, was held in midsummer and at the time of the simultaneous ripening of the corn, or maize, throughout the nation. When the corn was found ripe, a messenger was despatched to gather seven ears, bring them back to the counselors, and assemble the people. A 6-day hunt was decreed for the hunters and the seven prime counselors fasted for 6 days at the national heptagon. When the hunters had shot the first buck, they cut a small piece from the right side of the end of the tongue. On the evening of the sixth day, the populace assembled at the national heptagon bringing in fresh ears of corn while the hunters brought in fresh meat. This night was spent in an all-night vigil and religious dance. On the seventh day, the festival began with the delivery of the seven ears of corn to the *uku*. New fire was made by a fire-maker on the alter from bark of seven selected trees. Leaves of old tobacco were sprinkled on the fire and omens were taken from this. The *uku* placed the seven ears in the fire also with the piece of deer's tongue and then prayed that the sacrifice might be acceptable. After this rite the *uku* and his seven counselors fasted for seven more days [43] and the populace then assembled for another general day fast which completed the second festival.
>
> The third great feast was the Mature, or Ripe Green Corn Feast, and was held in September 40 or 50 days after the preceding festival. First, the seven counselors summoned the honorable women for a religious dance and then fixed the festival for some time later. The usual pattern of behavior occurred, the hunters being sent out and special officers appointed to order the festival. An arbor of green boughs was framed in the sacred square of the national heptagon wherein a beautiful shade tree was located. A large booth was erected and seats laid out. On the evening prior to the festival day, the hunters and the people assembled and everyone took a green bough for the rites of the next day. All then retired early. On the ensuing noon the people paraded with green boughs held overhead. The *uku* who presided at this rite was given the special ceremonial title of *Netagunghstah* and was elevated on a platform held up by carriers and was dressed in a white robe with leggings, moccasins, otter skins on the legs, and a red cap on the head. Altogether this festival lasted 4 days and women were excluded from the sacred square during the dances. In the evenings they might mingle in the social dances, however. This festival was the most deeply rooted rite that the Cherokees had and lasted the longest. It is said to have been connected at one time with a festival of green boughs which was more distinctive and exclusive in its characteristics.[256]
>
> The two Green Corn Feasts resemble each other and both were concerned with the ripening and harvesting of the corn and the rite of eating it. The details of these rites do not seem to have been well recorded but there was some fasting before the ceremonial partaking in the new corn.[257]
>
> In the capital town of the tribe there was a national council consisting of the *uku*, his town attendants together with the white chiefs of the lower towns and their attendants.

---

[256] *Ibid*, pp. 329-30.
[257] *Ibid*, p. 326.

This national council was convened by the newly elected *uku* before a Green Corn Feast, and on emergency occasions, through the raising the *uku*'s standard; ... [258]

The two festivals described here may represent a preliminary feast given when the corn is first eaten, and a later one when the green corn is abundant. Hicks's brief sketch, previously [44] quoted, would suggest such a division, and there is some modern evidence of a similar first corn observance and later major celebration. Data derived from Will West Long, however, might indicate a recent splitting up of an older festival equivalent to the Creek ceremony, hereinafter discussed, into several parts in the process of disintegration of Cherokee culture, as I have suggested elsewhere:

> ... it appears that the Cherokee in aboriginal times celebrated a major community festival when the green corn first became mature enough to eat; this festival persisted, probably in an abbreviated form as late as 1887. Portions of this ritual became separated from the obsolescent Green Corn Festival and at present are found as two separate survivals, a Green Corn Feast held for curative purposes whenever it may be required and a Green Corn Medicine, which is prepared in the separate households of the more conservative Cherokee and administered to all members of the family as a prerequisite to eating the green corn. Continued adherence to this medicine ritual indicates the strong conservatism of a certain minority of "full-blood" Cherokee households.[259]

The green corn medicine, referred to above, possibly the survival of Payne's preliminary festival, is still observed by some of the Qualla Cherokee. The following account of this medicine is extracted, with some additions, from my previous article on this ritual.[260]

At present, In addition to the green corn feast, which is performed when required, the Cherokee has also preserved one other fragment of extreme importance. This is the green corn medicine, called both *sɛ•lu' djwa'nigę'•i da•nisdi' gisgą' n'i* ("corn soft, for they are eating") and *sɛ•lu'itsehi'danisdi' gi•sgą'n'i* ("corn, new or green, for they are eating"). Mooney's data on the 1913 observance, already quoted, would indicate that other features had survived as a part of the family ceremony until at least that date.

This green corn medicine, according to tradition, was a feature of the green corn festival and is probably represented in Hicks's account by the reference to "wild horehound". It is [45] now no longer preceded by a purge, however, and is made and administered by the head of each household to his family; it is an individual, not a community function, and is performed whenever the family's green corn is ready to eat. According to Mollie Sequoyah, of the Big Cove, it is intended to prevent colic caused by eating corn, the primary food resource of the Cherokee, and one which is much relished. The people have been unaccustomed to eating green corn since the previous year, and its latency for harm or benefit is believed to be strong. Children especially require prophylactic treatment to avert sickness resulting from the first seasonal use of corn. Will West Long stated that it is intended to prevent the increase of stomach and intestinal worms, which otherwise would flourish on this choice food and do great damage to the person so rash as to eat of it without the medicinal preparative. None of the really conservative Indians of the Big Cove settlement would even taste green corn if they had not

---

[258] *Ibid,* p. 323.
[259] Witthoft, 1946*b*, p. 219.
[260] *Ibid.*

previously partaken of the medicine. I have seen Will look wistfully at "roasting ears" on the table of a neighbor with whom he was dining, but refuse the corn because his was not ready and he had not taken the medicine. Under similar circumstances, Mollie decided that she could eat the corn only because it was not a variety grown by the Indians, but "white man's corn," and so did not require this preventive measure.

The use of this medicine to inhibit the growth of parasitic worms from corn is not unparalleled, for Bartram noted a somewhat comparable prophylaxis for the same cause of illness among the Creeks:

> The hooping cough is fatal among their children, and worms very frequent. But (besides their well-known remedy, *spigelia anthelmentica*), to prevent the troublesome and fatal effects of this disease, they use a strong *lixivium* prepared from ashes of green stalks of beans and other vegetables, in all their food prepared from corn *(zea)*, which otherwise, they say, breeds worms in their stomachs.[261] [46]

The medicine itself is made up of the leaves of four or more different plants. Apparently, the recipe varies somewhat from family to family, but I do not have sufficient data to indicate how great the differences may be. These leaves are crushed in the hands, pounded together in the mortar used to crush corn into meal, and then steeped in warm water. The solution is drunk by all the members of the family. Then they are free to eat the unripe corn for the remainder of the season.

The plant ingredients used by Will West Long are listed in Table I. The use of the first three plants is obligatory, and any one of the remainder may be used as the fourth Ingredient, the others being added if available. Will West Long explains that these plants are rampant cornfield weeds and are thus, he supposes, able to overcome the generative power of the corn Imparted to the worms. The volunteer corn and the plant "resembling corn," are used because they appear to be dwarfed and weakly plants of the same sort as corn. Any other cornfield weed leaves may be added to the medicine if the preparator so desires. A vermifuge, such as *Artemesia,* might be as good, the informant suggests, but is not used in this association.

The medicine as prepared by Mollie Sequoyah consists of the leaves of four plants, used in exactly the same fashion. This medicine is required to prevent colic, which would plague anyone eating the new green corn without previously taking the medicine. It is especially necessary for children. The ingredients are as follows: *galų⁺•na'* ("gourd"), *sɛ•lu'kwoyα'* ("bearded wheat grass"), *walelu'unig'egtsti'* ("Jewelweed"), and *u•wαgα'* ("volunteer corn").

There are several observances in force concerning the eating of the unripe corn. The corn is the gift of a culture heroine, whose name is *sɛ•lu'*, the same name as that applied to corn, and the corn came from her body. These rules for treatment of the green corn and their explanation, as offered by Mollie Sequoyah, have their basis in the myth of the origin of corn, as do some of the features of the green corn festival.

One must not blow on a roasted ear of green corn in order to cool it, for this would cause a thunderstorm. The Thunders are the sons and husband of *sɛ•lu'*, the Corn Mother, and would [48] resent such disrespectful treatment of her. After the green corn has been eaten, the cobs must be kept in the house for four days, because *sɛ•lu's* body lay outdoors on the ground for that length of time after she had been killed by her son. The all-night dancing and wakefulness of the green

---

[261] Bartram, 1853, p. 43. Swanton (1928*a*, pp. 553, 608) mentioned use of vermifuges at Creek green corn ceremonies.

corn festival are the observation of the original admonition that they should stay awake all night and dance, so that the corn would grow and mature overnight. Seneca informants also told me that corn and other crops grow at night.

According to Will West Long, a medicine of the steeped leaves of the hog peanut, *Apios tuberosa* L. (*tuya'^{i}yusti'*, "like a bean"), was drunk in the usual manner before the first green beans were eaten, but this medicine was last used in the Big Cove about 1890. Hicks's account, previously quoted, mentions this medicine. The Creeks of *Cowassawday* also held some festival at this time.[262] [47]

TABLE I

CONTENTS OF THE CHEROKEE GREEN CORN MEDICINE

Indian Name	Translation	English Name	Latin Name
se·lu'kwo·ya'*	"Resembling corn"	Bearded wheat grass	*Apopyron caninum* (L.) R. & S.
		Adam's needle	*Yucca filamentosa* L.†
tol^{i}'diy'usti'	"Sticks on you, like"	Spiny amaranth	*Amaranthus spinosus* L.
awosą·ul'si'yenehi'	"Itself splitting or growing leaves"	Volunteer corn‡	*Zea mays* L.
unighis'o gohast'i'		Wild lettuce	*Lactuca biflora* Walt.
walelu'unig''legisti'	"Humming bird, taking sap out of flower"	Jewelweed	*Impatens biflora* Walt.§
galu^{t}na'		Gourd‖	*Cucurbita lagenaria* L.
wat'ska'		Green amaranth	*Amaranthus retroflexus* L.
ųgwas'ta'lu^{ya}da'		Ragweed	*Ambrosia trifida* L.
ųnistelę^{ye}sti'¶	"Sticking on"	Wild comfrey	*Cynoglossum virginianum* L.
nistelę'·histi'	"Sticking out"	Ragweed	*Ambrosia elatior* L.
^{d}ʐi^{d}ʐiyusti'	"Thistle like"		Not identified
uni'^{d}ʐi^{d}ʐi.igo^{hu}s'di'	"They are thistles scattering all over"		Not identified

* This name is used for both of the plants here listed, and either may be used in this medicine.

† According to Will West Long, the roots and leaves of the yucca are also soaked in warm water, and the potion drunk as a medicine for "sugar diabetes."

‡ This is merely corn that has seeded itself in a pasture or fallow field.

§ Leaves and flowers of this plant are also used, according to Mollie Sequoyah, as one ingredient in a tea that is given to a woman in childbirth to "make the child come quickly"; it is so used because of the explosive way in which the seeds fly out o their pods.

‖ According to Mollie Sequoyah, gourd seeds are mashed and soaked in hot water, and the potion is drunk to cure inability to urinate. This is probably related to the white peoples' use of pumpkin seed for the same purpose.

¶ This name is the general Cherokee term for bur-bearing plants, but the plant specimen was collected with the informant (as also in other cases). This plant is used as one ingredient in several compound medicines recorded by Mooney and Olbrechts, 1932, pp. 119, 174.

According to Moses Owl, and Jimsie and Takwat Wallace, of Birdtown (another community of Qualla Reservation), the green corn festival and the green corn medicine have not been used at Birdtown in the last century. The recipe for the medicine is lost, but it is said that it included cornstalks and the leaves of the barren strawberry, *Waldstemia* (*antą^{i}yusti'*, "like a strawberry"), and was drunk before the green corn festival.

Moses Owl offered some information that he had obtained from his grandmother, who had attended green corn festivals at Governor's Island, North Carolina, prior to the removal (1838). These ceremonies were held at or near the mound on the Ferguson Farm at Governor's Island and were attended not only by Cherokee but also by Creek and other Indians. One festival culminated in a vicious brawl between Creek and Cherokee participants. In this account earth was carried to the dance ground and spread on a rectangular area, and Moses supposed I that the mound had been built up by such accumulations. He has heard that only persons who died during the green corn festival were buried in this mound.

The carrying in of fresh earth to cover the ceremonial ground [49] is typical of the Creek ceremony, but is not noted for Cherokee. Bartram saw no such prepared squares in use in the Cherokee country, whereas they were abundant in the Creek territories.[263]

---

262 Swanton, 1928*a*, p. 568.

263 Bartram, 1853, p. 36.

The Cherokee green corn festival, as known from recent accounts, has survived as two rituals. A preliminary ceremony concerned with the prevention of illness which may result from eating green corn, is followed by a major ceremony intended to propitiate the corn and to be allegorical of the functions of men and women in Cherokee cultural life. There is some evidence from modern ethnology that these two ceremonial procedures were originally parts of one festival, but their separate observances are noted in the earlier accounts. The modern preliminary ritual consists mainly of the administration of an herb medicine; in Payne's account both green corn ceremonies are very similar in content. The preliminary ceremony shows some resemblance to the busk (the green corn ceremony of the Creeks). Later phases of the busk resemble somewhat the Cherokee second green corn festival. The parallels will be indicated in the discussion of the Creek ritual.

Certain features of the Cherokee ceremonies may be noted as distinctive. The attention in the ritual to the number seven, symbolic of the seven Cherokee clans, is noteworthy in Payne's description. The townhouse was seven-sided, the preliminary festival lasted seven days, seven ears of corn were sacrificed, and the fast was of seven days' duration. The square ground is described,[264] and Gilbert's summary indicates that an arbor of green boughs was included in this square, and possibly a tree. The division between sacred and social dances is noted. In later accounts these features are not recorded, and very little correlation exists between Payne's account and the modern observations; Hicks's and Foster's accounts check better with modern data than does Payne's account. A seven-sided ceremonial ground has been noted for several Oklahoma Cherokee communities, but I have no information on the associated [50] ceremonies.[265] More data from both historic and living sources of information would no doubt bridge the spaces between Payne's data and recent North Carolina Cherokee observations.

The Southeastern Siouan Tribes

ALTHOUGH the southeastern Siouan-speaking peoples may quite possibly have stressed ceremonial observances concerned with various phases of an agricultural year-cycle, there is little evidence of the existence of maize ceremonies among these tribes, either from the sparse historical material or from the surviving Catawba. Lawson has left two references which merely suggest the possibility of a green corn ritual. In his journal under an entry made between September 15 and November 17, 1700, he mentioned a Waxsaw ceremony:

> It happened to be one of their great Feasts, when we were there: ... This feast was held In commemoration of the plentiful Harvest of Corn they had reaped the summer before, with an united Supplication for like plentiful Produce the Year ensuing.[266]

This would appear to have been a harvest festival, but this Is the only certain reference to any maize ceremonialism among these people. If a green corn ritual were also observed, no evidence of it now exists. Another note of Lawson's may refer to either some group of Siouan or

---

[264] Squier (1851, pp. 239-40) quoted Payne's description of the Cherokee townhouse and square ground.

[265] Swanton, 1928*a*, p. 603.

[266] Lawson, 1714, p. 36.

Algonktan peoples of the Carolinas, or perhaps to the Tuscarora; it may represent a generalization derived from all of the tribes of this area. It possibly refers to a harvest festival: They have a third of Feasts and Dances, which are always when the Harvest of Corn is ended, and in the Spring. The one, to return Thanks to the good Spirit, for the Fruits of the Earth; the other, to beg the same Blessings for the succeeding Year.[267]

The only data from the surviving remnants of the southeastern Siouans comes from the Tutelo descendants of Six Nation's Reserve, Ontario, Canada, where Speck recorded some [51] ethnological data on Tutelo rituals and recorded songs associated with a harvest ritual.[268] Whether this observance represents a green corn or harvest festival, or both, is not certain. The ritual lasted for four nights and included the following dance songs:

Four nights songs. These have been adopted by the Cayuga, Onondaga, and Seneca longhouses as social dances and are known as the four nights songs.[269]

Bean dance. This has been adopted by the Sour Spring Cayuga, and seems to be the same dance as the bean dance or linking-arms dance among the Coldspring Seneca, discussed earlier.

Feather dance. This is apparently a Tutelo adoption of one of the four sacred ceremonies of the Iroquois, with Tutelo songs.

Adōnwa'. This is another of the Iroquois sacred ceremonies, adopted by the Tutelo and fitted out with songs in the Tutelo language.

This ceremony, held in October when all the crops were harvested, lasted four nights, each night being spent at the house of a different family. The four nights songs constituted a thanksgiving for all the crops and were sung during most of each night, only the women dancing. The bean dance was for men and women, who danced in two rings, the women forming the outer circle. The participants represented the growing corn and beans. This pattern suggests the Iroquois women's rite discussed previously, but not enough data are available for adequate comparison.

This festival has some curious relationships to the Iroquois ceremonies. All of the dances noted in its content are performed by the Sour Spring Cayuga and doubtless by other Iroquois communities; two of these ceremonial features were borrowed from the Iroquois four sacred ceremonies. The other two ceremonies may be Tutelo in origin. It would appear that this ceremony has been vastly modified by Iroquois influence, and it would be unwise to draw any conclusions as to the original agricultural ceremonies of the Tutelo. Even more significant [52] is the probability that this was a late harvest festival; the other Siouan reference would also indicate the emphasis on this time of the year for the ritual thanksgiving for the crops. It should also be noted that the content suggests the Iroquois harvest as much as the green corn festival for the Iroquois model. From the scant data available, the Iroquois harvest festivals would seem to be very similar in content to the green corn festivals.[270]

The data from the southeastern Siouan peoples are too inadequate to venture any conjecture as to the significance of their maize ceremonialism. The only modern data on such an observance reflect little except Iroquois ritual. Poverty of material does not indicate the

---

[267] *Ibid*, p. 174.

[268] Speck, 1942, pp. 18-20.

[269] Fenton, MS*a*.

[270] Morgan, 1851, pp. 206-7.

insignificance of such ritual among these peoples, but it is possible that these Siouans were peripheral to more agricultural peoples in the Southeast and that their economy did not stress agriculture to the same extent.

The Creek Indians and Their Neighbors

THE green corn festival as observed in the towns of the Creek Nation and their neighbors of the Southeast is generally called the busk (Creek *posketa,* a "fast").[271] It has probably attracted more attention than any other ceremony in the East. Several good descriptions were written by persons who witnessed these extended rituals, yet no complete study of the busk of any single town of the Creek Nation exists. No ethnologist has attempted to interpret any large part of the phenomena observed in one of these ceremonies through the medium of texts or through interpretations and explanations given by native ~~informants~~. This situation reflects greater emphasis by students of Southeastern ethnohistory on historical documents than on ethnographic studies. As a result one may expect to find some confusion in the data on agricultural ceremonies in this area, and one can only interpret the green corn festival by piecing together fragments of information from various localities and times. This is especially dangerous, because recent data from the Oklahoma Creeks and [53] from the Florida Seminole indicate that considerable modification may have taken place in the content and function of these festivals. Nevertheless, sufficient material exists to give at least as good a picture of Creek green corn ceremonialism as could be drawn for any other ethnic group.

Earlier students of the American Indian took great interest in the busk because it was the most conspicuous ceremony in this area and because the content, functions, and time of occurrence of this festival suggested that it was a broken-down survival of the Hebrew Passover. Thus, they recorded many more specific details of the ritual than most observers of this period were inclined to do. John Adair, a trader for some years among the Creek, Cherokee, and {especially} Chickasaw towns, in his ambitious attempt to demonstrate the origin and ethnic relationships of the American Indian, recorded much specific data, selected, however, by his emphasis on Hebrew and Tartar parallels. He has left the first significant account of the busk, although it is not known whether he described the busk as performed at Coosa, or whether, more likely, his account is a synthetic description made up of various observations from different towns and tribes of the Creek-Cherokee-Chickasaw region. His notes are spread over twenty-five pages of his book, interspersed with other data and with many fanciful interpretations. This busk would appear to have been a four-day festival, but the account is confused.

Adair's account of the preliminary procedure mentions the painting of the "war-cabin" with red clay, or blood-root, and the "white temple" with white clay (two of the sheds at the sides of the square), the cleansing of these structures, and the placing of new cane mats on the seats. The hearth was rebuilt; roots of button snakeroot, leaves of Indian tobacco, and ears of corn were enclosed in it. Presumably, the square ground was prepared at this time.[272]

After these preparations had been made, the materials for making the new fire were gathered, and a three-day fast began. Dry scratching was administered as a punishment (for having eaten green corn or breaking other taboos?). The "drivers" [54] (policemen) were placed in their positions on the square ground, and the participants partook of a purge made of the

---

[271] Loughridge and Hodge, 1890, pp. 28, 175.

[272] Adair, 1930, pp. 103-7.

button snakeroot and chewed and ate the Indian tobacco. This purging continued for three days, while the priest secluded himself in a separate hut.[273]

Apparently, on the third day the fast was broken with a meal of last year's food (corn bread, etc.). The people retired, and the new fire was made with a fire drill, caught in shavings, fanned to flame with a swan's wing, and carried to the hearth in an old pottery vessel. This fire is called *esakaata emishe*, "breath master"[274] (a term in the Chickasaw language?).

When the new fire has been started, the first fruits (green corn?), bear oil, meat, button snakeroot, and *Ilex cassena* were sacrificed to the fire. Offerings of the drinks were poured over the red and white seats.[275] Omens were drawn from the burning of the meat.[276]

The cassena was parched brown on the "altar'" boiled, and served in consecrated conch shell vessels; "of this they drink now and then, till the end of the festival, and on every other religious occasion from year to year." Some old men purged themselves very severely by drinking to excess. Salt was tabooed until the fourth day of the festival.[277]

The altar, or hearth, to which the new fire was carried, at which the sacrifices were made, and where the black drink was prepared, may have been the hearth in the square ground.[278]

Adair's brief description of the conclusion, probably the fourth day of the festival, mentions a men's dance with pot drum and gourd rattles in which the participants were dressed in martial array; they carried white feathers or feather wands, and danced in three circles. Then these men repainted, dressed, and held a mock battle, which was followed by a grand mixed dance of three circles. The participants then painted themselves white and "went to water" (the ceremonial equivalent of the Cherokee water-ordeal ritual previously described).[279] [55]

In another section Adair gives a more complete description of the last dance ritual of this sequence:

> While their sanctified new fruits are dressing, a religious attendant is ordered to call six of their old beloved women to come to the temple, and dance the beloved dance with joyful hearts, according to the old beloved speech. They cheerfully ,obey, and enter the supposed holy ground in solemn procession, each carrying in her hand a bundle of small branches of various green trees; and they Join the same number of old magi, or priests, who carry a cane in one hand adorned with white feathers, having likewise green boughs in their other hand, which they pulled from their holy arbor, and carefully place there, encircling it with several rounds.
>
> The beloved men have their heads dressed with white plumes; but the women are decked in their finest, and annointed with bears grease having small tortoise-shells, and white pebbles, fastened to a piece of white-drest deer-skin, which is tied to each of their legs.
>
> At the end of this notable religious dance, the old beloved, or holy women return home to hasten the feast of the new sanctified fruits. In the meanwhile, everyone at the temple drinks very plentifully of the Cassena and other bitter liquids, to cleanse their

---

273 *Ibid*, pp. 107-9.
274 *Ibid*, pp. 110-111. {Creek: *hasi:kitamisi* Breat Holder, God, cf p. 99}
275 *Ibid*, pp. 121.
276 *Ibid*, pp. 114-15.
277 *Ibid*, pp. 116-17.
278 *Ibid*, pp. 101-2.
279 *Ibid*, pp. 103-4.

sinful bodies; after which, they go to some convenient deep water, and there, according to the ceremonial law of the Hebrews, they wash away their sins with water. Thus sanctified, they return with joyful hearts in solemn procession, till they enter into the holy ground to eat of the new delicious fruits of wild canaan, etc.[280]

In the speeches preliminary to the dancing and feasting of the last day, the priest charges the people not to eat any "unsanctified, or impure food, otherwise they will get full of worms, and be devoured by famine and diseases,"[281] thus rationalizing the green corn ritual in the same terms as do the modern Cherokee.

John R. Swanton has fitted all of Adair's scraps together into a continuous narrative, which Is easier to follow than the original.[282]

Adair, however, does not indicate the exact sequence of the features of this festival and has omitted any mention of certain [56] parts of the ceremony. His description is not so much an outline as a compilation of fragments that one would like to fit into a demonstrable sequence. Other accounts may supply this outline, but different procedures were no doubt followed in different towns, and Adair's account cannot be interpreted strictly in the light of other data.

The most revealing sketch of the busk as performed in the eighteenth century in the Creek town of Little Talasi (*Otciapofa*) was written by Alexander M'Gillivray, noted chief of the Creek nation, and was included in Charles Swan's *Position and State of Manners and Arts in the Creek, or Muskogee Nation in 1791.*[283] This author did not give a miscellany of observations, but he was sure of his data and gave a brief outline, including the features that were to him the most significant. This is the only early account of the busk written by a Creek, and is the most dependable early source:

The ceremony of the busk is the most important and serious of any observed by the Creek Indians.

It is the offering up of their first fruits, or an annual sacrifice, always celebrated about harvest time.

When corn is ripe, and the cassina or new black-drink has come to perfection, the busking begins on the morning of a day appointed by the priest, *or fire-maker* (as he is styled) of the town, and is celebrated for four days successively.

On the morning of the first day, the priest, dressed in white leather moccasins and stockings, with a white dressed deer-skin over his shoulders, repairs at break of day, unattended, to the square. His first business is to create the new fire which he accomplishes by much labor by the friction of two dry sticks. After the fire is produced, four young men enter at the openings of the four corners of the square, each having a stick of wood for the new fire; they approach the new fire with much reverence, and place the ends of the wood they carry, in a very formal manner, to it. After the fire is sufficiently kindled, four other young men come forward in the same manner, each having a fair ear of new corn, which the priest takes from them, and places with great solemnity in the fire, where it is consumed. Four young warriors then enter the square

---

[280] *Ibid*, p. 116.

[281] *Ibid.*

[282] Swanton, 1928*a*, pp. 590-601.

[283] Schoolcraft, 1860, 5: 251-83.

in the manner before mentioned, each [57] having some of the new cassina. A small part of it is given to the new fire by the priest, and the remainder is immediately parched and cooked for use. During these formalities, the priest is continually muttering some mysterious jargon which nobody understands, nor is it proper for any inquiries to be made on the subject; the people in general believe that he is then communicating with the *great master of breath* {*hasi:kitamisi*}.

At this time, the warriors and others being assembled, they proceed to drink black drink in their usual manner. Some of the new fire is next carried and left on the outside of the square, for public use; and the women were allowed to come and take it to their several houses, which have the day before been cleaned and decorated with green boughs, for its reception; all the old fire in the town having been previously extinguished, and the ashes swept clean away, to make room for the new. During this day, the women are suffered to dance with the children on the outside of the square, but by no means suffered to come into it. The men keep entirely by themselves, and sleep m the square.

The second day is devoted by the men to taking their war-physic. It is a strong decoction of the button snake-root, or *senneca*, which they use in such quantities as often to injure their health, by producing spasms, etc.

The third day is spent by the young men in hunting or fishing, while the elder ones remain in the square and sleep, or continue their black drink, war-physic, etc., as they choose. During the first three days of busking, while the men are physicking, the women are constantly bathing. It is unlawful for any man to touch one of them, even with the tip of his finger; and both sexes abstain rigidly from all kinds of food or sustenance, and more particularly from salt.

On the fourth day, the whole town are assembled in the square, men, women and children promiscuously, and devoted to conviviality. All the game killed the day before by the young hunters, is given to the public; large quantities of new corn, and other provisions, are collected and cooked by the women over the new fire. The whole body of the square is occupied with pots and pans of cooked provisions, and they all partake in general festivity. The evening is spent in dancing, or other trifling amusements, and the ceremony is concluded.

N.B. All the provisions that remain are a perquisite to the old priest, or fire-maker.

ANTHONY. ALEX. M'GILLIVRAY[284]

Le Clerc Milfort, [58] a French adventurer, spent about twenty years in the Creek Country as a friend and follower of Alexander M'Gillivray during his rise to power; he married M'Gillivray's sister. His memoir, a book of slightly dubious value, contains a notable account of the Creek busk, probably that of Otciapofa:

Ils n'ont pas une religion déterminéd; quoi-qu'ils reconnoissenc le grand maitre du souffle, ils n'ont aucunes cérémonies religieuses. Chaque année, au mois d'aout, ils s'assemblent par habitation pour célébrer la fete des moisons; alors its renouvellent tout ce qui leur a servi dans le courant de 1'année qui vient d'expirer; les femmes cassent et

---

[284] *Ibid*, pp. 267-68.

brisent tout ce qui compose leur ménage, et le remontent à neuf. C'est ce meme jour que l'on mange, pour la première fois, du bled nouveau, et que le pretre ou médecine du canton allume un feu nouveau, et distribue à tous les hommes assistans la nouvelle medécine de guerre. Les Sauvages sont si religieus observateurs de cette cérémonie, que celui d'entr'eus qui n'auroit pas de maïs ancien pour se nourrir jusju'a cette epoque, mangeroit de racines plutot que de toucher au nouveau maïs. C'est également l'epoque ou 1'on oublie et pardonne tous les motif des querells. Un Sauvage qui, après la fête, rappeleroit une ancienne querelle, seroit blamé par tous les autres.[285]

{ They don't have a set (organized) religion, while recognizing the grand master of all breath (*hasi:kitamisi*), they don't have any devotional religious ceremonies. Each year, in August, they gather by town (talwa) to celebrate the annual harvest festival (Busk New Year). Then they renew everything they had used during the past year that just expired; women break and shatter everything that composed their household, and replace it. That same day, we eat, for the first time, new maize corn, and the priest or medicine man of the district lights a new fire, and dispenses to all men attendees the new war medicine. The Natives (Savages) are very fervent adherents (observers) of this ceremony, so that the each would not have any ancient corn to eat until this interval, would rather eat roots than touch the new maize. This is also the time when we forget and forgive every reason for disputes. Any native (Savage), who, after this celebration would recall an old quarrel, would be blamed (faulted) by all the others. }

William Bartram's notes on the busk are apparently at second hand and are mainly concerned with the new fire rite:

They venerate *Fire,* and have some mysterious rites and ceremonies which I could never perfectly comprehend.
They seem to keep the *Eternal Fire* in the Great Rotunda, where it is guarded by the priests.
In their great annual festival, called the *Busque* or feast *of First Fruits,* they put out all the fires of the nation or town; and then the high priest, by friction of dry woods, and the addition of *resin,* produces new fire in the Great Temple or Rotunda, from whence the whole town is supplied. But so far are the Muscogulges from having a corps of consecrated virgins to guard and keep this fire, that the women are not allowed to step within the pale of the Rotunda, and it is death for any to enter it. None but a priest can carry the fire forth.[286] [59]

Bartram's description of the busk of one of the upper Creek towns, perhaps Atasi, varies considerably from other accounts.[287] The fasting and medication lasted three days, the new fire and the feast of new corn were prepared on the fourth day, and the feasting and dancing continued for three days, followed by four days of entertainment of friends from neighboring towns. They collected all their old clothing, pots, furniture, grain, and all old things while cleaning their households, and burned them in a common heap, a radical finish to the old year.

---

[285] Milfort, 1802, pp. 216-17.
[286] Bartram, 1853,pp. 26-27.
[287] Bartram, 1791, p. 508.

Another description of a Creek busk is a well-known outline by Benjamin Hawkins, an Indian agent in the last part of the eighteenth century. He described the eight day busk of Kasihta, as observed, apparently, in the 1790's; his account is the only full outline of the eight-day ceremony:

Boos-ke-tau
{Poskitv}

This annual festival is celebrated in the months of July or August. The precise time is fixed by the Mic-co and counsellors, and is sooner or later, as the state of the affairs of the town, or the early or lateness of their corn, will suit for it. In Cussetuh, this ceremony lasts for eight days. In some towns of less note, it is but four days.

First Day

In the morning, the warriors clean the yeard of the square, and sprinkle white sand, when the a-cee (decoction of the cassine yupon) is made. The fire-maker makes the fire as early in the morning as he can, by friction. The warriors cut and bring into the square, four logs, as long each as a man can cover by extending two arms; these are placed in the centre of the square end to end, forming a cross, the outer ends pointed to the cardinal points; in the centre of the cross, the new fire is made. During the first four days, they burn out these four logs.

The *pin-e-bun-gau* {*pinobānka ~ penopvnkv*} (turkey dance) is danced by the women of the turkey tribe; and while they are dancing the possau is brewed. This is a powerful emetic. The *possau* is drank from twelve o'clock to the middle of the afternoon. After this, the *Toc-oo-yule-gau* {*tokyolka opānka ~ tokyulka opvnkv*} (tadpole) is danced by four men and four women. (In the evening, the men [60] dance *E-ne-hou-bun-gau*, the dance of the people second in command.) This they dance till daylight.

Second Day

This day, about ten o'clock, the women dance *Its-ho-bun-gau*, (gun dance). After twelve, the men go to the new fire, take some of the ashes, rub them on the chin, neck and belly, and Jump head foremost into the river, and they return into the square. The women having prepared the new corn for the feast, the men take some of it and rub it between their hands, then on their face and breasts, and then they feast.

Third Day

The men sit in the square.

Fourth Day

The women go early in the morning and get the new fire, clean out their hearths, sprinkle them with sand, and make their fires. The men finish burning out the first four logs, and they take ashes, rub them on their chin, neck and belly, and they go into the water. This day they eat malt, and they dance *Obungauchapco* {*opanka capko ~ opvnkv cvpo*}(the long dance).

Fifth Day

They get four new logs, and place them as on the first day, and they drink *a-cee*, a strong decoction of the cassine yupon.

Sixth Day

They remain in the square.

Seventh Day
Is spent in like manner as the sixth.

Eighth Day

They get two large pots, and their physic plants, 1st. *Mic-co-ho-yon-e-juh.* 2. *Toloh.* 3. *A-che-nau.* 4. *Cup-pau-pos-cau.* 5. *Chu-lis-sau*, the roots. 6. *Tuck-thlau-lus-te.* 7. *Tote-cul-hil-lis-so-wau.* 8. *Cho-feinsuck-cau-fuck-au.* 9. *Cho-fe-mus-see.* 10. *Hil-lis-hut-ke.* 11. *To-te-cuh chooo-his-see.* 12. *Welau-nuh.* 13. *Oak-chon-utch-oo.* 14. *Co-hal-le-wau-gee.*

These are all put into the pots and beat up with water. [61] The chemists (*E-lic-chul-gee*, called by the traders physic makers) they blow in it through a small reed, and then it is drank by the men, and rubbed over their joints till the afternoon.

They collect old corn cobs and pine burs, put them into a pot, and burn them to ashes. Four virgins who have never had their menses, bring ashes from their houses, put them in the pot and stir all together. The men take white clay and mix it with water in two pans. One pan of the clay and one of the ashes, are carried to the cabin of the Mic-co, and the other two to that of the warriors. They then rub themselves with the clay and ashes. Two men appointed to that office, bring some flowers of tobacco of a small kind (*Itch-au-chu-le-puc-pug-gee*) of, as the name imports, the old man's tobacco, which was prepared on the first day, and put in a pan on the cabin of the Mic-co, and they give a little of it to every one present.

The Mic-co and counsellors then go four times round the fire, and every time they face the east, they throw some of the flowers Into the fire. They then go and stand to the west. The warriors then repeat the same ceremony.

A cane is stuck up at the cabin of the Mic-co with two white feathers in the end of it. One of the Fish tribe (*Thiot-lo-ul-gee*) {*łałoalki ~ rvrovlke*}) takes it just as the sun goes down, and goes off towards the river, all following him. When he gets halfway to the river, he gives the death whoop; this whoop he repeats four times, between the square and the water's edge. Here they all place themselves as thick as they can stand, near the edge of the water. He sticks up the cane at the water's edge, and they all put a grain of the old man's tobacco on their heads and in each ear. Then, at a signal given, four different times, they throw some into the river, and every man at the like signal plunges into the river, and picks up four stones from the bottom. With these they cross themselves on their breasts four times, each time throwing a stone Into the river, and giving the death whoop; they then wash themselves, take up the cane and feathers, return and stick it up in the square, and visit through the town. At night they dance *O-bun-gau Haujo* (mad dance), and this finishes the ceremony.

This happy institution of the *Boos-ke-tuh*, restores man to himself, to his family and to his nation. It is a general amnesty, which not only absolves the Indians from all crimes, murder only excepted, but seems to bury guilt itself in oblivion.[288] [62]

Adam Hodgson, about 1820, jotted down some information he had from a trader, apparently referring to the busk at Kasihta:

Before the corn turns yellow, the inhabitants of each town or district assemble; and a certain number enter the streets of what is more properly called the town, with the war-whoop and savage yells, firing their guns into the air, and going several times around the pole. They then take emetics, and fast two days; dancing around the pole a great part of the night. All the fires in the township are then extinguished, and the hearths cleared, and new fires kindled by rubbing two sticks. After this, they parch some of the new corn, and, feasting a little, disperse to their several homes. Many of the old chiefs are of opinion, that their ancestors intended this ceremony as a thank offering to the Supreme Being, for the fruits of the earth, and for success in hunting or war.[289]

Here is a Creek reference to what appears to be a centerpole. The date is noted, and a good observation of the function of the ceremony occurs. This busk appears to have been a four-day ceremony, and the sequence does not agree with that of Hawkins; the observations were probably from some other settlement than Kasihta.

My last description of a busk held east of the Mississippi is also the most thorough and best report on Creek ceremonialism. In 1835-36 John Howard Payne traveled in the Creek and Cherokee country; he had an intense interest in Indian customs, and he carried a small ledger into which he had copied a manuscript, William Bartram's letter to Benjamin S Barton, later published as *Observations on the Creek and Cherokee Indians*. He attended the busk at the Creek town of *Tukabatchie* and kept a diary containing an account of the proceedings; this amounted to some twenty pages in the center of the notebook. He also incorporated some very interesting data and interpretations derived from Indian ~~informants~~. This was Payne's first excursion into the Indian country, earlier than his Cherokee studies discussed above, and his enthusiasms and his artist's [63] attention to detail are admirably displayed. Later, this account was incorporated into a letter to a relative in New York, cut out of the notebook, and sent by means of another traveler. A one-page postscript, dated August 12, 1835, in which Payne noted that he has substantiated all of his observations by careful questioning of Indians, was not separated from the notebook. The letter which had been removed was published in 1862.[290] The

---

[288] Hawkins, 1848, pp. 75-77.
[289] Hodgson, 1823, p. 268.
[290] Payne, 1862.

remaining manuscript was among Payne's effects when he died in Tunis and is now preserved in the Pennsylvania Historical Society Library, Philadelphia.[291] This may be the source of Squier's published version, although differences are evident. Swanton discovered the published account too late for inclusion in his major works and republished it separately, with a brief introduction and a few notes.[292] The neglect of Payne's study is unfortunate, for he clearly described distinctive features which have been overlooked in other sources and by later students of the Southeast. Other Creek data gathered by Payne exist in the Ayer Collection in Chicago[293] and may include material of primary significance, but I do not yet have access to this source. Payne apparently gathered data and recorded observations after a fashion typical of good modern ethnography. It is unfortunate that his literary remains were distributed at his death and have not been accessible to later students.

The account as written by Payne is an indispensable document to any student of the Southeast, but is far too long to reproduce here. A resume of the description, however, seems worthwhile.

The Creek year began with the green corn festival (Payne seems to have been the first to use this term), and it was considered Infamous to taste the corn before this ceremony. Chiefs of all the towns forming any particular clan met prior to the green corn season, to give orders for the manufacture of pottery vessels for the medicines. A second meeting was held to order new mats for the seats of the assembly. At a third meeting the date was apparently set, and bundles of sticks for a day-count [64] were distributed to representatives of the families involved, who removed one stick each day until the set date, when everyone appeared at the square ground.

An ample square with four log sheds, one at each side, was formed far from any habitation. These four shelters, which were built of logs and wattle and were open only on the inside toward the square, were built up chin-high on the outside, and roofed; they contained broad benches or "beds," covered with matting. A thick, notched "mast" was attached to the inner side of each house, and during the festival each "mast" supported a bundle of tall canes hung with black and white feathers. The posts and roof beams of the four houses were decorated with "rude paint-daubs." At each angle was a broad open space between the house structures. Outside of one of these corners was the "council house" (townhouse), a high, conical, circular building with a low door apparently below ground level. Next to this was another square, sided by cornfields, backed by an earth ridge, and fronting on one of the house structures. In the center was a high circular mound, composed of sweepings and scraped-off earth from the annual preparation of the square ground. Each year the old surface of the square ground was removed and fresh earth strewn over it, after which all strangers and persons who had not observed the dietary and other taboos were excluded from this sanctified area. Just outside one corner of the second square was another small mound made up of the accumulated ashes of the busk fires, which were required to be gathered and carefully preserved. Women, strangers, persons who broke their fast or tasted liquor, and anyone touching a white man were excluded from the square g   Before the festival began and prior to the preparation of the square ground, a women's dance was held in the square, after which the women separated from the men until the conclusion of the fast. After the square was prepared, all of the fires in the district were extinguished, and all dwellings swept and washed. This ritual end of the old year was marked by the cessation of

---

[291] Payne, MS*a*.

[292] Swanton, 1922.

[293] Payne, MS*b*.

all enmities and the pardon of all sentenced criminals who could slip into the gathering at the beginning of the ceremonies. The fire was started by fire chiefs, with a square board, tinder, and [65] stock twirled in a hollow in the board. The original name was carried to the center of the square, where a fire was lighted and the medicines were prepared in the new pottery vessels; brands were carried to all the households of the community. Drinking gourds were set on a bench, and officers guarded and prepared the black drink with great formality and ceremony.

The people were seated in the buildings; the chiefs stood at the edges of the square. The long-drawn-out, single-note refrains noted by Adair and others as specific to the black drink ceremony were repeated thrice, and the chiefs formed two diagonal lines across the square, with their backs to opposite corners. In succession they each took a draught of the black drink and after a few seconds ejected what they had swallowed, without moving a muscle; then two attendants passed gourds of the liquor to other persons, who remained in their places. A chief made a speech from his place, charging the participants to continue faithful to their traditional rituals and explaining some of the ritualistic features which were to follow.

Another chief walked around giving directions; gourd rattles, painted white, were produced by men who took stations on mats. All of the men participated in a dance in which feather fans were carried, and each person raised his hands over the fire at a special point in the dance circuit (feather dance of recent accounts?). The pace of the dance increased until all uttered a loud whoop, stopped, and then, running from the square, went to the river and performed the "going to water" ritual. They returned to the square and performed other dances; one dance pertained to the ball game and some appear to have been animal dances.

Here Payne, noting the inability of the interpreters to understand the content of some of the speeches and dance songs, made an observation reminiscent of Hicks's and M'Gillivray's comments about the use of an esoteric language on these occasions, and, incidently, touched upon the slight knowledge of their kinsfolk displayed even by the professional interpreters:

But even their language, on these occasions, seems, by their own admission, beyond the learning of the "linkisters" (linguists). It is [66] a poetical, mystical idiom, varying essentially from that of trading and of familiar intercommunication, and utterly incomprehensible to the literal minds of mere trafficking explainers. Even were it otherwise, the persons hovering upon the frontiers most ingenuously own, when pressed for interpretations of Indian customs, that they care nothing for the Indians excepting to get their lands, and that they really consider all study concerning them as egregious folly, save only that of finding out how much cotton their grounds must yield and in what way the greatest speculations can be accomplished with the smallest capital.[294]

The last ceremony consisted of a scratching ordeal for boys and young men; this rite was held at the backs of the four buildings and at the back of the council house. The scratching was restricted to the legs; the blood was scooped off by those submitting to the ordeal and dashed against the outside of the back walls of these buildings.

A shed of loose boards on posts, covering a raised platform, was provided in a field near by, and Payne slept here in preference to staying in the adjacent white town of *Tallasse*. The dancing (apparently social dances), and stirring of the medicine (with sung incantations) continued all night.

---

[294] Payne, 1862, p. 23.

On the morning of the second day the whole black drink ceremony was repeated, and two ancient circular shields of copper and steel were now borne in the dance, sacred paraphernalia produced only on great occasions. Ears of green corn had previously been brought in and presented to a chief, who repeated an invocation that the corn might continue plentiful throughout the year and then returned them.

The gun dance sequence followed. A procession of women entered the square and seated themselves in one of the houses, where they sang to the accompaniment of two men seated in front of them shaking gourd rattles. Two warriors with tomahawks danced halfway around a circle. The women then went to the mound in the center of the outer square, covered the mound, and resumed their chant. A stuffed figure was placed in each [67] corner of the outer square enclosing the mound. Two parties of armed warriors crept up on the lateral sides of this "battle square," and the two warriors who had previously danced in the square ground crept up on the third side. These two men snatched two of the puppets, stabbed and scalped one, and carried off the second. The other two parties began a mock battle, In which a third puppet was shot and the fourth tomahawked, and finally both sides burst into the square. Disorder then subsided into a dance around the central mound on which the women were; they plunged into the square ground, ran around it lashing spectators with corn stalks, rushed back to the mound square, and then went to the river for the "going to water" ritual. Peace and a feast on the green corn ensued, and Payne noted considerable use of alcohol.

The third day, during most of which Payne was not present, "consisted, I was told, in the display of wives urging out their husbands to hunt deer."[295] When Payne returned toward evening, he saw the men returning with deer to present to the priests; the skins were returned with a prayer that these deer would be only a harbinger of abundance of game. Some dances were performed in the square ground that night.

On the fourth morning the medicine pots were no longer in the square ground. The first feature was a dance by all of the women dressed in their finest clothes; some of them wore terrapin-shell leg rattles under their long skirts. These women slowly danced around the central fire, and the last part of the line, consisting of women wearing the rattles, stopped facing the men and kept time for the rest. The first and last woman, each carrying a stick decorated with two pendant feathers, left the three circles of dancing women and danced in a fourth circuit outside of them. The old men made comments intended to surprise the women into laughter. At one point in each circuit the women turned to face the men. The women left the square at the end of the dance, but repeated the same performance in about an hour. The final phase of the ceremony, a rapid mixed [68] dance, the dance of the olden time, concluded the festival, and Payne took his leave, having witnessed a ceremony that would next be performed on the alien soil of Indian Territory.

All of the previous references are to busks held before the removal of the Creeks to Oklahoma. The various towns continued to hold their green corn festivals, and a number of later accounts exist. In no case, however, has any observer made a complete study of the busk of any single town. The recent material has all been gathered and analyzed by Swanton[296] and shows little variation from the older data, except for some shortening and simplification of the rituals. The same variations in procedure that exist in the earlier accounts are noted. Rather than duplicate Swanton's material, I intend to limit this study to busks held east of the Mississippi and

---

[295] *Ibid*, p. 27.
[296] Swanton, 1928*a*, pp. 534-621; 1928*b*, pp. 170-312.

draw only on his information for some explanation of the concepts and symbolism underlying these ceremonies.

There are indications that certain features were always [present in these ceremonies. Such traits include the square ground, the new fire ritual, the feather dance, the old dance, the gun dance, the preparation of the square ground, and the cleansing of the households, ritual disposal of earth removed from the square ground, the granting of amnesty to criminals, the use of herb medicines and purges, the priest's blowing into the medicine, fasting, the prohibition against salt, the taboo against eating green corn prior to the busk, the "going to water" ritual, all-night ritual observances, scarification (scratching) for punishment and as a ritual feature, animal dances, the seclusion of men in the square ground at certain times, direction and color symbolism, the appointment of "drivers" (as policemen), the erection of "sheds" on the sides of the square ground, a concluding feast on new corn and other foods, the use of gourd rattles, women's turtle-shell leg rattles, and water drum, the use of ibis or heron (?) wings, the setting of the date by male officials at a preliminary meeting, and a ceremonial hunt. These seem to be features which were always present in the busk. More than half [69] of these elements are also noted m the Cherokee data, and several occur among the Delaware.

These features are also conspicuous in the recent accounts collected by Swanton. The tremendous amount of symbolism implicit in the busk has not been carefully or systematically studied by means of native ~~informants~~, but has attracted some attention among later students, notably Speck and Swanton. From their data one may conclude that the square ground is a world symbol, often called "the big house" and "the rainbow." Such an interpretation would seem to equate the square ground with the ceremonial grounds of the Iroquois and Delaware areas; this idea and the direction-color symbolism of the square would sharply distinguish these rectangular structures from the round community structures used by Creek and Cherokee and noted by archaeologists in the Ohio Valley and other areas.

The busk is also referred to as a "peace time"; not necessarily in the sense of freedom from war but in the sense of peace within the community and between the community and supernatural powers. The dance content and specific features of the Creek and Cherokee green corn festivals suggest that one function of this ceremony is the placation and propitiation of the whole pantheon, including the sun, the fire, the thunders, the corn spirit, the spirits of plants, and the spirits of the animals upon which man preys. In the ceremonial inauguration of the new Creek year man renews his worn and strained spiritual relationships with his environment. Man's and woman's participation in Creek cultural life would also seem to be enacted in allegory. Thanksgiving, in the Iroquois sense, is not very conspicuous in available Creek data.

One notable feature is the injunction against eating the new corn prior to the festival, and the threat of disease as a punishment for the violation of this taboo. This not only determines the date for the ceremony, but may give a clue as to a primary and early significance of green corn ceremonialism; unfortunately, no information as to the existence of this taboo has survived in most areas. [70] The small amount of data available for the Tuskogee and Yuchi would indicate the essential Creek nature of their busks.[297] J Francis Le Baron's Lake Pierce, Florida, note of 1881 contains some interesting references to the Seminole busk, which was doubtless very similar to the Creek ritual:

---

[297] Speck, 1907; 1909b.

They have a semi-religious annual festival in June or July, called the green corn dance, the new corn being then ripe enough to be eaten. Plurality of wives is forbidden by their laws. Tom Tiger, a fine-looking Indian, is said to have broken this rule by marrying two wives, for which misdemeanor he was banished from the tribe. He traveled about one hundred miles to the nearest tribe in the Everglades, and jumped unseen into the ring at the green corn dance. This procured him absolution, conformably to their laws.[298]

Although it has been claimed that the Choctaw were more agricultural than the Creek and other peoples of the South-east,[299] there is remarkably little data on their ceremonialism. One of the authorities, Gideon Lincecum, who wrote a lengthy account of his Choctaw observations, mentioned a green corn dance,[300] but Alfred Wright, in 1828, denied that a green corn ritual was ever practised among the Choctaw.[301] Swanton's information from Choctaw ~~informants~~ indicates that the green corn ceremony, held in August, was primarily a time of law making and regulation, and lasted three days.[302] It seems probable that a festival somewhat like the Creek busk may have been observed among the Choctaw, but I have no data. The Chickasaw may also have held a green corn ceremony, but there is no information on this point, unless some of Adair's data about the busk pertain to Chickasaw.

The Natchez and Tribes Outside Of
the Eastern Woodlands Area

INFORMATION concerning the Natchez, although indicating a political and religious organization somewhat of the nature of a [71] climax development, is drawn almost exclusively from the early French observers in Louisiana and consists mostly of accounts of the more spectacular aspects of Natchez life. Swanton has collected and discussed accounts of the green corn festival from five early sources.[303] His collection contains all of the data on this ceremony among the Natchez. It is not even certain whether some of this data actually pertains to the green corn festival. It is known from these accounts that a ceremony, generally observed in July, included a feast of first fruits and that certain traits were noted in its content. These include the use of a rectangular ceremonial ground, a new fire ceremony, four-direction symbolism, red and white symbolism, the use of special cabins on the sides of the square ground, all night dancing, the ball game, the use of a centerpost in the middle of the square, and the leaving of gifts at this post. The length of time noted for the ceremonies varies from one day to ten days.

After the destruction of the Natchez nation by the French in the early eighteenth century, some of the Natchez settled in the Creek and Cherokee country, and their descendents still exist among the Cherokee in Oklahoma. George Stiggins, a Creek of Natchez descent, wrote of these Natchez survivors in the latter part of the nineteenth century: "They keep the Busk festival in a

---

[298] Gatschet, 1884, p. 73.
[299] Swanton, 1931, p. 46.
[300] *Ibid*, p. 21.
[301] *Ibid*, p. 221.
[302] *Ibid*, pp. 225-26.
[303] Swanton, 1911, pp. 110-23.

107

very devout and sacred manner."[304] There seems to be no other data on the Natchez green corn festival, nor is there any indication of the influence the Natchez may have had on the busks of their neighbors, either before or after the Natchez settlements were located among other tribes. The little information which we do possess indicates strong resemblances between the Creek and Natchez green corn ceremonies.

The Quapaw and the Osage, Siouan tribes to the north of the Natchez, observed a green corn festival, according to Nuttall's information of 1819,[305] and Hunter suggested an Osage green corn festival,[306] but I can find no later information pertaining to these rituals. According to Joutel, the Caddoan Cenis of [72] Texas also held some ritual at this time.[307] It might be expected that similar ceremonies occurred among the other agricultural tribes of the lower Mississippi Valley and Red River Valley, and among such more northerly agricultural tribes as the Hidatsa, Crow, Mandan, Arikara, Dakota, Penca {Ponca}, Pawnee, and Cheyenne, but no definite data on such ceremonies have been noted in the literature about these peoples. It seems impossible to say whether the Hako rite of the Pawnee might have had any relationship to the ceremonies I have discussed.

Whitman's Oto report would indicate that a green corn ritual, held when the tribe returned from its early summer buffalo hunt, was a primary concern of the red bean medicine lodge-Members of this society ate the green corn and other crops only after holding a ritual, most details of which have not survived. Wilson noted, however, that all night dancing and the use of the red bean for a purge and purifying medicine preceded a feast on the new crop and the first buffalo meat of the season; these features have close parallels in the southeastern rites.[308] The buffalo-corn association and the general patterns of the society suggest the prairie corn complex, but the use of a corn medicine and the little information on the sequence suggest that a very modified version of the southeastern ritual existed here as a survival or as a restricted rite which had diffused from that direction. The red bean, widespread on the plains and prairie in other associations, may have been substituted here for the *Ilex* and other herb ingredients of the southeastern green corn ceremonies.

According to Schoolcraft, a Sioux group on the upper Mississippi held a green corn ceremony on August 1, 1820.[309] Later sources contain no clear information on such rituals in adjacent areas. In recent years the tremendous culture changes which were in process on the eastern plains and near-by regions in the period between the time of first European influence and the date of recent ethnographies have been noticed. Earlier students [73] of the cultures of these areas could perhaps have still salvaged much data on the agricultural complexes of the plains and prairie regions, but with a few exceptions they emphasized the spectacular buffalo-hunting, military plains culture aspects of the unstable transitional cultures of these areas. The accounts of the Pawnee Hako are good examples of an extinct rite inadequately recorded and interpreted, and, as with much of the Osage data, the descriptions are largely out of context and defy analysis. Will and Hyde, in a most satisfactory study of the agriculture of the Upper Missouri area, concluded that "the elaborate ceremonies which marked the opening of the green corn season among many tribes appear to have been lacking among the Upper Missouri Indians."[310]

---

[304] Swanton, 1922, p. 315.

[305] Nuttall, 1821, pp. 96, 101.

[306] Will and Hyde, 1917, p. 260.

[307] *Ibid*, p. 259.

[308] Whitman, 1937, pp. 120-21.

[309] Schoolcraft, 1825, p. 319.

[310] Will and Hyde, 1917, p. 116.

Their data indicate that the green corn season was a time of feasting and plenty and that the extensive use of green corn in this area, both fresh and preserved for later use, is like that of the woodland peoples.[311] This preference throughout the eastern areas for foods prepared of unripe corn seems basic to the eastern maize complex and may be closely correlated with the general ritual emphasis in the East.

Jedidiah Morse, in 1820, wrote a lengthy account of the Miami, apparently from information supplied by Jean Baptiste Richardville, chief of the Miami nation.[312] Some of this is apparently a reliable record of Miami and Shawnee tradition, but more than half of it is plagiarized, with only the slightest alteration, from Hawkins' *Sketch of the Creek Country,* a work which was not published until eighteen years later (from a manuscript in the Alabama Historical Society). Possibly Morse was hoodwinked by some scholar in American ethnology; perhaps Morse used this manuscript material to swell out his account. Either theory seems unlikely, and this strange Miami description will no doubt remain a mystery. Of the sections copied from Hawkins, one describes the *"Green Corn Dance,* or, [74] more properly speaking, "the ceremony of thanksgiving for the first fruits of the earth'."[313] It is a description of a Creek busk by a person who had Hawkins' account at hand, but who had never seen the observance. Richardville was *Peschewah* ("the Lynx"), chief of the Miami nation, who died in 1841.[314] This account is perhaps copied from one of the several manuscript copies of Hawkins' paper which circulated among traders in the Creek area.

There is no information on similar rituals on the western Gulf coast. Gatschet and Swanton's Atakapa linguistic data might indicate such a festival among these people, but the reference is too vague to constitute even a suggestion.[315] In the Southwest the material available would indicate only slight resemblances between Pueblo agricultural ceremonialism and any eastern ritual complex.

The Mexican data would require more study than the Eastern Woodlands material to permit any comparisons. Ralph Beals has ventured some suggestions as to the possibilities of such comparative studies, and, although he seems more optimistic than his facts would warrant, his conjecture should be kept in mind:

A number of ceremonial dances having similar purposes are found in northern Mexico. As suggested already, the ceremonies or dances may not themselves be the same or even of the same derivation, but the underlying idea may be from the same source. How close together they may actually be has been suggested by Fewkes's comparison of a Hopi and Aztec ceremony with the same object. (J. Walter Fewkes, "A Central American Ceremony Which Suggests the Snake Dance of Tusayan Villagers," *American Anthropologist* 6 [1893]: 285-305). Rain making and maize ceremonies are the most obvious and the most frequently referred to. They are, of course, rather obviously connected with agriculture and may have diffused along the track of the agricultural complex.[316]

---

[311] *Ibid*, pp. 115-23, I47-58.

[312] Morse, 1822, pp. 96-106.

[313] *Ibid.,* p. 105.

[314] Hodge, 1911, 2: 234.

[315] Gatschet and Swanton, 1932, p. 23.

[316] Beals, 1932, p. 133.

In another place he listed his references to maize ceremonies as follows: Natchez, Tarahumare, Acaxee, Huichol, Tamaulipas, [75] Tarascans, Mexico, Maya, and Lacandone.[317] Again, the Mexican data do not indicate any relationships.

One may note that even in the Southeast, about which there seems to be an abundance of reliable information, an adequate understanding of aboriginal life can only be arrived at with much careful study of all available data. The place of the busk in the cultural life of the Southeast has not been carefully denned by earlier students. Recent conclusions of Swanton's illustrate the confusion that exists in the Southeast and sometimes contradicts the best source material on the area:

Roughly the economic life of these Indians resolved themselves into a summer horticultural and fishing season and a winter hunting season. They had to return to their towns in time to plant the fields, after which some Indians continued to remain about the towns to keep watch over them, but the others dispersed in small parties to live upon fish, shell-fish, small game animals, berries, roots, and so, on. The early corn also served to carry them over until July or August, when the new flour corn was ready to eat, the so-called green corn ceremony was held, and there was for a time abundance of food.[318]

Swanton said of roasted green corn:

The late varieties of corn were eaten in this way only after the annual ceremony usually called the "green corn dance," the busk of the Creeks, had been celebrated.[319]

Throughout the rest of the Southeast – except perhaps for a few bands living near the larger tribes, who are said to have specialized on hunting – corn, beans, pumpkins, and a few other vegetables were raised, and the fields where these grew usually determined the sites of the towns. This was because they required labor and protection and because most of the crop was stored for later consumption. Dried meat was also stored there, but it was never possible to tell where game animals were to be found, while the location of the field was definite. This, of course, meant that the people were generally in or near their villages in summer. They had to return to them in spring to plant, and a certain amount of cultivation was also necessary during the growing season, though the Indians did not worry themselves on this point [76] as much as our farmers. However, It was also necessary to have someone watch the fields during the sprouting season to keep the ubiquitous crow and other birds in check. Between planting and harvest they did, however, often get time for a shorter hunt. After harvest they would remain in town until well toward winter to enjoy the produce of their fields and thus place it beyond the reach of human or animal depredation. This determined the period when the greatest feasts and ceremonies were held, the people being together and the maximum amount of food being available, the time of plenty was usually inaugurated by a special ceremony known to English-speaking people popularly as "the green corn dance,"

---

[317] *Ibid*, p. 219.

[318] Conference on Southeastern Pre-history, 1935, p. 15.

[319] Swanton, 1946, p. 351.

though it might be more accurately defined as a feast of first fruits, the ceremony being intended to insure continued supplies of plant and animal food during the ensuing year and along with them the health and prosperity of the partakers.

As the harvest was seldom sufficient to last – nor was it expected to last – until another crop came in, the Indians were obliged to seek natural food supplies elsewhere and, since such supplies were not usually concentrated, this meant that the people themselves scattered about in camps where they remained until planting time. Along the coast food supplies were usually more plentiful, though the same scattering took place in search of favorite fishing grounds. Here the annual spring runs of herring and other fish brought about concentrations of population at fishing stations on the rivers, particularly those at the edge of the Piedmont Plateau. But as these took place near the planting season, the interruption of the winter hunt occasioned by them was relatively small. Among littoral people, however, fishing tended to take the place of the summer hunt. Nevertheless, even the inland tribes were not without opportunities to enjoy a fish diet in summer, for they had fish traps led to by converging lines of rocks, and it was then they resorted to the poisoning of fish in pools In the shrunken streams, or dragged them for the same purpose.[320]

One short description written by Benjamin Hawkins is of considerable interest because it suggests far better the role of agriculture and the maize complex in the sedentary town life of the Creeks.

I chose the river path that I might have a view of the Indian fields, their mode of culture and the quality of the lands. The first [77] 4 miles were high and open sound low grounds, subject to inundations only in the seasons of floods which happen once in 15 or 16 years, the river is also subject to annual overflowings, but always in the winter season, generally in March, the next 8 miles is mostly canebrake land, very rich, much of it under cultivation, the corn planted in hills, not regular, about 5 feet from each other, and from 5 to 10 stalks in a hill, near every small division of corn they have a patch of beans stuck with cane. The margins on the river under cultivation is from one hundred to 200 yards wide, then the land becomes a rich swamp for 400 to 600 yards, this when reclaimed must be valuable for rice or corn, the river never subject to freshets in the spring or summer. I saw one conic mound in this low land 30 feet diameter, ten feet high, it stands near the river. The towns standing on the right bank of the river, there are at several places large peach trees, and a few summer huts to shelter the labourers in summer against rain, and the guards who watch the crops whilst it grows to protect it against every thing that may be injurious to it. Many of them move over their families, reside in the fields whilst the crop is growing and when it is made they gather the whole and move into town.

During this season, they show in a particular manner their hospitality, they call to all travelers, particularly white travelers and give them fruit, melons and food. If there is a necessity the women and children eat of the young corn before the busk, but the men do not.[321]

---

[320] Swanton, 1946, pp. 256-57.
[321] Hawkins, 1917, pp. 41-42.

Corn Origin Myths

IN the Southwest corn is either considered as always having been in existence or accounted for in the emergence stories, and a number of female spirits, the corn maidens, are known in the folklore and literature. In the Eastern Woodlands a mythical, premaize period is recognized, and one myth of the origin of corn is told with considerable uniformity throughout the area.

According to some traditions the corn was carried from the South in the ear of a crow. This story is recorded for the New York City area and for the Narranganset and Iroquois,[322] but is not recorded for the rest of the area. In Tuggle's version of the [78] Creek story of the Corn Mother,[323] the birds carried off and ate the corn which the Corn Mother's son had hidden in a corn crib, but the crows dropped some, which people found and planted.

Throughout most of the Eastern Woodlands, however, the Corn Mother was the mythical being who was transformed into the maize. Swanton, in a recent discussion of the ethnological problems of the Southeast, has suggested the significance of this folktale:

There are traces also of a worship of the Corn Mother and certain other spirits of a general character associated particularly with the Busk. This busk was always held when the flour corn of the new crop was first fit for use, and practically every tribe in the Southeast had some special ceremony connected with this event, while the Creeks and Natchez, at least, seem to have had an extended series of ceremonies lasting all summer.[324]

Swanton has collected several versions of this tale from Creek ~~informants~~ and several from persons of Natchez descent who still had some knowledge of the Natchez language.[325] Although most of these represent clipped versions of what must have been a more complete story, there is little difference between the Creek and Natchez variants, and both are probably derived from the same tradition. Whether this indicates the near identity of the Creek and Natchez Corn Mother tales, or whether all of these stories are of Creek origin, is a difficult question, but the latter explanation seems more probable.

These stories contain a central narrative in which the son of the Corn Mother tends to be disobedient. She obtained corn and beans from a corn crib whenever it was needed, and he became curious about her source of supply. He watched her through a crack in the wall of the 'crib and saw her shaking the corn from her body into a basket. He thought the food was merely excrement and refused to eat it. She realized what had happened and sent him out hunting for food. He looked beyond [79] the mountains and felt an urge to travel into the marvelous land beyond. His mother made him a flute and a headdress of snakes and bluejays (and sometimes parakeets). She told him that he must kill her and burn her body in their house. After disposing of her, he set out into the world, where he engaged in a series of adventures in which he overcame the trickster rabbit and women with toothed vaginas, and found a wife. He demonstrated certain magical powers (and showed some traits of the culture hero) and returned with his wife to harvest the corn. The same story occurs without the corn-origin motif.[326] In some versions the

---

[322] Williams, 1827, p. 8; Wolley, 1902, p. 42; Converse, 1908, p. 63.

[323] Swanton, 1929, pp. 16-17.

[324] *Conference on Southeastern Pre-history*, 1935, p. 19.

[325] Swanton, 1929, pp. 9-17, 230-34.

[326] *Ibid*, pp. 17-19, 234-39.

Corn Mother's son was the orphan born from a blood clot or "thrown away" blood,[327] and in one version the Corn Mother's body is dragged on the ground, from which corn springs up.[328]   In none of these versions do the twin culture heroes play the role of the orphan in this tale. The twins play major roles in other tales; the orphan of the Corn Mother tale definitely suggests the afterbirth boy or the blood-clot boy of the twins, but is not identified with him in the available material.

An interesting dichotomy is indicated in the Creek area. Farther north in the Eastern Woodlands the twin culture heroes are instrumental in the origin of corn; on the plains and in other areas twin culture heroes function in similar ways, but the Corn Mother story is absent. In the Creek area, and also among the Seminole, the two features exist side by side, but are not incorporated into one tale.[329]

Several versions of the Cherokee tale have been published, and although there is some disagreement in detail between different versions, a generalized résumé of the story is possible.[330] A man and his wife (*kanati'*, "the hunter," and *sɛ•lu'*, "corn") monopolized all of the game and vegetable crops in the world. A son was born to them, and his wild twin was transformed from [80] the thrown-away placenta or from blood. The wild boy was finally captured and the two boys were raised together; the "tame" boy being well-behaved, the "wild" boy demonstrating the well-known perversities of the trickster culture hero and taking the lead in their escapades.

The twins, apparently by accident, released all of the game which their father had impounded in a cave, thus making it available for man. They spied on their mother in the corn house and saw her shaking the corn from her body. The boys, believing that she was tricking them into eating excrement, killed her. When her body was dragged about in the clearing, corn sprang up. Originally, the corn grew and matured overnight, provided that the people stayed awake all night and danced, but this requirement was once overlooked, and ever since corn has taken much longer to grow. The two boys set off in search of their father, who fled to the West when he learned of the death of his wife. In their journey they overcame a number of menaces to humanity, and, finally arriving at their father's abode, assumed their duties as the Thunders.

I have found no record of this story among the Delaware and their neighbors, but the Corn Mother story is a major Iroquois explanation of the origin of corn. Whereas the Cherokee tale exists as an isolated myth, the Iroquois version has been incorporated into a cosmogenic myth cycle, all the parts of which do not occur together in any single published version (thus probably indicating some flexibility in the content and sequence). The Iroquoian Corn Mother story has also been recorded separately in other contexts.[331]

According to the usual Iroquois version, maize grew from the body of the woman who gave birth to the Creator and his evil-minded twin.[332] This Corn Mother, in turn, was the daughter of a pregnant woman who was let down from heaven, and for whom the earth was formed by the animals (the earth-diver story). The Corn Mother was impregnated by a man from the [81] heavens, who, according to my Cayuga ~~informants~~, laid a sharp arrow and a blunt arrow on her body, these forming the good and bad brothers. When the twins were ready to be born,

---

[327] *Ibid*, pp. 10, 13-14, 16-17.
[328] *Ibid*, p. 14.
[329] *Ibid*, pp. 2-7, 133-34, 222-30; Greenlee, 1945, p. 141; Reichard, 1921.
[330] Mooney, 1888, p. 98; 1900, p. 242-45, 248, 431-34; Witthoft, 1946*b*, pp. 217-18.
[331] Hewitt, 1918, pp. 642-63.
[332] Parker, 1910, pp. 36-37; Cornplanter, 1938, pp. 26-30.

the evil-minded one went in the direction of a beam of light, so killing his mother, but the Creator was born naturally. The maize sprang from her body. Flint, the evil-minded brother, and the Creator grew up together, always engaged in struggle. The Creator made man and many useful animals and plants; Flint made carniverous animals and enemies to man. Finally, the Creator overcame his brother (in the bowl game, according to some variants), and thus ensured the continuance of man and his world.

One may note here that the Creator and his brother actually are the twin culture heroes and are equivalents of the Cherokee Thunders. The specific modifications of the theme of this tale in various areas present a most interesting subject of study. Similar twin culture heroes played a comparable role in the mythology of southern New England,[333] but I have no data on equivalent corn origin stories from this area.

In northern New England beyond the area of green corn ceremonialism appears the last dim outline of the Corn Mother myth. This story, recorded for both Malecite and Penobscot, may be a recent accession from the Iroquois; at any rate, it seems to mark the limit of the diffusion of the Corn Mother belief. According to Speck's and Mechling's data,[334] a woman who magically produced corn from her body grew old and was about to die. She told her husband that he should clear land around their cabin and then drag her body over the cleared ground. He did this after she died and was dismayed to find her body torn off in shreds by the stumps. The maize grew in the area where the body had been dragged.

Will and Hyde have collected together the data on corn origin stories from the tribes of the Upper Missouri and adjacent [82] regions and have pointed out characteristic features of the corn origin stories of these areas.[335] The corn people origin tales in this region suggest the southwestern corn traditions; the female corn spirits and the Corn Mother suggest the Eastern Woodlands belief, although the twin tales do not occur in this association. The Corn Mother contrasts sharply with the male corn spirit of the central Algonkian area, who is an actor in tales suggestive of prairie traditions. Central Algonkian social patterns are reflected in the corn traditions and usage as are those of the prairie and Eastern Woodlands cultures. It is curious to note that the central Algonkian corn origin legends have diffused to the Iroquois and are found as isolated tales in the collections.

Conclusion

ONE of the recurrent features of the maize complex of the Eastern Woodlands is the correlation of a major ritual with the ripening of corn. Such green corn ceremonies were generally more important than planting or harvest rituals and in the Southeast and among the Iroquois are known to have marked major divisions of the annual cycle. Such rituals appear to be specific to the Eastern Woodlands, roughly to coincide with the distribution of other traits characteristic of the Eastern Woodlands maize complex, and to differ significantly from any aspects of southwestern or Mexican ceremonialism. Available data indicate the distribution of this trait from the southern New England tribes to Seminole, and west to Natchez, Quapaw, Osage, and eastern Dakota. It is not recorded for many groups within this area, however, and, in

---

[333] Information personally supplied by Eva Butler, who is engaged in a study of the mythology of southern New England.

[334] Speck, 1940, pp. 194-95; Mechling, 1914, pp. 87-88.

[335] Will and Hyde, 1917, pp. 210-36.

view of the sparse data for many tribes, the boundaries cannot be accurately determined. Emphasis on this specific rite seems to be correlated with the extensive utilization of green corn within this area.

Green corn ceremonies have survived to the present, often in attenuated form, among Iroquois, Cherokee, Creek, and Seminole. The Cherokee ritual seems to have been subject to the [83] most extensive modification in recent years, but there are indications that considerable change may have occurred in the ceremonies of other groups in the past century or two of European contact. Observations on such trends in Creek busks have been previously noted. The general poverty of information for other ethnic groups is the major obstacle to a trait distribution study of green corn rituals.

Within the Eastern Woodlands, the largest part of the area is linked by such traits as the correlation of the ritual with the stage of maize ripening at a preliminary meeting, the rectangular ceremonial area as a stratified world symbol, new fire ceremonialism, the burning of tobacco, the use of tally sticks or tally notches to set the date in advance, a four-day ritual, all night dancing, calendric significance of the ritual, the distinction between ritual and social dances, the Corn Mother myth as the origin story for the ceremony, and separate men's and women's parts as well as mixed functions.

In the Southeast the green corn festival is most conspicuous and most elaborate. Variation between the rituals of Yuchi, Tuskigee, Alabama, and Creek is no greater than variation between those of various Creek towns. The Cherokee ritual is very closely related, and data from the Cherokee-Southeastern area indicate the closest correspondences in detail for any sizeable area of the Eastern Woodlands. Some of the traits shared between the Creek busk and the Cherokee ceremony are the open square ground surrounded by sheds, use of an emetic followed by herb medicines, belief in the production of intestinal worms from corn and the use of herb medicines as prophylaxis during the ritual, injunction against the eating of corn prior to the ceremony, taboo against salt during the ritual, green corn festival as the new year rite, vegetable and animal burnt offerings, a ritual hunt, fasting, direction – color symbolism, gourd rattles, women's turtle-shell leg rattles, animal dances, a gun dance, some dances held outside of the square ground, the square ground consecrated, swept, or covered with fresh earth and restricted, the "going to water" ritual, the ceremony as a [84] time and place of amnesty, use of ritual jargon and archaic forms, appointment of "drivers" or policemen, green tree branches carried in ritual.

In the Southeast animal dances are conspicuous features in green corn rituals. These dances are apparently concerned with the propitiation of the spirits of hunted animals and are comparable to the hunting and medicinal songs and formulas which also serve this function.[336] Other first fruits rites were held, for example, a bean ritual. Animal dances are also a part of the Delaware ritual, but are unimportant in the Iroquois ceremony. Animal foods were apparently sacrificed in the Delaware ceremony, as in the Southeast, but not in the Iroquois (and southern New England?) rites. The Delaware and New England and coastal Algonkians held first fruits rites which were not concerned with agriculture; venison, fish, and other animal foods were involved in separate ceremonies initiating their seasonal usage. The green corn festival seems to be the sole Iroquois first fruits rite and is only incidentally concerned with nonagricultural economic activities. The southern Algonkian first fruits observances are curiously reminiscent

---

[336] Speck, 1907, pp. 135-36, gives the best discussion of this important aspect.

of northern Algonkian animal ceremonialism;[337] they also suggest specific animistic attitudes toward the animal world which are characteristic of Creek and Cherokee but not strongly developed in Iroquois.

Like many other traits of the Eastern Woodlands maize complex, green corn ceremonialism apparently was not derived from the Southwest or from Mexico. In terms of importance and complexity, its place of origin and strongest development would appear to be in the Southeast. Rituals involving the first seasonal usage of each major animal food are present in both non-agricultural and agricultural areas of the Eastern Woodlands and may provide the substratum for agricultural rites. The Indians of the Southeast still preserve elements of such animal rituals within green corn festivals, and the southern Algonkians [85] held both corn and animal first fruits rites. The Iroquois, further from the presumable center of the maize complex, held only a green corn festival not directly concerned with hunting. Possibly, green corn ritualism may in part represent a transference and remodification of earlier hunting ceremonialism in the Southeast, rather than a part of an agricultural complex which diffused to the Eastern Woodlands.

Literature Cited

ADAIR, JAMES

1930 History of the American Indians. Johnson City, Tenn: Watauga Press.

BARTRAM, WILLIAM

1791 Travels Through North and South Carolina. Philadelphia: James and Johnson.

1853 Observations on the Creek and Cherokee Indians. (E.G Squier, ed.) Transactions of American Ethnological Society, 3, Pt. 1: 1-81.

BEALS, RALPH

1932 Comparative Ethnology of Northern Mexico before 1750. Ibero-Americana, Berkeley, California: University California Press.

BEVERLEY, ROBERT

1705 The History and Present State of Virginia. London: R. Parker. 4 vols.

BRICKELL, JOHN

1844 Narrative of John Brickell's Captivity Among the Delaware Indians. *In:* American Pioneer. Cincinnati: Logan Historical Society, 1842 I: 43-56.

CARTER, GEORGE F

1945 Plant Geography and Culture History in the American Southwest. Viking Fund Publications Anthropology 5.

CHAMBERLAIN, M

1904 Indians. Acadiensis, 4: 280-95.

---

[337] Flannery, 1939, pp. 135-36,184, 192; 1946, p. 267.

Conference on Southeastern Pre-history. Birmingham, Alabama, Dec. 18-20, 1931.

   1935 Washington: National Research Council.

CONVERSE, HARRIET

   1908 Myths and Legends of the New York State Iroquois. (Ed. by A.C Parker.) New York State Museum Bulletin, 125.

CORNPLANTER, JESSE J

   1938 Legends of the Longhouse. Philadelphia: J.B Lippincott Co.

DENTON, DANIEL

1937 A Brief Description of New York. New York; Facsimile Text Soc. [86]

Explorations and Field Work of the Smithsonian Institution for 1913.

   1913 Smithsonian Misc. Coll., 63, Pt. 8. *Ibid.,* 1914, 65, Pt. 6.

FENTON, WILLIAM N

   1936   An Outline of Seneca Ceremonies at Coldspring Longhouse.   Yale University Publications Anthropology 9.

   1941 Tonawanda Longhouse Ceremonies Ninety Years after Lewis Henry Morgan. Bulletin Bureau American Ethnology, 128*:* 140-66.

MS*a* Green Corn Festival at Coldspring Longhouse. MS in possession of Dr. Fenton.

MS*b* Green Corn Festival at Newtown Longhouse. MS in possession of Dr. Fenton.

MS*c*   Outline of Onondaga Ceremonies, Six Nations Reserve, Ontario, Canada.   MS in possession of Dr. Fenton.

FLANNERY, REGINA

   1939   An Analysis of Coastal Algonquian Culture.   Catholic University, of American Anthropology Series 7.

   1946 The Culture of the Northeastern Indian Hunters: A Descriptive Survey. *In* Frederick Johnson, Ed., Man in Northeastern North America. Papers Robert S. Peabody Foundation, Archeology, 3: 263-71.

FOSTER, GEORGE E

   1885 Se-quo-yah, the American Cadmus and Modern Moses. Philadelphia: Indian Rights Association.

FROBENIUS, LEO

   1909 The Childhood of Man. (Trans. by A.H. Keane.) Philadelphia: J.B Lippincott Co.

GATSCHET, ALBERTS

   1884 A Migration Legend of the Creeks. Brinton's Library of Aboriginal American Literature. Philadelphia: D.G. Brinton. No. 4.

GATSCHET, ALBERT S., and JOHN R. SWANTON.

   1932 A Dictionary of the Atakapa Language. Bulletin, Bureau American Ethnology, 108.

GILBERT, WILLIAM H

   1943 The Eastern Cherokee. Bulletin, Bureau American Ethnology, 133: 169-413.

GREENLEE, ROBERT F

1945 Folktales of the Florida Seminole. Journal American Folklore, 58: 138-44.

GROVER, THOMAS

1904 An Account of Virginia. (Reprinted from the Philadelphia: Transactions of Royal Society, June 20,1678.) Oxford.

GYLES, JOHN

1850 Captivity. *In:* Samuel G. Drake, Indian Captivities or Life in the Wigwam. Auburn, NY: Derby and Miller. Pp. 75-109.

HARRINGTON, M.R

1921 Religion and Ceremonies of the Lenape, Museum American Indian, Heye Found, Indian Notes and Monographs, Miscellaneous, No. 19. [87]

1938 Dickon among the Lenape Indians. Philadelphia: John G. Winston Co.

HARIOT, THOMAS

1895 Narrative of the First English Plantation in America. (Reprint) London: Bernard Quaritch.

HAWKINS, BENJAMIN

1848 A Sketch of the Creek Country in 1799. Col. Georgia Hist. Soc., Pt. i:3.

1917 Letters of Benjamin Hawkins, 1796-1806. *Ibid,* 9.

HECKEWELDER, JOHN

1876 History, Manners, and Customs of the Indian Nations. (Ed. by W.C. Reichel) Memoirs, Historical Society of Pennsylvania, 12.

HEWITT, J.N.B

1918 Seneca Fiction, Legends, and Myths. Ann. Report Bureau American Ethnology, 32.

HICKS, CHARLES

1818 Manners, Customs, etc. of the Cherokee Indians. Published in the Raleigh Register and clipping preserved in Bureau American Ethnology, Scrapbook, 1: 354.

HODGE, FREDERICK W

1911 Handbook of American Indians North of Mexico. Bureau American Ethnology, Bull., 30.

HODGSON, ADAM

1923 Remarks During a Journey Through North America. New York: J. Seymour.

Indian Papers I. MS in Connecticut State Library, Hartford, Conn.

JAMESON, ANNA M

1839 Winter Studies and Summer Rambles in Canada, New York: Wiley and Putnam. 3 vols.

LALEMANT, JEROME

1898*a* Relation of 1640. *In:* R.G. Thwaites, The Jesuit Relations and Allied Documents. Cleveland: Burrows Bros. 19: 77-267.

1898*b* Letter of 1645. *Ibid,* 28: 39-101.

LAWSON, JOHN

1714 The History of Carolina. London: W. Taylor and J. Baker.

LINTON, RALPH

1924   The Significance of Certain Traits in North American Maize Culture.   American Anthropology, n.s, 26; 345-49.

LOSKIEL, GEORGE H

1794 History of the Mission of the United Brethern among the Indians in North America. (Trans. by C.I LaTrobe) London: Brethren's Society for the Furtherance of the Gospel.

LOUGHRIDGE, R.M, and DAVID M HODGE

1890 English and Muskokee Dictionary. St. Louis: J.T Smith. [88]

MECHLING, W.H

1914 Malecite Tales. Memoirs, Canadian Department of Mines, 49.

MILFORT, LE CLERK

1802 Memoir du coup d'oeil rapide sur mes differens voyages et mon sejour dans la Nation Creek. Paris: Giguet et Michaud.

MOONEY, JAMES

1888 Myths of the Cherokees. Journal American Folklore,1i: 97-108.

1900 Myths of the Cherokee. Ann. Report Bureau American Ethnology, 19: 5-548.

MS*a* MS 2235, Bureau American Ethnology, Archive

MS*b* MS 3848, ibid.

MOONEY, JAMES, and FRANZ OLBRECHTS

1932 The Swimmer Manuscript. Bulletin Bureau American Ethnology, 99.

MORGAN, LEWIS H

1851 League of the Ho-de-no-sau-nee, or Iroquois. Rochester: Sage and Brother.

MORSE, JEDIDIAH

1822 Report to the Secretary of War of the United States, on Indian Affairs. New Haven, Conn: Howe and Spaulding.

NUTTALL, THOMAS

1821 A Journal of Travels into the Arkansa Territory During the Year 1819. Philadelphia: T.H Palmer.

PARKER, ARTHUR C

1910 Iroquois Use of Maize and Other Food Plants. New York State Museum Bulletin, 144.

1913 The Code of Handsome Lake, the Seneca Prophet. *Ibid,* 163.

PAYNE, JOHN HOWARD

1862 The Green Corn Dance. Continental Monthly, I: 17-29.

MS*a* Manuscript including copy of Bartram's Observations, untitled. Pennsylvania Historical Society Library, Philadelphia.

MS*b* Manuscript relating to southeastern Indians, 14 vols, Ayer Collection, Newberry Library, Chicago.

PENN, WILLIAM

1852 A Letter from William Penn, Proprietary and Govenour of Pennsylvania in America to the Committee of the Free Society of Traders of that Province, Residing in London. Reprinted in Samuel M. Janney, The Life of William Penn. Philadelphia; Lippincott, Grambo, and Co, Pp. 227-38.

REICHARD, GLADYS

1921 Literary Types and Dissemination of Myths. Journal American Folklore 36: 269-307.

Rhode Island Historical

1829 Collections 2. Providence, R.I.

RITCHIE, WILLIAM A

1944 The Pre-Iroquoian Occupations of New York. Rochester Museum Mem., 1. [89]

RUTTENBER, E.M

1872 History of the Indian Tribes of Hudson's River... Albany, NY: J. Munsell.

SCHOOLCRAFT, HENRY R

1825 Travels in the Central Portions of the Mississippi Valley. New York: Collins and Hannay.

1860 Historical and Statistical Information, Respecting the History, Condition, and Prospects of the Indian Tribes of the United States. Philadelphia: J.B. Lippincott and Co. 6 vols.

SKINNER, ALANSON

1915*a* Indians of Manhattan Island. American Museum Nat. Hist. Guide Leaflet, 41.

1915*b* Indians of Greater New York. Little Histories of North American Indians, Cedar Rapids, Ia.

SMITH, JOHN

1907 Generall Historic of Virginia, New England, and the Summer Islands. Glasgow: J. MacLehose and Sons, 2 vols.

SPECK, F.G

1907 Creek Indians of Taskigi Town. Memoirs, American Anthropology Assn., 2: 99-164

1909*a* Notes on the Mohegan and Niantic Indians. Anthropology Papers, American Museum Nat. Hist., 3: 181-210.

1909*b* Ethnology of the Yuchi Indians. University Pennsylvania. Anthropology Publications, University Museum, 1.

1924 Ethnic Position of the Southeastern Algonkian. American Anthropology, n.s., 26: 184-200.

1928 Native Tribes and Dialects of Connecticut. Annual Report Bureau American Ethnology., 43: 199-287.

1937 Oklahoma Delaware Ceremonies, Feasts and Dances. Memoirs, American Phil. Soc., No. 7.

1940 Penobscot Man. Philadelphia: University Pennsylvania.

1942 The Tutelo Spirit Adoption Ceremony. Harrisburg, Pa: Pennsylvania Historical Commission.

1945 The Celestial Bear Comes Down to Earth. Reading Public Museum, Science Publications, 7.

MS*a* Eastern Cherokee Songs and Dances, MS in possession of Doctor Speck.

MS*b* Cayuga Ceremonies. In press, University of Penna. Press.

SQUIER, E.G

1851 Antiquities of the State of New York. Buffalo; Geo. H. Derby and Co.

STILES, EZRA

1916 Extracts from the Itineraries and Other Miscellanies. (Ed. by F.B Dexter.) New Haven: Yale University Press. [90]

SWANTON, J.R

1911 Indian Tribes of the Lower Mississippi Valley and the Adjacent Coast of the Gulf of Mexico. Bulletin Bureau American Ethnology, 4, 3.

1922 Early History of the Creek Indians and Their Neighbors. *Ibid.,* 73.

1928a Creek Social Organization and Usages. Annual Report Bureau American Ethnology., 42: 23-472.

1928b Religious Beliefs and Medical Practices of the Creek Indians, *Ibid.,* pp.473-672.

1929 Myths and Tales of the Southeastern Indians. Bulletin, Bureau American Ethnology, 88.

1931 Source Material for the Social and Ceremonial Life of the Choctaw Indians. *Ibid.,* 103.

1932 The Green Corn Dance. Chronicles of Oklahoma, 10: 170-95.

1946 The Indians of the Southeastern United States. Bulletin, Bureau American Ethnology, 137.

THOMAS, GABRIEL

1900 An Historical and Geographical Account of the Province and Country of Pennsylvania. Reprinted in Liberty Bell Leaflets, 5, 6. Philadelphia: Sower.

TUTTLE, SARAH

1833 Letters and Conversations on the Cherokee Mission. 2d ed.; Boston: American Sabbath School Union.

WASSENAER, NICOLAES VAN

1850 Description and First Settlement of New Neatherland. *In* E.B O'Callaghan, Documentary History of New York. Albany, NY 3: 27-48 (trans. Wassenaer, Historic van Europa. Amsterdam, 1621-32).

WAUBUNO, CHIEF (John B Wampum)

n.d. The Traditions of the Delaware, as Told by Chief Waubuno. London.

WEBB, WILLIAM S, and C.S SNOW

1945 The Adena People. University Ky. Publications Anthropology, 6.

WHITE, JOHN

Photographs of the original drawings (British Museum) issued by the Bureau American Ethnology.

WHITMAN, WILLIAM

1937 The Oto. Columbia University Contributions to Anthropology., 27.

WILL, GEORGE F, and GEORGE E. HYDE.

1917 Corn among the Indians of the Upper Missouri. Little Histories of North American Indians. St. Louis. No. 5.

WILLIAMS, ROGER

1827 A Key into the Language of America. Rhode Island Historical Collection, 17-165.

WISSLER, CLARK

1922 The American Indian. New York: Oxford University Press. [91]

WITTHOFT, JOHN

1946 Cayuga Midwinter Festival. New York Folklore Quart., 2: 24-39.

1946 The Cherokee Green Corn Festival and the Green Corn Medicine. Journal Wash. Academy of Science, 36: 213-19.

WOLLEY, CHARLES

1902 Two Years' Journal in New York. Cleveland; Burrows Bros.

ZEIZBERGER, DAVID

1910 History of the Northern American Indians. (Ed. by A.B. Hulbert, and W.N Schwarze.) Columbus, Ohio: Ohio State Archaeological and Historical Society.

THE Occasional Contributions from the Museum of Anthropology of the University of Michigan are issued at irregular intervals as opportunity permits and are numbered serially.

The subject matter of the individual contributions prepared by staff members, associates, and friends of the Museum, includes descriptions of museum collections and field work, results of research in various anthropological fields, and discussions of field and museum techniques.

The Occasional Contributions and other publications of the Museum may be purchased from the University Press, 311 Maynard Street, Ann Arbor, Michigan.

JAMES B. GRIFFIN
Director of the Museum of Anthropology

Lenape Delaware Ritual Contexts

According to AFC Wallace (same: 3 #4), the major ritual series of the protohistorical Delawares did not include the Big House or Gamwing: "Witthoft in his study of Green Corn ceremonialism in the eastern woodlands found that the Green Corn dance, rather than the Big House ceremony, was the ritual described by observers of the Delaware in early contact times.... the Big House was a 'new religion' dating from 1805 ... a reorganized form of the Green Corn, with innovations both in ritual detail and in over-all pattern." During the succeeding decades many scholars have accepted Wallace's strongly worded claim that the Gamwing emerged from the Green Corn, despite his own references and Delaware statements about the continuity of both rites among the Unamis in Oklahoma (see Speck 1937: 79-90). Indeed, the chain of sources cited by Wallace to derive the Gamwing from the Maize rite calls his claim into question, for it seems that he misread Witthoft, who in turn had never finished reading a novel by Harrington.

In his famous study of the Green Corn throughout the eastern woodlands, John Witthoft did not derive the one ceremony from the other; on the contrary, he cautioned against doing so. Specifically, Witthoft (1949: 15) criticized Alanson Skinner, another anthropologist celebrated for his comparative Algonquian work, for having "carelessly equated such rituals." Moreover, while Witthoft (same: 16) was silent on the antiquity of the Delaware Green Corn rite, he erred in reporting that MR Harrington "included no data pertaining to such a festival in his published accounts" of the Delawares.

In Harrington's (1963: 135) superb novel set among colonial-era Delawares, John Dickon, the protagonist, initially comments that "green corn time was always a happy time in Lenape land, with much feasting; yet I never saw a public dance to celebrate the occasion, as I hear is the custom among many other tribes." Later on, however, several pages are devoted to describing a Green Corn dance, after a woman has explained that "of course you [Dickon] would not know, because the Smearer's Corn Dance was over last fall before you came to the village, and nobody thought to tell you" (same: 182). Thus the plot of the novel accounts not for the lack of the ritual but for the initial denial of it. Once Dickon has been adopted and has spent a whole year in the town, he observes both the Green Corn ceremony and the Gamwing (same: 48-53). By the end of the book Dickon has received a vision and has recited it in the big house (same: 223-26).

For Harrington as for other scholars, therefore, the Green Corn and the Gamwing were parallel, not derivative, rites. Most have agreed that the Gamwing, in some form, was aboriginal among the Delawares. In particular, Paul Wallace (1975: 66), father of Anthony FC Wallace, argued, "It is, of course, probably true that the precise form in which this twelve-day ritual has come down to us does not antedate 1805, when the revelations of a Munsee prophetess gave it final shape; but its central symbol, the World Tree (imaged in the Center Post), is very old." Yet the elder Wallace left unstated the role of the world-tree center post as the touch point of Delaware creation, the sacred spot between the post and the eastern fire marking the place where woman first appeared.

While Witthoft overlooked important information in Harrington and was himself misconstrued by Anthony Wallace, he did assemble useful comparative information that helps us interpret the Gamwing as a distinctively Delaware rite. For example, Witthoft (1949: 22) reported that William Fenton had discovered that an abbreviated version of the Green Corn rite was included in the Iroquois Midwinter rite (Tooker 1970; Speck 1949). This ceremony, as reworked by the Seneca prophet Handsome Lake, summarized Iroquois belief about the world and was analogous to the Gamwing. Thus, for the Delawares the Big House rite did much the same under the influence of different prophets at different times and places. While the Green Corn of necessity was a separate event, the Gamwing began to incorporate features of Maize preharvest and other rites, because it was the culmination of the ritual year, epitomizing and all-inclusive to encompass the cosmos. Therefore, during the nineteenth century the Gamwing subsumed some features of the lapsed Green Corn and, at the very end, actually reversed the process proposed by Wallace.

Since the Green Corn was a celebration of the maturing harvest, and since Mother Corn was believed by the Delawares to be extremely jealous, all of the foods served were from plant crops; meat was excluded. Therefore, when the serving of both meat and maize is mentioned, the likelihood is that the Gamwing rather than the Green Corn is being described.

Lastly, although Harrington's opinion seldom figures in arguments about the antiquity of the Gamwing, he did make the following observation:

> That these concepts are not new among the Lenape may be seen from the fact that most of the early writers who treat these people have noticed such beliefs among them, which can be traced back as far as 1679....
>
> It therefore seems likely that the rites, in spite of the differences noted, probably have a common origin, and hence date back to a period before the separation of the Unami and the Minsi [Munsee]. Indeed we have an historical account which seems to refer to this kind of ceremony as early as 1683, while under date of 1779 there is a description of the rites practiced as enacted as late as 1920 (Harrington 1921: 192, 197-98)

So while Wallace presented his evidence for historical changes in Delaware religion carefully and well, his treatment of the Gamwing as a new religion of 1805 does not stand close scrutiny.

As Frank Speck, the best-known scholar of the rite and a mentor of Wallace, observed, the Gamwing was celebrated by all major groups of Delaware refugees, whether they went to Oklahoma as Unamis or to Ontario as Munsees. Further, their diverse observances of the rite suggest its great antiquity both in the homeland and in numerous resettlements:

> For, indeed, the ceremony shows itself to have a complex capitalization, its ritual extending through every form of worship, including individual, family or "clan rites," that we have mention of in any of the Delaware accounts. The Big House capitulates the elements of certain minor feast ceremonies held on special occasions by families. The great annual ceremony seems to stand as an entity, one that does not submit to any assumption of recent origin in its present form of organization (Speck 1931: 17).

> While it is one truth that the annual Big House ceremonies of the various divisions of the widely diffused Delaware Nation show specific differences in their performance, it is also true that they coincide in the basic purpose of the performance and in the essentials of worship addressed to the Creator (Speck and Moses 1945: 83).

Annual Rituals

For over half a century, however, after settling in Oklahoma, traditional Delaware families continued to celebrate not only the Gamwing, but a full series of traditional rituals, which have been recorded by scholars. These annual rituals included family sponsored Grease Drinking Rites in honor of (1) Otter or (2) Bear and the (3) Doll Dance, all three probably held in the spring; and tribal sponsorship of (4) "Indian Football" games held from the first budding of vegetation (April) until mid-June, (5) the Məsing Dance held every fall and whenever else the need for it arose, (6) the Maize Preharvest (Green Corn) held when the crops first ripened, and, finally, (7) the Big House Rite celebrated when the leaves began to change color in mid-October.

Aside from the Big House Rite or Gamwing, the other six rituals once celebrated in Oklahoma can be viewed as forming two triads of Family or of Tribal rites. Each will be discussed in turn.

It is interesting that the Family Rites were held in the Spring when, aboriginally, people were returning from winter camps to the summer farming town, and reintegrating themselves into a community in which those families able to sponsor rites would be quietly able to assert positions of leadership. The Tribal Rites were mostly held in the Fall, when food was plentiful before groups left to winter in hunting territories.

Family Rites

The Grease Drinking Rites (called in Lenape, "repeatedly rising up") for Otter and Bear belonged to certain matrilines, as did the responsibilities associated with the inheritance of certain carved dolls.

Otter

Nora Thompson Dean would have inherited one of the Otter Rites if her mother had not sold the necessary bundle to Harrington, acting for the Museum of the American Indian, Heye Foundation, which preserves a receipt for the sale of the bundle but lacks any notes on the ceremony itself. These collections now belong to the Museum of the American Indian in DC. Chief Elkhair told Michelson (ms.) that Nora's brother Jesse died at 16 because his mother had sold the bundle, but Nora always said that Jesse died of appendicitis and the bundle was sold because no one could remember all of the songs, thus placing the family in great danger because the Otter Spirit would be offended by such neglect. By selling the bundle, this onus fell on the buyer. Even so, family members still avoid contact with otters or otter pelts. This family's version of the Otter Rite was last held when Sarah Wilson Thompson's oldest son was two years old.

According to Nora, the rite was held every two years, usually on a spring afternoon in the open air. The speaker on the last occasion was Billy Wilson, Sarah's father, who began the rite by facing east, praying, and explaining the purpose and procedure of the ceremony. The bundle was an otter skin with a long slit in the neck area (cf. Pawnee warrior garb, below). The service involved visionary recitations by men, each of whom, in turn, wore the sacred pelt with the head resting on the chest and the tail hanging down the back, as illustrated by Harrington (1921: 178).

Each recitation duplicated those done in the Big House, using the turtle shell rattle with strap handle. Among these men, one was memorable because his dog walked around the fire with him and every time he shouted "Hoooo, Hoooo, Hoooo", the dog barked an echo. Meanwhile, a kettle of meat cooked over the fire, probably bear or deer in the old days, but pork in Oklahoma. Two men served as cooks, appointed by the host family to butcher the hog and make the watery soup. Toward the end of the recitations, one of the visionaries carried the hog head on a plate around the fire. After several circlings, he threw the head into the fire as an offering to Otter. Women and "empty" (visionless) men sat at the edges of the cleared area, offering their own personal prayers.

When the food was ready, a gifted man moved one way around the fire and one of the male cooks circled the opposite way, carrying the kettle full of greasy meat. When they met, the visionary would sometimes take a ladle of this soup and give it to a clansman, who had to drink all of it immediately. Towards dark, after the recitations finished, everyone was served a feast of hog meat. Finally, the two cooks were each given a yard of wampum for their efforts.

Speck (1937: 46) reported another version of the Otter Rite, but it seems doubtful since it included an unroofed brush arbor, probably a confusion with the den of the Bear Rite. Also, no otter pelt was used. Speck said this version of the rite passed from Colonel Jackson to his daughter Lizzie Half Moon, but elders are sure that the rite, whose details were forgotten, had been properly transmitted from mother to daughter.

Bear

The Bear Rite was similar to that for Otter, and both were regarded as Grease Drinking Rites (Harrington 1921: 171, Speck 1937: 30). Jake Parks, husband of Annie Brown Parks and a Big House singer, said that Jackson and Old Mrs. Frenchman shared one type of Bear Rite, but it did not use a brush arbor. This is confusing because in other versions the enclosure represented the bear's den. Modern Delaware have not witnessed this rite, so I have relied on Harrington, who was generally a reliable source. The Delaware Bear Rite has added significance because it was a southern example of the circumpolar distribution known for such ceremonialism (Hallowell 1926).

The Bear Rite was held every two years within the confines of a brush arbor shaped like a small version of the Big House, 14 by 30 feet. A meat pole was put up to hold fresh bear meat before it was cooked. After bears became scarce, a black hog was used, then a decision was made to use any hog available so the rite could continue. Held at night, gifted men recited, wearing a string of wampum about the neck and using a turtle shell rattle. The hog head had two ribs stuck in its mouth and was placed on a platter near the center. At the end of the recitations, the head was thrown into the fire.[338]

After the service, everyone feasted on cooked pork. Any remaining fat or broth was added to the fire, while six women were asked to move apart and recite the prayer word "Hoooo" six times [at the meat pole?], a significant act for determining its inclusive character when compared to the use of that sound by men in other rituals. Its use by women also indicated that bear and hog were more womanly meats than venison. The rectangular arbor probably represented an assimilation to the form of the Big House. Earlier, it may have been circular, more like a den and the earth. Among Algonkians generally, bear is a symbol of the earth.

Bear and Otter Rites had similar tales of origin. A child had a pet bear or a young girl had a pet otter that was released into the wild with wampum tied around its neck. Later, the child became deathly ill and a shaman diagnosed the cause as the animal being unable to care for itself and making the child sick in order to receive periodic offerings of food from its former keepers.

---

[338]. There is no explanation for these ribs in the mouth, but, given the legendary accounts of cannibal monsters, it may be that the rite also symbolized the triumph of Delaware ancestors over fierce beings like the naked bear.

Doll

The third rite in this triad was the Doll Dance, related to the Bear/Otter pair in complex ways (Miller 1976b). The dance ground had a fire in the middle of a cleared space and, on the edge, a tent where the doll(s) were dressed. Participation was open to all, gifted and empty. Speck (1937: 66, note 6) placed the Unami ceremony in the fall, when the Munsee ritual was held, but both Harrington and Nora Dean said it was held in the spring. It may be that various families held their versions of the rite at different times.

According to Nora Dean (Miller 1976b), the Doll Dance was held in the dusky dark. Each doll, tied to a stick, was passed along the line of dancers. Dolls were alive and sometimes dangerous, so the sticks must have provided mediating protection. Dancers were accompanied by singers using special songs and beating on a folded deerskin drum. Families who inherited one or more dolls kept them stored in trunks, which were opened once a year to provide each one with a new set of clothing. During the previous year, their clothing had become worn and frayed because they were believed to wander out at night. Dolls were inherited as a single female addressed as "Grandmother" or as male + female pairs addressed as "Grandfather" and "Grandmother", exclusively female or inclusively paired.

During the dance, normal gender patterns were reversed. Men danced as the inside ring near the fire, passing a Grandfather Doll from one to another, starting at the front of the line, at each verse change. Women in the outside line did the same with the Grandmother(s). During lulls, sticks holding the dolls were stuck into the ground in front of the tent.[339]

After twelve rounds of dancing, people feasted on corn gruel that had been cooked over the fire. Afterward, all night long, Delaware did social dances. Early the next day, a "scramble" was held. Everyone gathered around an area covered with leaves and tried to catch oversized cornmeal biscuits and a special large loaf called "Bear", which were thrown to the spectators by the doll owners. It was a feat to catch these biscuits in the air as they were so hard they hurt on impact. Most people waited for them to hit the ground and gathered them from the leaves.

Together, the Bear, Otter, and Doll Rites formed a set with closure, representing the elements of land, water, and air. In this triad, Bear was of the land, Otter of the water, and the Doll was the mediator, carved from wood and sharing the associations of trees with sky. As the Doll Dance was inclosive, so the Otter was inclusive and the Bear exclusive.

Speck (1937: 61) said the Doll Dance was intended to appease Mother Maize, mentioning cornhusk dolls. Harrington, Nora Dean, and my own inspection of a doll indicate that they were made of wood, much like those of Great Lakes tribes (Skinner 1925). Rather than being emblematic of maize, these dolls represented trees, the World Tree, and the link between earth and sky. This was vividly displayed at the end of the rite when the corn biscuits and Bear loaf were thrown into the air to land among the leaves, as though they were falling from a tree. The bread evoked both plants and animals, maize and bear, while tying the dolls onto sticks placed them along the vertical dimension between earth and sky. Since only corn gruel was served at a Doll Dance, plant associations were particularly strong.

The extensive power of this rite is confirmed by the decision to hold the last Doll Dance in 1933. During a severe drought in northeastern Oklahoma, elders met at Chief Elkhair's home to

---

[339] Apparently, Vincenzo Petrullo was the only anthropologist to ever witness a Doll Dance, held in 1929. The last one of 1933 was reported to Frank Speck in a letter from Charlie Webber.

decide how to bring rain. Elkhair had a rainmaking charm of dried frogs that came alive when a ritual was performed, but, instead, they held the 1933 Doll Dance with a Grandfather and two Grandmothers.[340] As Webber noted in a letter to Speck,[341] the dance was held on a Monday and the next Sunday there was a full day of rain. As a mediating and inclosive rite, the Doll Dance proved itself to be the better selection, calling down a rain storm to save the crop.

Lastly, there was a suggestion in the account of the Doll Dance by Silas Longbone to Michelson (ms.a) that there were clan-based versions of this rite. Longbone remarked that the special loaf thrown up at the end could be in the form of a turkey, bear, turtle, or human, each linked with a "band", by which he meant a matriclan. This gives further support to the mediating role of the Doll as a nexus for several opposed categories.

Tribal Rites

While the Family Rites were transmitted by women of elite families, the tribal rites involved the whole community, focusing on the economic cycle that started with the football games and culminated at the Məsing and Maize Rites.

Football

Oklahoma Delaware football was played men against women, using an eight inch oval made of deerskin stuffed with deer hair. The playing field, about 180 feet long, had pairs of goal posts set six feet apart at opposite ends. Before the game, a bet string was taken around and wagers were added to it of money (singles or change knotted in a cloth), ribbons, cigarettes, and handkerchiefs.

The game began when a respected elder took the ball out to the center of the field, prayed, and threw it into the air. Whichever player caught the ball started the game. If a man, he started kicking the ball from the men's goal posts, but if a woman, she began play from the posts at the women's end. At the now-abandoned field on the Falleaf farm, men were on the south side and women on the north. At the White Oak Shawnee ground, currently in use, men are on the east and women on the west. To score, the ball had to pass between the posts of the opposite sex; the first goal won the game. Then, a new game would start. Total scores for all games, for both men and women teams, were kept by a man using counting sticks. The Delaware limited play to 12 games, on rare occasions to 24, and the side that won the most games was declared the winner for that day.

Lacking referees, players settled their own disputes, minimizing the need for judges by using certain strategies to handicap the men and keep the play friendly. Men could only kick the ball, while women could hold, run with, and throw the ball. Women would never kick the ball because that was considered immodest. As Nora Dean said, it was as though men were playing soccer and women football. The most a man could do was slap the ball out of the hands of a woman. If he became rough, grabbing or holding a woman, the other women would mob him to teach the men a lesson in manners. Therefore, a man avoided touching a woman during the game, putting males at a disadvantage. Sometimes, women would deliberately mob a man if the game were going against them, but the men dared not retaliate. At decisive moments, the ball was sometimes given to an ancient and vulnerable dame who was slowly and carefully guided by the

---

[340.] These three dolls were buried together with a brother of the last owner.

[341.] American Philosophical Society, ms. # 932.

women down the field and through the goal posts. The men could only stand by, never obstructing such a frail and defenseless opponent.

After the last game of the season, an elder prayed on the field before splitting open the ball and scattering the deer hair stuffing. The hide covering was kept in trust by a respected person or couple until the next year. The night after the last game, a stomp dance was often held. Games went on during the first few months of the spring to encourage the growth of vegetation, particularly crops. During the 1970s, traditional elders were confounded, however, because younger Delaware played football (at the Copan powwow grounds) all summer long, an excess harmful to healthy growth.

During a game, the exclusiveness of Woman allowed the female team to monopolize the field because men had to abide by restrictions applying to women. Speck (1937: 73) recorded that the games were held to advance vegetation, a womanly purpose, but otherwise his description was much less informative than that provided by Nora Dean.

Məsing

The Məsing outfit and bundle, sold to Harrington and never replaced, had been kept in a tiny house in the yard of a respected old man. After the annual rites lapsed, he would occasionally hear the sound of Məsing's snapping turtle rattle, like those used by the Iroquois in their rituals, but no one went near the tiny house because they had neglected Məsing. After a time, the custodian went "berserk" (lost his senses). An Indian doctor diagnosed the cause as Məsing insisting that his dance be revived. This was done and the man was cured, but no one wanted responsibility for the bundle so it was passed from one elder to another, each one concerned about the consequences that might befall his family for avoiding the rite. Its last keeper was George Bullitt and the circumstances of the sale to Harrington are discussed by Speck (1931: 43).

The bundle contained the entire outfit, a jacket and pants of bearskin, together with a wooden mask painted half red and half black, a snapping turtle rattle holding corn kernels, a walking stick, and a pouch, said to hold "snakes". Children proved their bravery by going up to Məsing and giving him tobacco to put into this pouch. Shy or weak children were especially encouraged to do so. When fully dressed, the impersonator held the mask in front of his face, gripping it through the mouth opening with the left hand. In his right hand were the cane and rattle. The fitted cap securing the mask over the face, as described by David Brainerd in 1745, apparently did not continue in use.

The Delaware loved Məsing because he was uniquely their own. In Oklahoma, many Delaware were angered by the sale of the Məsing bundle, but, in hindsight, most have decided it was safer for everyone because any danger was transferred to the new custodians, much as Sarah (Sally) Thompson decided to sell her Otter bundle to Harrington for $20.

Other tribes have also sold sacred goods to collectors or museums, preserving a source of mystical power while shifting any adverse consequences to the new keepers. Ever a concern was the danger in passing powerful items on to a younger generation, if they were unprepared to accept them or unwise in their use.

In some cases, the Delaware buried bundles or dolls with the last owner, but this could be dangerous because the residual potency of the bundle might be used by the dead to harm the living. Delaware believed in several souls (Miller 1992), one of which lurked on the earth. Any harm it intended would be worse if a bundle shared its coffin. In short, there were several ways of disposing of sacred items. Destroying them, usually in a fire, ended their utility, so this was often too extreme a solution; placing them in graves gave the dead a potentially dangerous advantage; while selling them to outsiders preserved them for the future while deflecting any harm.

The Məsing Rite was held in the fall (Speck 1937: 50) or in May (Harrington 1921: 152). More likely, it was probably held during the hunting season and whenever else the custodian felt it was needed. A dramatic figure, Məsing left a lasting impression on those who saw him. The mother of Charlie Dean saw the rite once and for the rest of her life talked about the "Devil Dance". This was not unusual because Məsing could be frightening, as vividly recalled by older Delaware and early Oklahoma settlers. At least once, while the messengers and Məsing were going around to announce the camping day for the Big House, the sight of him caused the horses of an on-coming buggy to bolt in terror.

The Məsing Dance was held at midnight in a forest clearing, accompanied by special hunting songs and a folded deerhide drum stuffed with dried grass. A water drum, with a hide cover drawn over a hollowed log partially filled with water, may have also been used since Nora had such a drumstick with a Məsing face carved at the end. A fire burned at the center of a clearing, with the men dancers forming an outside ring and women an inside one. Məsing danced "outside the circle of people, not with them. When they have finished, he dances twelve changes alone, which occupies the time until morning" (Harrington 1921: 154). At the end, everyone feasted on hominy.

For an earlier period, Richard Adams (1906: 299) reported

> Across the fire and inside of the ring is a long hickory pole supported at each end by wooden forks set in the ground. On the east of this pole the singers stand; on the west end is a venison or deer, which is roasted. About daylight, when the dance is nearly over, all the dancers eat of the venison. They have a dried deer hide stretched over some hickory poles, and standing around it beat on the hide and sing. The dancers proceed around the fire to the right, the women on the inside next to the fire. After the dance is under way the Messingq comes from the darkness, jumps over the dancers, and dances between the other dancers and the fire. He makes some funny and queer gestures, kicks the fire, and then departs... He is a terror to little children, and when he comes to a house or tent the man of the house usually gives him a piece of tobacco, which the Messingq smells and puts in his big pouch, after which he turns around and kicks back toward the giver which means "thank you", and departs.

Məsing also appeared in the Oklahoma Big House Rite during the days of the hunt, while the Munsee parallel, called Mazink, appeared during the last half of the Bear Sacrifice. Instead of a single masked figure, the Munsee had a Mazink guild, limited to 12 members, which functioned like an Iroquois Falseface order (Harrington 1921: 158ff).

Speck and Moses (1945: 27, 29) also mentioned other feasts and rituals in the Munsee series, such as the Maple Sugar and Strawberry, which agree with or follow Iroquois practice. Delaware and Iroquois cultures were indeed very close, but their similarities were buffered by deliberate reversals. Thus, they could adopt features from each other without cultural dissonance, as the Munsee adopted the masking sodality. The same also applied to Delaware and Shawnee parallels, aided by their common Algonkian background.

Maize

Contrary to A.F.C Wallace's claim (1956: 3; Miller 1996), the Maize (Preharvest Green Corn) Rite did not lapse until shortly after the Delaware settled in Oklahoma. As a young man, Jim Thompson encountered two Excrement Daubers, wearing cornhusk masks, as they were going around announcing that the rite would begin in four days. They had to be given a gift immediately, otherwise they were at liberty to smear the ungrateful with a fecal mixture from their container. Jim quickly gave them his neck bandanna.

At the actual dance, the men dancers were led by the Daubers wearing cornhusk masks, while the women were led by two women without special attire. At the feast, only hominy and cornbread were served, exclusively made from maize. Drums and rattles accompanied the songs. All other sources describe Dauber masks as made of cornhusks, so the set of wooden ones made for Speck (1937: 80) by Joe Washington reflect a creative imagination (and assured sale). While Harrington (1921; 43) said "little remembrance of the details of her worship can now be found among the Oklahoma Lenape, his novel (1963: 179) detailed that the Daubers wore "ugly little masks of wood with cornhusk hair and their clothes were made of cornhusks: sleeveless jackets, leggings, and shoes coarsely woven".

Since their own Green Corn lapsed, faithful Delaware have danced with the Shawnee at White Oak, Oklahoma, but the Shawnee had no Daubers. Throughout the East, the ceremony was held preharvest, while the corn is still alive in the fields, allowing "her" to receive thanks directly.

According to Speck (1937: 79), the daubing with human excrement was a "punishment", but this was an overly fastidious explanation. Generally, human cultures used feces to represent disjunction, separation, chaos, and disorder. Often, it symbolized a switch in time. Therefore, the Daubers were not just announcing the rite, they were marking the end of an old year and the beginning of a new one, a time of uncertainty well represented by the symbolism of feces.

While the Green Corn marked the end of the agricultural year, the Gamwing was the summary of the entire annual round. Their functions were distinct, refuting Wallace's (1956) attempt to derive the Big House Rite from the earlier Green Corn. Further, the two ceremonies continued, side by side, until Delaware reached Oklahoma. There, the Big House steadily incorporated other rites, not all of them Delaware, including the Maize Rite.

Other Rites

Comparative study of such external and intertribal influences can shed light on the rest of the ritual series. For example, Speck (1937: 67) and Harrington (1921: 182) disputed that the Buffalo Dance was integral to the Delaware ceremonial cycle. This dance is still performed at White Oak by Shawnee and participating Delaware, much as described by Speck.

At the 1975 White Oak Bread Dance, men danced the inside ring and women the outside one, moving around cornbread loaves and garden vegetables piled in the center. Afterward, everyone feasted on meat, bread, and corn on the cob. A week later the Buffalo Dance should have been held, but drought had killed the maize crop, so the dance was cancelled. Ordinarily, the dance involved men (impersonating bison bulls) guarding two kettles of mush and "butting" the women (acting as bison cows) out of the way. Everyone tried to grab some of the mush. The Bread and Buffalo Dances were reciprocal, the first held for harvested plants and the second for products of the hunt and farm. Delaware say that both these dances were like their own had been.

The Delaware Buffalo Dance seems to have been part of another matrix of rituals concerned with killing: Buffalo, War, and Opossum. The Buffalo Dance was "intended for fighting men and hunters" (Speck 1937: 67), "usually given before starting on the chase" (Adams 1906: 299), with both men and women dancing. The War Dance was held by men and a few unique women before departing for raids and battle, or later to commemorate their deeds of valor. The Opossum Dance, named for an animal that "plays dead", emphasized women, since it featured a vision recitation by a woman, singers using a pottery water drum, and a row of female dances. "Other women, we are told, formed a line of followers behind her, and there is no mention of men in the column" (Speck 1937: 58). The indications, then, are that the Opossum Dance was exclusive, the War Dance inclusive, and the Buffalo Dance inclosive.

Of the best known tribal rites, The Maize Preharvest Rite was womanly and exclusive, linked with Mother Maize, who was believed to be jealous and very sensitive (Speck 1937: 61). She was set apart, treated carefully, and somewhat feared because her wrath would ruin the harvest if she thought any disrespect was being shown to her fields, crops, or bounty.

The ballgame was inclusive, played men against women for the part of a year transitional between hunting and farming. The game encouraged the spring growth of plants, in sympathy with the rapid movement of people along the field. The game used a ball made of deer products which was itself a mediator, passing between men and women, sky and earth, and the standing wooden goal posts. Tribes of the Southeast and the Lakota equated a ball game with the quest for knowledge and wisdom. Although this was not a ready Delaware explanation, it accords well with their attitude.

The Məsing Rite was inclosive, associated with sky and earth, animals and plants, hunting and farming. In all, the tribal triad of Ballgame (Məsing) Maize parallels that for the Family Rites of Otter (Doll) Bear.

Speck equated Məsing with a widespread belief in a Game Boss (Owner), although he was more like a Keeper or Warden in that he did not "own" the resources or species, he only managed them. Məsing was believed to live in a mountain range floating above the earth. Anciently, he was probably the lowest one of the 12 skykeepers represented on the Big House posts. He received particular attention because he lived closest to the earth, and initiated the upward movement of prayers to the Creator. Unifying this chain of beings was the Mind they shared in common.

An unexpected reversal occurs between the Məsing and Maize Rites. Both rites used masks, a wooden one for Məsing and two husk ones for the Daubers. We should expect a single mask for the womanly rite and two for the manly one, but this was not the case, probably to emphasize the value of reciprocity, exchange, and complementarity among all the rituals. As Nora Dean said, "Just because it was called the Green Corn didn't mean that people did not also take time to give thanks for everything else". Thus, while directed to the approaching maize harvest, prayers were also addressed to all interrelated beings. In Canada, of course, there were 12 Mazink, each representing a skykeeper, so there was no reversal.

Big Moon Peyote

Oklahoma also had its own prophets. Foremost among them was John Wilson (Moonhead, *Nishkantu* in Caddo), an Anadarko Caddo with a Delaware father who was related to Nora Dean's mother (Speck 1933). Moonhead was profoundly interested in religion, serving both as an advocate for Catholicism and as a leader in the Ghost Dance. About 1895, he began to preach the virtues of the sacrament of peyote, a thornless cactus long important in the rituals of tribes in northern Mexico. His teachings formed the Big Moon Rite, now limited to the Quapaw and Osage. While Wilson is still acknowledged as the revealer of peyote ritual, the modern form originated with the Lipan Apache, Comanche, and Kiowa. Sometimes called Little Moon, it counted among its converts such prominent Dewey Delaware as Chief Charlie Elkhair. Incorporated as the Native American Church and granted legal status in various states, this modern form of Little Moon recognizes Quanah Parker as its founder. Anadarko and other Delawares, nevertheless, continue to revere the teachings of Nishkantu.

Sources

Adams, Richard C
  1890 Notes On The Delaware Indians. Report on Indians Taxed and Not Taxed. 1890 United States Census, Volume 10.
  1904 Ancient Religion of the Delaware Indians: Observations and Reflections. Washington, DC: Law Reporter.
  1906a Legends of the Delaware Indians and Picture Writing. Washington, DC: Law Reporter.
  1906b A Brief History of the Delaware Indians. 59th Congress, 1st Session, Senate Document 501. June 22. US Government Printing Office, Washington, DC.
Harrington, Mark R
  1913 A Preliminary Sketch of Lenape Culture. *American Anthropologist* 15: 208-35.
  1921 *Religion and Ceremonies of the Lenape.* Museum of the American Indian, Indian Notes and Monographs # 19.
  1963 *The Indians of New Jersey: Dickon among the Lenapes.* 2d ed. New Brunswick, NJ: Rutgers University Press.
  nd Draft on Delaware Social Organization and Ethnography. MS on File at the Museum of the American Indian, Heye Foundation, New York.
Miller, Jay
  1972 The Priority of the Left. *Man* 7: 646-7.
  1974a The Delaware As Woman: A Symbolic Solution. *American Ethnologist* 1 (3): 507-514.
  1974b Why The World Is On The Back Of A Turtle. *Man* 9 (2): 306-8.
  1974c The Unalachtigo? *Pennsylvania Archaeologist* 44 (4): 7-8. :
  1975a Delaware Alternative Classifications. *AL* 17 (9): 434-44.
  1975b Addendum On Ethno-Taxonomic Congresses. *AA* 77 (4): 887.
  1975c Delaware clan names. *Man in the Northeast* 9: 60-63
  1976 The Delaware Doll Dance. *Man in the Northeast* 12: 80-84.
  1977 Delaware Anatomy, With Linguistic, Social, and Medical Aspects. *Anthropological Linguistics* 19 (4): 144-166.
  1979 A Strucon Model of Delaware Culture and the Positioning of Mediators. *American Ethnologist* 6 (4): 791-802.
  1980a A Structural Analysis of the Delaware Big House Rite. University of Oklahoma, *Papers in Anthropology* 21:107-33.
  1980b High Minded High Gods in North America. *Anthropos* 75: 916-19.
  1980c The Matter of the (Thoughtful) Heart: Centrality, Focality, or Overlap. *Journal of Anthropological Research* 36: 338-42.
  1982 People, Berdaches, And Left-Handed Bears: Human Variation In Native North America. *Journal of Anthropological Research* 38 (3): 274-287.
  1989a Delaware Traditions from Kansas, Nahkoman to Isaac McCoy. *Plains Anthropologist* 34 (123): 1-6.

1989b   The Early Years of Watomika (James Bouchard), Delaware and Jesuit. American Indian Quarterly 13 (2): 165-188.

1990   *Delaware Integrity* ~ The Ritualization of Culture in the Gamwing (Big House Rite). Amazon.

1994a *The Delaware*. Chicago: Childrens.

1994b   The 1806 Purge among the Indiana Delaware: Sorcery, Gender, Boundaries, and Legitimacy. *Ethnohistory* 41: 245-66.

1996 Changing Moons: A History of Caddo Religion. *Plains Anthropologist* 41 (157): 243-259.

Miller, Jay, and Nora Thompson Dean

1978 A Personal Account of the Delaware Big House Rite. *Pennsylvania Archaeologist* 48 (1-2): 39-43.

Morgan, Lewis Henry

1959 *The Indian Journals 1859-1862*. Leslie White, ed. University of Michigan Press, Ann Arbor. Originally published 1859.

1972 *League Of The Iroquois*. Secaucus: The Citadel Press.

Petrullo, Vincenzo

1934 *The Diabolic Root*: A Study of Peyotism, the New Indian Religion among the Delawares. Philadelphia: University of Pennsylvania Press.

Speck, Frank

1931   *A Study of the Delaware Big House Ceremony*. Publications of the Pennsylvania Historical Commission 2. Harrisburg.

1933 Notes on the Life of John Wilson, the Revealer of Peyote, as Recalled by His Nephew, George Anderson. *General Magazine and Historical Chronicle* 35: 539-56.

1937   *Oklahoma Delaware Ceremonies, Feasts and Dances*. Memoirs of the American Philosophical Society 7. Philadelphia.

1945 *The Celestial Bear Comes Down to Earth*. Reading, PA: Reading Museum Scientific Publications # 7.

1945 *The Iroquois* ~ A Study In Cultural Evolution. Cranbrook Institute of Science Bulletin 23.

1946   The Delaware Indians as Women: 377-389. *Pennsylvania Magazine of History and Biography*. October.

1948   Critical Comments on "Delaware Culture Chronology. *American Anthropologist* 50: 723-2.4.

1949 *Midwinter Rites of the Cayuga Long House*. Philadelphia: University of Pennsylvania Press.

APS   Archived materials stored in the Library of the American Philosophical Society, Philadelphia. Delaware material in boxes 8 and 9. Manuscript numbers given in the text.

Speck, Frank G, and Jesse Moses

1945 *The Celestial Bear Comes Down to Earth*. Scientific Publication # 7. Reading, PA: Reading Public Museum and Art Gallery.

Tooker, E

1968 Masking and Matrilineality in North America. *American Anthropologist* 70 (6): 1170-1177.

1970 *The Iroquois Ceremonial of Midwinter*. Syracuse, NY: Syracuse University Press.

Wallace, Anthony FC
1947 Woman, Land, and Society: Three Aspects of Aboriginal Delaware Life. *Pennsylvania Archaeologist* 17 (1): 1-35.
1949 *King of the Delawares*: Teedyuscung 1700-1763. Philadelphia: University of Pennsylvania Press.
1956 New Religions among the Delaware Indians, 1600-1900. *Southwestern Journal of Anthropology* 12: 1-21.
1957 Political Organization and Land Tenure among the Northeastern Indians, 1600-1830. *Southwestern Journal of Anthropology* 13: 301-21.
Wallace, Paul AW
1975 *Indians in Pennsylvania.* Harrisburg: Pennsylvania Historical and Museum Commission.
Witthoft, John
1949 *Green Corn Ceremonialism in the Eastern Woodlands.* Occasional Contributions #13. Ann Arbor: University of Michigan, Museum of Anthropology.

CHEROKEE SUMMER DANCES[342]
Green Corn Ceremony and Dance

Legend relates that a branch of the Cherokee tribe compressed their infants' heads laterally. The method was for the mother to warm her hands and press on the child's temples every day until it was grown. For this reason the people of this group were called Di:ni:kɔhɛ̆hã, "big foreheads projecting out people." Like the rest of the Cherokee they had a Green Corn Dance, but they were given to performing it with great devotion at the harvest. So the other Cherokee came to refer to the dance by the name of this group, whence akɔhã̆dĩ: Green Corn Dance (literally, "big foreheads in motion").

The dance, which lasts all day and the following night, has four periods. The men's and women's parts are performed separately but concurrently. The dances are sponsored by some person who wishes to make a ceremonial donation from which he gains prestige and spiritual benefit, as do the participants.

First stage: Men's part (uli'sĩ). — The leader is followed by a column of men (ten, twelve, sixteen, or twenty) carrying guns. They circle counterclockwise at the dance station, which is several hundred yards from the main dance ground and feasting place.

First movement (see Pl. XVII, *a,* and fig. 4). — The company of selected men dancers circle counterclockwise behind the leader, who sings to the accompaniment of a gourd rattle. Guns are discharged at intervals throughout the morning, beginning with the man at the head of the column, followed by a shot from the next, and so on to the end man, who fires twice. The shots are given at signals in the leader's song and at a rapid shaking of the rattle. The reports from the guns symbolize thunder.

Second movement (see fig. 4). — The men dance two abreast, starting from the remote dance station and moving to the main dance ground, with the leader at the head. At the signal asi:hu'yakã they turn suddenly and go back across the space to where they started. This movement takes place about noon, and the men rest from dancing for half an hour to eat food provided by the women of the settlement. There are no food restrictions.

That the use of an explosion is a modern innovation to the rite is denied by the informant, who explained it as follows. Formerly a medicine man was called upon to exercise his magic power to produce a report to accentuate the intervals of the song and dance. As the men danced around, he would sit beside a "big white rock," put charcoal on the rock, spit on the charcoal, and, at the words hi':ha':hi', strike it with a club (stone). An explosion with a sharp report would result. Later, by the end of the seventeenth century, when the white traders had supplied European arms to the Cherokee, "they substituted guns" for the chemicals. This is a rather interesting example of rationalization in technology. A similar vulcanic feat was reported in 1934 by Deskaheh, a Cayuga ceremonial informant.

---

[342] Frank Speck and Leonard Broom, with Will West Long, Cherokee Dance and Drama, California, 1951; Oklahoma, 1983.

Women's Dance part (*atɑhon'*, literally, "make wood," Women's [47] Dance or Meal Dance; i:ł:tsã, literally, "meal," Women's Dance song). — The women dancers (volunteers) gather in the center of the main dance ground at some distance from the men dancers. They are lined up side by side before the main singer and shuffle with short steps. They are accompanied by a man[16] at some distance with a drum and the woman leader, who uses tortoise shell leg-rattles. The Women's Dance may be detached from its ritual context and performed in other dance series such, as the Booger Dance.

First movement (see fig. 5). — The dancers advance a few feet toward the singer, then retreat. The first part of the movement is in slow time. The last part is accelerated and the file turns right about, advancing and retreating to the singer.

Second movement (see fig. 5). — The women follow their leader, who is wearing turtle leg-rattles, circling counterclockwise once around the dance ground. The stanzas of the women's song elicit formal responses from the leader of the men's song group.

Third movement (see fig. 5). — The women resume formation abreast, as in the first movement, all holding hands. The woman wearing turtle leg-rattles dances at the left of the row of dancers.

Combined part. — *At* the conclusion of the separate dances for men and women the following takes place.

First movement (see Pl. XVII, &, and fig. 6). — Starting from the separate dance ground, the men dancers with guns are led by the leader with a rattle in a shuffling trot, two abreast, to the main dance ground. First they surround the women dancers in a large circle, dancing clockwise, then close in tightly around the women's dance line until they merge with it. This repeats the action of the second movement of the men's part.

Second movement (see fig. 7). — Men dancers combine with the women's dance column led by the men's dance leader, and mingle with the women, circling counterclockwise.

Third movement (see fig. 7). — The man drumming and singing for [51] the women's party resigns his station to the men's leader with the gourd rattle, who then takes both parties through to the finish, as in the second movement of the women's part.

Although the symbolic value of these movements is not clear, there [52] is implied a fertilization of vital elements, specifically the grains. A short notice of the Green Corn Dance was given by Chief Hicks in 1818.[17]

The green corn dance, so called, has been highly esteemed formerly. This is held when the corn is getting hard and lasts four days, and when the national council sits — a quantity of venison being procured to supply the dance. It is said that a person was formerly chosen to speak to the people on each day in a language that is partly lost — at least there is very little of it known now. At such times as the above, a piece of land is laid off and persons appointed to occupy it—no others being allowed to use it while the feast continues.

Second stage: feasting interval. — At the conclusion of the first stage of dancing the entire gathering partakes of the feast provided by the women of the home settlement. "Everyone is invited to share," both strangers and people from other Cherokee towns.

Third stage. — This is timed to take place just before sundown. The men and women dancers begin dancing in separate groups as in the first stage. The man singing for the women dancers uses a gourd rattle, but no drum is heard at this time. The women's dance leader wears tortoise shell leg-rattles.

First movement. — The men's leader conducts the dancers, who carry guns on their shoulders,[18] toward the women's dance circle, as in the third movement of the combined part. They surround the women and, moving clockwise, close in about them.

Second movement (gañã'ni:, "along the path or trail"). — The men dancers mingle with the women dancers, circling counterclockwise and zigzagging, and the men's leader resigns leadership to the women's male leader and singer. This movement continues for about half an hour, until the sun has set.

Fourth stage. — The night following the feast is spent in dances chosen from the series of animal rites, with the exception of the Booger, Bear, and Eagle dances. The dances begin with the [53] Friendship Dance and end just before dawn with the Round or Running Dance, which is preceded by the Corn Dance, an intrinsic part of the harvest ceremony. Mooney's informants related that in old times every fire in the settlement was extinguished just before the Green Corn Dance and all the people came and got new fire from the town house."

The performance of the corn rite in the morning has symbolic significance, according to West Long. It represents "early spring planting" through the analogy of morning and the springtime of the year. It is also believed to have been a necessary preparation for planting; the medicine man had an important part to play in offering prayer so that the corn would grow fast. Another purpose of the rite was to prevent the illness believed to result from eating green corn. Like all the tribes of the Southeast, the Cherokee feared the consequences of eating corn before the performance of placatory rites. The drinking of certain medicine in the form of an infusion is also remembered. Though the full particulars of the older Cherokee ceremony are not now known, this portion has been described by Witthoft. From his material it appears that the festival was a major community rite celebrated in August, when the green corn first became mature enough to eat, that it persisted as late as 1887, and that aspects of it are found as two separate survivals, the green corn feast and a green corn medicine. The latter is prepared and administered in the separate households of the conservatives as a prerequisite to eating green corn. West Long did not identify specimens of *Ilex cassine,* source of the "black drink" used on similar occasions by the Creeks and Yuchi, as the ingredient called for in the Cherokee prophylaxis; but the details of the rite might be clarified if they were supplemented by information culled from the narratives of such eighteenth-century travelers as Timberlake, Brickel, and Adair, *Ilex cassine* does not grow in the region now occupied by the eastern Cherokee. [54]

A Moravian account of a Green Corn Dance in August, 1803, is given by Schwarze:"

While awaiting the session of the Council at Oostanaula, lodged with Standing Turkey near the Town House, the Brethren had opportunity to observe some of the Cherokee dances. They saw five different varieties of Indian dances, all very simple, but some distinguished by great regularity. Each dance was accompanied by the song of two men who also beat time with calabashes filled with small stones. Their principal dance was the "Green Corn Dance," really intended to be a religious exercise of Thanksgiving to "the Man above," for the new crop of corn. Men and women were decked out in their best for these dances, at which good order prevailed. The dancing ground was in front of the Town House, a large, level place swept clean. In the center stood a high pole with green boughs tied to it to afford some shade. At the pole stood a bench upon which were seated those who beat time. One dance is carried out by two groups of men who appear out of the bushes on opposite sides of the dancing ground with loud shouts and advance towards the pole in the center around which they dance in opposite directions. Another dance is done by one group of men who are led by their singer. They carry guns and after they march a little distance to calabash time, the singer quickly turns and bows down to the earth. The whole group then sing with him and likewise bow to the ground and begin to dance around the singer; next, the guns are fired and then they begin all over again! A third dance, in which men and women assist, is carried out in a slow movement around the pole. The singers dance in front and somewhat to one side of the ring, looking very serious and solemn. Another dance employs about sixty Indians who start dancing at the pole and then widen the circle more and more with an interwoven, spiral movement until they reach the limits of the ground, then closing up to the pole again. The last dance the missionaries witnessed was done by women only, dancing around the pole, the men beating time. The female leader of this dance wore leather shoes with turtle backs fastened thereto with which she mightily rattled!

An Analysis of the First Salmon Ceremony[343]
by Erna Gunther

A CEREMONY marking the advent of the first salmon run of the season is general among North Pacific Coast Indians.

Many of the ceremonial features are similar throughout the area, yet the question remains in how far these common elements are dependent on the salmon run and how far they represent a diffused ceremonial complex.

The majority of tribes on the coast make salmon one of their principal foods. This is true of tribes as far inland as the Rockies, that is, wherever they live on streams which have connection with the ocean. Several varieties of salmon (*Oncorhynchus*) are abundant from Monterey, California to Bering Sea. When these fish run up the rivers in enormous numbers to spawn, the great fishing season commences for the Indian. In most localities there are no salmon in the streams during some seasons of the year, or if any are to be found the quality is so poor that the Indians do not use them. Hence the coming of the first salmon is a real event, for it means not only a change from the diet of dried meats and fish, but in many instances saves the people from imminent starvation.

I will give a description of four typical first salmon ceremonies and then deal with the following questions: first, is the distribution of this ceremony co-extensive with the use of salmon? Second, what is the relation of this ceremony to the ceremonial complex of the tribe, especially to other first-fruits ceremonies? Finally, what is the attitude toward the salmon as shown by this ceremony and by myths and taboos?

The northernmost people practising the ceremony are the Tsimshian. When the first salmon of the year is caught, four old shamans are called to the fisherman's platform, bringing a new cedar bark mat, bird's down and red ochre. They spread out the mat and a shaman puts on the fisherman's clothing. He holds a rattle in his right hand and an eagle's tail in the left. The shamans [606] put the salmon on the mat and taking it up at the four corners, carry it to the chief's house, the shaman dressed in the fisherman's clothing leading the way and shaking his rattle. All young people who are unclean are ordered to leave. The old people enter the house in front of the procession. After the procession has passed in, all the shamans of the village dressed in ceremonial regalia enter. The salmon is placed on a cedar board and the shamans march around it four times. Then the shaman wearing the fisherman's clothes calls two old shamans to cut the fish. The head is cut off first, then the tail is cut, never broken, with a mussel-shell knife. A stone or metal knife would cause thunderstorm or disaster. While cutting the fish they call it honorary names. They cut along the ventral side and remove the stomach.[344]

The second area is that of the Kwakiutl-speaking peoples. The Kwakiutl are justly famous for their complete ritualization of life. In regard to the salmon ceremony they have lived up to their tradition, for where most tribes have one ritual they have at least three. The first is really an individual ritual. Every wise salmon fisher has prayers which belong to him personally. These prayers are offered when the first catch of salmon is made with the hook. When some are

---

[343] Read before the British Association for the Advancement of Science, Toronto, August, 1924 605606 American Anthropologist n.s, 28, 1926: 605-617.

[344] Franz Boas, Tsimshian Mythology, 31st Report, Bureau of American Ethnology, 1916, p. 450.

caught, the fisherman goes to the river house and prays to the fish to be good while he is drying them. He prays:

> Swimmer, I thank you because I am still alive at this season when you come back to our good place, for the reason why you come is that we may play together with my fishing tackle, Swimmer. Now, go home and tell your friends that you had good luck on account of your coming here, and that they shall come with their wealth bringer, that I may get some of your wealth, Swimmer; also take away my sickness, friend, supernatural one, Swimmer.[345]

The other ceremonies are the collective rituals used elsewhere. As soon as the first four silver salmon of the run are caught the wife of the fisherman meets him on the beach. She prays to the silver salmon, picks them up and lays them on the beach before their house. She cuts them with a fish knife so that the head and [607] tail are left on the backbone. She sets up roasting tongs on the beach and fastens the salmon so that the eyes project on the tongs. Later the tongs are carried into the house and placed by the fire. As soon as the eyes blacken, the fisherman calls together his family group to eat them for if roasted eyes are kept in the house overnight, the silver salmon will disappear from the sea. The guests who are called sit behind the fire. The hostess spreads new food mats and places the tongs with the eyes before the guest. She gives them water to drink before eating. The guest of the highest rank prays to the food before it is eaten. The fisherman's wife picks up all bones and skin, wraps them in a food mat and throws it in the sea. The guests rub their hands, but do not wash them, and wipe them on shredded cedar bark as they usually would do.

At the ceremony for the first dog salmon the wife of the fisherman again officiates. She prays to the salmon:

> O Supernatural Ones, O Swimmers, I thank you that you are willing to come to us. Don't let your coming be bad, for you come to be food for us. Therefore I beg you to protect me and the one who takes mercy on me, that we may not die without cause, Swimmers.

The woman replies "Yes" to herself. She goes up the bank and there cuts the fish. The intestines of a speared salmon are broken off at the anal fin, while those of a salmon caught on the hook are cut. If these rules are not followed the fisherman's line will break. The entrails are gathered in a basket and poured into the sea at the mouth of a river for it is believed that various kinds of salmon at once come to life when the intestines are put into the water.[346]

Among the Lower Lillooet the ceremony is preceded by watching and praying at the fishing-places, a feature that also occurs in northern California. When the salmon have passed up the river the chief under whose supervision the ceremony is performed sends a boy to pray at each fishing-place for a heavy run. Just before the catch the tops of the weir poles are decorated with owl, hawk, red-wing, flicker or eagle feathers. At fishing places without weirs, poles are decorated with feathers and set up. Then the chief orders a man to go out in a canoe and make

---

[345] Franz Boas, Ethnology of the Kwakiutl, 35th Report, Bureau of American Ethnology, 1921, p. 1318-1319.

[346] Boas, *Ibid.* p. 609-611.

the first catch. Before taking [608] the salmon from the water it is rolled up in a mat, for if it saw the ground, no more fish would come. They wait until it is dead on the shore; then rolled it in leaves and branches of a bush with red berries. They carry it to the place where a new kettle stands ready to receive it. New stones for boiling are used and are first dipped into a new basket of water to clean them. The salmon is boiled whole, then lifted out with sticks and laid on a new mat in order to pull off the fins and take out the backbone. It is boiled again until it is reduced to a mush. Then it is divided with a new spoon and put into two new dishes. Now the people are all assembled to eat the fish. Unmarried adult women, menstruating women, orphans, widows or widowers are not allowed to eat the first salmon. All others must eat some of it, the men from one dish, the women from the other.

If the first salmon were cut with a knife, there would be no run. The humpback is regarded as the chief of the salmon and is believed to lead all other salmon away from the sea, so if he is prayed to, the salmon will come quickly. He is frequently treated with as much reverence as the first salmon caught earlier in the seasons.[347]

Hill-Tout records another Lillooet salmon ceremony, specifically for the sockeye which according to him was regarded as the chief of the salmon. It is conducted in much the same way but adds an elaborate introduction of the salmon to the elders of the village by laying the right fin of the salmon on a series of rods, each named for one of the elders. In this way the salmon is welcomed into the tribe. After a feast of salmon cooked to a mush there is a ceremonial dance. After the feast, the bones are thrown into the water so they can revive.[348]

These ceremonies differ radically from those to the south, for in the Puget Sound region and beyond the ceremonial eating of the salmon is practically the whole ceremony.   The Snohomish at the mouth of the Snohomish River on Puget Sound allowed [609] nobody to step over the first salmon. The man who caught the first fish invited all his friends to a feast at which everyone except the host ate some of the fish.[349] From this point southward the ceremony always centers around the eating of the salmon. The ritual is generally very simple. Sometimes the mode of cutting the fish and the persons who are to partake of it are specified. The southernmost ceremony occurs among the Northern Maidu.[350]

The first question is whether all Pacific Coast people who use salmon, perform this ceremony for the first catch of the year. The northernmost people who have the ceremony are the Tsimshian, whose neighbors the {Nuxalk} Bella Coola share their type of ritual, whereas the salmon runs as far north as the Yukon where the dogs salmon goes up the river in July.[351] There are no accounts of Tlingit or Haida ceremonies although both these people use the fish, hence it may be assumed that they lack the ceremony. The Tahltan have five varieties of salmon which

---

[347] James Teit, The Lillooet, Memoirs, American Museum of Natural History, part 5, 1906, vol. 5, p. 280-281.

[348] Charles Hill-Tout, Report on the Ethnology of the StlatlumH of British Columbia, Journal, Royal Anthropological Institute, vol. 35, 1905, p. 140.

[349] Hermann Haeberlin and Erna Gunther, Ethnographische Notizen tiber dieIndianerstamme des Puget-Sundes, Zeitschrift fur Ethnologie, 1924, p. 17.

[350] Roland B Dixon, The Northern Maidu, Bulletin, American Museum of Natural History, vol. 17, 1905, p. 198.

[351] E.W Nelson, Eskimo about Bering Straits, 18th Report, Bureau of American Ethnology, 1899, p. 183.

begin running in June but here again no ceremony is noted.[352] Further inland, the Carrier and Chilcotin are quite dependent on salmon for food but no ritual has been described.[353] Among the interior peoples we find the Thompson, Shuswap[354] and Upper Lillooet,[355] who use salmon extensively, have no ceremony. The Shuswap and Thompson say that the salmon is a "hard fish" and does not have to be treated carefully. They claim that it has no real "mystery." The Cowichans of the Delta,[356] the StsEelis[357] and other tribes along the [610] Fraser River, share the elaborate first salmon ceremony of the Lower Lillooet. On Vancouver Island the Kwakiutl on the east coast and the Nootka on the west coast have much the same ceremony, but I could find no information concerning the Salish tribes of the island.

About Puget Sound the ceremony seems to be practiced generally. For the Klallam I have conflicting data.   An informant who was raised in the village where Dungeness, Washington, now stands, gives an account of a ceremony similar to that found elsewhere on the Sound, while another informant whose native village was about ten miles east of Dungeners tells me that salmon ran all year in the Dungeness River so that there was no ceremony to mark its coming in the spring.[358]

It is possible here that one village had the ceremony and the other did not. The Nisqually[359] and Puyallup,[360] who are closely related linguistically and culturally to the Snohomish, have similar simple ceremonies. All the Chinook tribes on the Columbia River from its mouth to the Dalles perform a salmon ceremony very similar to the Snohomish.[361] The Wishram, who live at the Dalles, suspend all fishing after the first spring salmon is caught until after the ceremony has been performed. The fisherman carries the fish to a shaman who cuts the fish lengthwise, taking out the head and backbone in one piece. The fish is baked in a depression

FIG. I. Map showing the distribution of the tribes with the first ceremony(underlined)
and the distribution of the salmon (cross-hatched). [612]   (see it enlarged on last page)

---

[352] George T Emmons, The Tahltan Indians, University of Pennsylvania Anthropological Publications, vol. IV, part 1,1911, p. 85.

[353] A.G Morice, Western Denes, Proceedings, Canadian Institute, 3rd Series, vol. VII, 1899, p. 128-129.

[354] James Teit, The Shuswap, Memoirs, American Museum of Natural History,vol. IV, part 7, 1909, p. 602.

[355] James Teit, The Lillooet, p. 280.

[356] Franz Boas, Indians of the Lower Fraser River, British Association for the Advancement of Science, Report, 1894, p. 461.

[357] Charles Hill-Tout, Ethnological Report on the StsEelis and Sk'aulits Tribes [610] of the HalkomelEm Division of the Salish of British Columbia, Journal, Royal Anthropological Institute, vol. 34, 1904, p. 330.

[358] Field notes gathered under the auspices of the Department of Anthropology, University of Washington.

[359] George Gibbs, Tribes of Western Washington and Northwestern Oregon, Contributions to North American Ethnology, vol. I, 1877, p. 196.

[360] Arthur C Ballard, Personal Communication.

[361] James G Swan, The Northwest Coast, 1857, p. 107-108; George Gibbs, loc. cit, p. 196; Gabriel Franchére, Narrative of a Voyage to the Northwest Coast of America, New York, 1854, pp. 26 & 261.

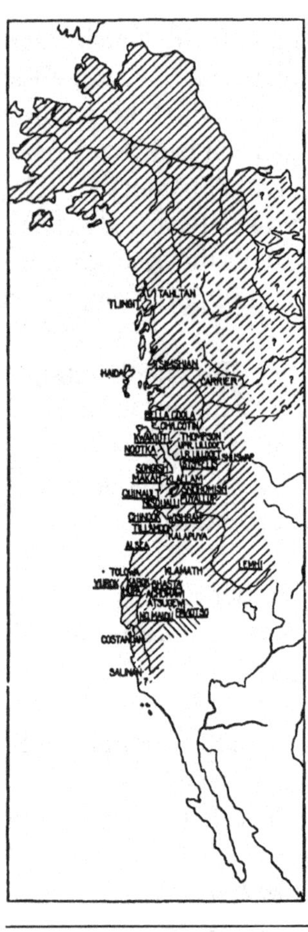

in the ground, which is lined with choke-cherry leaves and covered with mats. Everyone is invited and gets some of the fish. They pray at the feast. The bones are not returned to the river.[362] [611]

The Tillamook and Alsea honor the salmon by boiling the first catch with a simple ceremony.[363] The Kalapuya[364] however have no ceremony because the salmon cannot ascend the falls of theWillamette at the northern border of their territory. In northern California, the Tolowa, Karok, and Yurok[365] have a salmon dance which is said to be much like their deer dance. The Hupa[366] and Shasta have a ceremony which recalls that of the Lower Lillooet in that a person is sent out to watch for the first salmon. The Shasta allow this fish to pass, for this one was believed to lead the others upstream.[367] Salmon was used by the Achomawi andAtsugewi in quantity but there is no record of a ceremony.[368] The Northern Maidu of the foothills prohibit salmon fishing until a ceremony has been performed.[369] In his survey of California Kroeber makes the statement that wherever salmon abound in California there is a salmon ceremony.[370] Salmon are found as far south as Salinan territory, but at the southern boundary of this area they occur only in small numbers for there are few rivers to the coast.[371]

The two eastern outposts of the salmon ceremony are the Paviotso of Pyramid Lake who order a dance five days after the [613] fish come into the lake,[372] and the Lemhi Shoshoni who divide the first catch and feast on it, their faces being painted ceremonially for the

---

[362] Leslie Spier, Wishram Notes.

[363] Franz Boas, Notes on the Tillamook, University of California Publications in American Archaeology and Ethnology, vol. 20, 1923, pp. 9-10.

[364] Handbook of American Indians, Bulletin 30, Bureau of American Ethnology, 1907, p. 645.

[365] Stephen Powers, Indians of California, Contributions to North American Ethnology, vol. m, 1877, pp. 56, 67.

[366] P.E Goddard, Life and Culture of the Hupa, Univ. Calif. Publ. Amer. Arch. and Eth., vol. I, 1903, pp. 78-79.

[367] Roland B Dixon, The Shasta, Bulletin, American Museum of Natural History, 1907, pp. 430-431.

[368] *Id*, Notes on the Achomawi and Atsugewi, American Anthropologist, n.s, 10, 1908, pp. 212-213.

[369] Roland B Dixon, The Northern Maidu, p. 198.

[370] AL Kroeber, Handbook of the Indians of California, p. 467, Bulletin 78, Bureau of American Ethnology, Washington, 1925.

[371] J. Alden Mason, Ethnology of the Salmon Indians, Univ. of Calif. Publ. in Amer. Arch. and Eth., vol. 10, 1912, p. 124. At present the southernmost salmon are in the Carmel River near Monterey. Dean Cobb of the College of Fisheries said that they may have occurred as far south as the Salinan River in aboriginal times, for the distribution of salmon is very variable.

[372] Robert H Lowie, Notes on Shoshonean Ethnography, Anthropological Papers, American Museum of Natural History, vol. xx, p. 306. These people probably have a trout or red fish which is colloquially known as salmon. There is no true salmon in the Great Basin Area.

occasion.[373] The Kutenai and their neighbors certainly use salmon extensively for food yet they do not express their reverence for it by way of a ceremony.

The area in which salmon is caught extends beyond 'the area of the ceremony especially to the north and east. The presence of salmon in a particular place is somewhat variable from. year to year, for each group of salmon goes back to the place where it was spawned. If a river is avoided one year there may not be any fish in it for several years, depending on the age of maturity of the fish.[374] Even within the salmon area the ceremony is not performed by every tribe that uses the fish. The Klamath Indians, who use salmon sparingly, have no ceremony and none of the taboos that are current elsewhere.[375] The Costanoans who were on the southern margin of the salmon area could catch the fish during the winter months when the water was high.[376] Their culture so far as we know was very simple so that it may be logical not to expect a ceremony among them. The accompanying map gives the general distribution of salmon on the Pacific coast and indicates the distribution of the ceremony.

The procedure of the salmon ceremony has beyond doubt grown out of the regular procedure for handling a salmon catch; the interesting feature is the amount of ceremonial action with which it is garnished and the extent to which this ritual is taken from other ceremonies of the tribe. When the Tsimshian carry the salmon into the chief's house on a mat covered with cedar leaves {boughs} they are treating the fish as they would treat an honored guest, who is carried to the house on a cedar plank.[377] The Tsimshian [614] also greet the first olachen with a ceremony that consists of roasting and eating the first catch. The Lillooet have a bear ceremony which they share with many tribes to the north and east of them. The attitude toward the bear seems to be very much that which the coast people have toward the salmon. The Lillooet pray to the bear, just as the Kwakiutl pray to the salmon. Here arises the question whether the salmon has been substituted on the coast for the bear which is the object of reverence across northern North America and in many parts of eastern Asia.

Teit records that when the potato was first obtained, it was addressed as "chief" and the Lillooet danced to it four times before it was eaten.[378] When the berry crop is almost ripe the chief addresses the mountain tops and the people pick just enough for a day's supply; to keep them overnight would be unlucky. A similar taboo is found among many coast tribes with regard to the first salmon. The StsEelis on the Fraser River observe a similar ceremony for the first berries as they do for the first salmon. In northern California the salmon ceremony belongs to a whole group of dances which are given to produce more bountiful wild crops, abundance of salmon, prevention of flood, famine and earthquake.[379] The definitely local characteristic here is the recitation of esoteric formulas.

The pattern for the salmon ceremony seems to be based on a reverential attitude toward the fish and a desire to treat it in such a manner that it will come in great numbers. The actual

---

[373] Robert H Lowie, The Northern Shoshone, same series, vol. II, 1909, p. 218.

[374] John Cobb, Pacific Salmon Fisheries, Bureau of Fisheries Document, no. 902,1921.

[375] Leslie Spier, Personal Communication.

[376] Kroeber, Handbook.

[377] Boas, Tsimshian Mythology, p. 438.

[378] Teit, The Lillooet, p. 279.

[379] Kroeber, Handbook, p. 53.

[37a] John Swanton, Contribution to the Ethnology of the Haida, Memoirs, American Museum of Natural History, vol. VIII, pp. 48-49.

procedure is taken from the normal handling of the catch with such additional ceremonial features as have been pointed out above. The other first-fruits ceremonies in this area share with the salmon ritual a ceremonial eating of the product in many cases followed by a dance. The possibilities for developing something strikingly different are after all limited. It is clear, however, in spite of the meager information available, that some features of the general ceremonial life in each tribe have been infused in the procedure. Californian [615] tribes have a social dance where the Kwakiutl have a speech and a feast with guests sitting according to rank.

Finally, the attitude toward the salmon as expressed in mythology and taboo is the same feeling that underlies the ceremonial. The salmon myth on the Pacific coast has a much wider distribution than the ceremony, or rather it occurs among tribes for whom no data concerning a ceremony is available. The typical incidents of the salmon myth are: a boy comes to the salmon country and is told to kill some of the children for food. He is cautioned to save all the bones and throw them into the water so that the children may revive. Very frequently the boy returns home and brings plenty of fish to his village.

The Haida and Tlingit have such a myth but there is no record of a ceremony. Among the Haida is the belief that if a girl sees a salmon jumping in the creek, within a year of her puberty rites, all salmon would leave the creek. For five years after her puberty rites she is not allowed to eat The Chilcotin have the myth. The Quinault, who also tell such a story, express their attitude toward the salmon by the taboo that the first catch is never sold for fear that the hearts may be destroyed or fed to the dogs.[380]

Very frequently myths dictate ceremonial behavior. In this instance the feeling expressed in the myth and the ceremony maybe regarded as alike, but the only concrete feature carried from the story to the ritual is the instruction that the salmon bones be thrown back in the water, this being based on the theory that salmon revive when their bones are returned to the river. This belief is not limited to salmon. The Shuswap who have no such regard for the salmon throw beaver bones back into the streams that they may come to life again.[381]

Special relations to food animals are universal and the salmon comes in for a liberal share. Throughout the salmon area there is [616] some association between salmon and twins. The Tsimshian believe that twins have the power to call olachen and salmon.[382] The Kwakiutl believe that twins of the same sex were salmon before birth.[383] The Nootka believe the father of twins to be an instrument of the salmon world and during the fishing season he devotes his entire time to singing and performing secret rituals to propitiate the salmon so that there may be a maximum catch. The appearance of twins forecasts an unusually large run. A twin child will burst into tears if a salmon is mistreated.[384]

When Makah twins are born during the fishing season at Tatoosh Island the parents are sent back to Neah Bay and prohibited from eating any kind of fish.[385] Similarly, the Klallam do

---

[380] Cobb, Pacific Salmon Fisheries, p. 23.

[381] British Association for the Advancement of Science, Sixth Report on the tribes of Northwestern Canada, 1890, p. 646.

[382] Boas, First General Report on the Tribes of Northwestern Canada, Brit. Assoc. Adv. Science, 1889, p. 847.

[383] Brit. Assoc. Adv. Science, Sixth Report, p. 614.

[384] Edward Sapir, "Nootka" in Hasting's Encyclopedia of Religion and Ethics.

[385] James G. Swan, The Indians of Cape Flattery, Smithsonian Contributions to Knowledge, vol. 16, 1870, p. 82.

not allow the parents of twins to come near salt or fresh water for one year after the birth of the children. The Klallam from all the villages along the Straits of Juan de Fuca used to go to Hood Canal in the fall of the year to catch and dry salmon. On one occasion a woman from Clallam Bay gave birth to twins there. She and her husband had to carry the children overland instead of returning home by canoe on account of this taboo. The Klallam of Dungeness relate that one of the early white families on the river had twins and they besought the father of the children not to fish because he would spoil the run of humpbacks which was then in the Dungeness River. He disregarded their petition and as a consequence there were no humpbacks in the river for twenty years.[386] Here again the pattern is a relation between twins and salmon, but the relation differs from tribe to tribe. [617]

There is on the North Pacific coast a reverent regard for salmon which is one of the principal food animals. This regard shows itself in the rituals which are performed for the salmon, the taboos surrounding it, and in its place in mythology. The first salmon ceremony follows a pattern used in other first fruits ceremonies of the area, and draws on other ceremonial complexes of the tribe. The particular relation to the salmon is further akin to the attitude toward the bear in adjacent areas of North America and Asia. Within our area the fundamental and widespread feature of the first salmon ceremony is in the attitude toward the salmon, although its expression varies somewhat from tribe to tribe. This is of such a character as to suggest the diffusion of at least this basic idea. The diffusion of minor details among neighboring groups suggests possible historic connection in the borrowing of these ceremonial features.

SEATTLE, WASHINGTON

---

[386] These two incidents are taken from my recent field notes. In discussing the second incident with Dean Cobb of the College of Fisheries, University of Washington, I learned that it may be true that for many years there was no humpback run in the Dungeness River because through some accident they may not have been able to spawn there one season. After such an occurrence the fish may avoid the stream for a long time.

Tahltan
Tlingit

Tsimshian
Haida
Carrier

Bella Coola {Nuxalk}
Chilcotin
Kwakiutl Thompson
Nootka Upper Lillooet
Tsihalis Lower Lillooet Shuswap
Songish
Makah Klallam
Quinault Snohomish

Nisqualli Puyallup

Chinok Wishram

Tillamook
Kalapuya

Alsea

Tolowa Klamath Lemhi

Yurok Karok Shasta
Hupa Achomawi
Atsugewi
N Maidu Paviotso

Costanoan

Salinan

New Salmon '28

UNIVERSITY OF WASHINGTON PUBLICATIONS
IN
ANTHROPOLOGY

A Further Analysis of the First Salmon Ceremony

by
Erna Gunther

Submitted in partial fulfillment of the requirements for the degree of Doctor of Philosophy
under the Faculty of Philosophy, Columbia University, New York

University of Washington Press
Seattle, Washington
1928

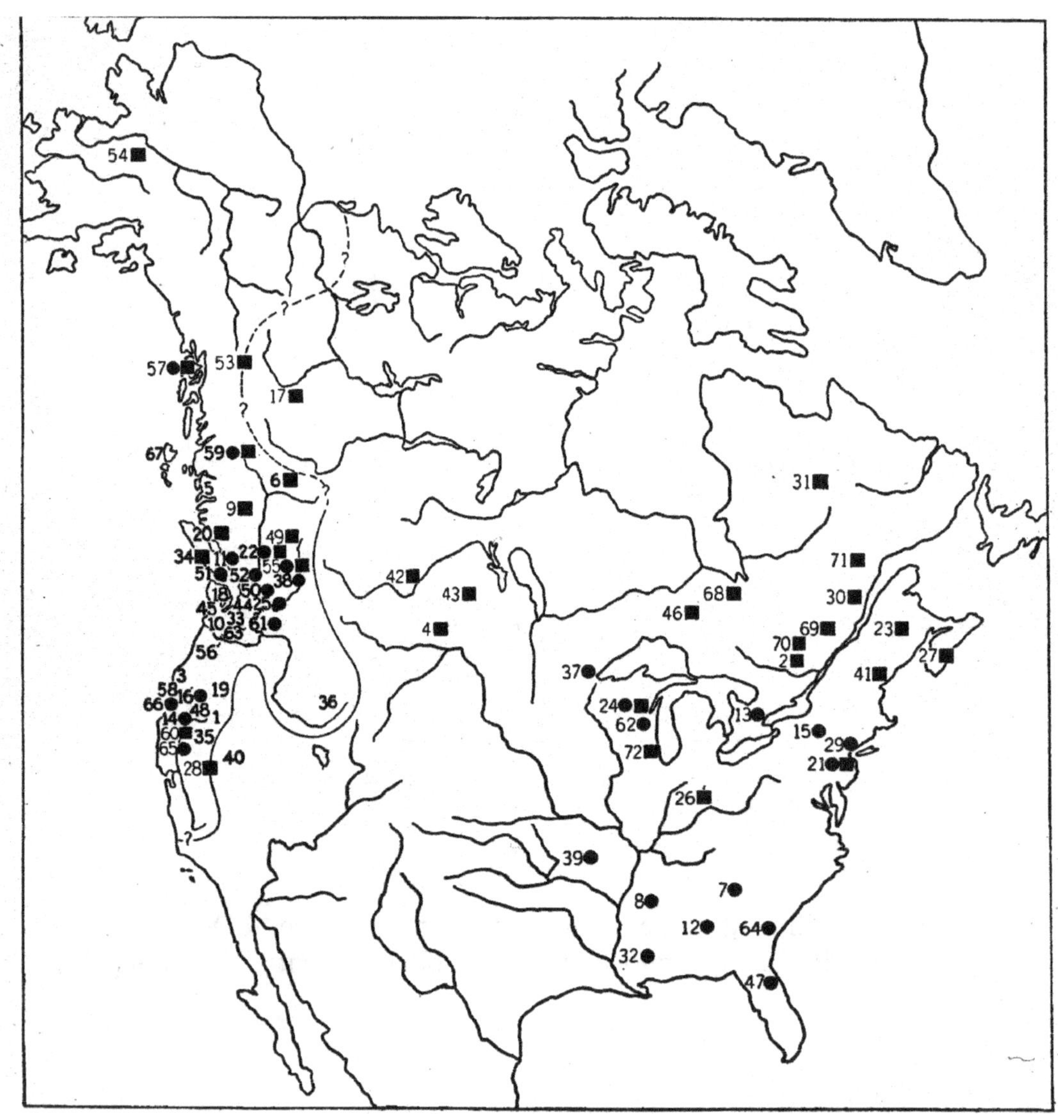

FIG. 1.—The Distribution of the First Salmon, First Fruits, and Bear Ceremony in North America (Bold face figures represent the First Salmon Ceremony; circles, First Fruits; squares, Bear Cult. The distribution of the salmon is included within the boundary line. For references see pp. 159-160.)

FIG. 1. — The Distribution of the First Salmon, First Fruits, and Bear Ceremony in North America

(Bold face figures represent the First Salmon Ceremony; circles, First Fruits; squares, Bear Cult. The distribution of the salmon is included within the boundary line. See references pp. 159-160.)

Contents

TABLES

TEXT FIGURE

A Further Analysis of the First Salmon Ceremony

A recent paper[387] gave briefly the distribution of this ceremony and indicated its significance in the ceremonial life of the tribes which participate in it. It became clear after the paper was finished that it touched on many points which are worth further investigation. It is the purpose now to discuss especially the integration of the ceremony with the ritual life of the people who practice it, and the relation of this ceremony and the attitude which fosters it, to similar rituals current in the same area, especially, the first fruits ceremonies and the bear cult.

The salmon ceremony is performed by a large group of tribes on the North Pacific Coast and as far inland as the salmon runs. The area covered by the ceremony is not entirely coextensive with the territory in which salmon is caught. None of the tribes who catch the salmon practice agriculture, but depend largely on fish. The fish is eaten fresh during the season and also dried for winter use. The salmon runs occur from early spring through the summer, varying according to locality; for instance, in the Yukon River the dog salmon runs in July; in the Klamath River the salmon comes upstream in large numbers in spring and fall, but there is so much water in the river that some variety of salmon can always be taken. This is true of many streams in this area but the winter salmon usually is of poor quality so that, even if the coming of the new run does not save the people from actual starvation, it gives a welcome fresh food supply. In most streams this spring salmon run comes in prodigious numbers, and is awaited with great eagerness. It presents an occasion for expressing the attitude of veneration which is held throughout the area toward the salmon.

When the first salmon comes upstream, each group, according to its ceremonial pattern, celebrates the first catch by ritualizing each step in handling the salmon from the catching to the eating. This ritual is simple or elaborate according to the tendency of the group. One of the major problems in analyzing this ceremony is its relation to the ceremonial pattern of each group that has adopted it.

Another problem involved is the diffusion of this ceremony. Its spread, as was stated before, is not coextensive with the salmon fishing area. Some of the gaps are probably due to lack of ethnographic knowledge, but there are other groups for which definite negative evidence is given. Why is this ceremony adopted by some groups and disregarded by others? Beyond the general diffusion of the ceremony, there is a more minute problem, namely; how many specific features of the ceremony are common to a number of tribes?

The salmon ceremony is based on a veneration for the salmon which is present even among groups where it has not been crystallized into a set of [136] rites. These groups, as well as those who practice the ceremony, have various taboos connected with the salmon which carry out this attitude. An analysis of these taboos will show to what extent the salmon has become the object of special behavior.

This attitude of veneration is a pattern of behavior toward many animals in a territory larger than the salmon fishing area. This is especially developed in relations to the bear, about which a cult has grown up that resembles the salmon taboos in many respects. Furthermore in the same area, there is a sporadic appearance of first fruits ceremonies, the only instance outside of agricultural groups in North America. The basic attitudes underlying these cults as well as the

---

[387] Erna Gunther, Analysis of the First Salmon Ceremony (AA, n.s, 28, 1926, 605-617).

actual ritual pattern so closely resemble one another that it seems profitable to consider their possible interrelation.

Finally, it was pointed out in the earlier paper that the mythology of these tribes bears out the attitude toward the salmon expressed in the ceremony, These myths may have some direct bearing on the ceremony. They may dictate the ritual or explain it. The types of myths and their position in the folktales of each group will also show their relative importance.

This problem involves a consideration of the mechanism of diffusion and the transformation of, a cultural trait as it is assimilated into each tribal pattern. Throughout the North Pacific Coast there is the feeling of veneration for the salmon which in some places has developed into a ritual and elsewhere has remained only a series of taboos regulating actions toward the salmon.

I ~ Additions and Corrections

The salmon ceremony which is to be discussed in the present paper is found on the Pacific Coast from the Tsimshian on the Skeena River to the Northern Maidu of north central California and eastward as far as the Lemhi Shoshoni and the Paviotso of Pyramid Lake, Nevada. Its distribution among the tribes of this area was discussed in the previous paper, but further work reveals some additions and a few corrections.

The ceremony, of which several detailed descriptions will be given in the course of the paper, celebrates the arrival of the salmon in its first run of the season and consists in handling-the fish ceremonially and eating the first catch in festivity. The details of this procedure vary according to the ritual pattern of each tribe. Among the marginal groups it is an open question whether to include their rituals with the first salmon ceremony. With more intensive analysis of the ceremony it becomes clear that these peripheral examples should be included. The Lemhi Shoshoni and the Paviotso do not have the true salmon but a salmon trout. They celebrate the first run of the season in the same way the salmon is celebrated on the coast; therefore they were included in the earlier study and allowed to remain in this one. It was stated in the first paper that the Klamath ate sparingly of the salmon and performed no ceremony. On being questioned again, the Klamath informant gave the ceremony which they perform for the first sucker saying that this fish was treated ceremonially instead of the salmon.[388] Suckers are found in Klamath Lake and the rivers that flow into it, in abundance. For this reason the Klamath ceremony will be included in this study.

In Northern California, the Achomawi were listed as one of the tribes without a ceremony, but on closer reading of Kroeber's *Handbook of California Indians* this brief statement is found:

> "There is mention of a first salmon ceremony, suggestive of the northwestern new year's rituals. Old men fasted in order to increase the run of fish, while women and children ate out of sight of the river. But no further details are known."[389]

Every observer of early Chinook life has commented on their performance of the salmon ceremony.[3a] Even when the tribe was fast disappearing they still clung to that part of their salmon taboos which seemed most important, burning the heart to prevent its mutilation by dogs. The localized salmon taboos are fully expressed in the mythology. Coyote in his progress up the

---

[388] 2 Spier, ms.
[389] Kroeber, BBAE 78: 313.
[3a] See appendix.

river institutes the taboos for each fishing place.[390]   A similar tale is told by the Kathlamet.[391] Their culture was probably as closely related to the Chinook 'proper as they were related linguistically.   On the basis of this evidence it is [138] perhaps legitimate to claim that the Kathlamet as well as the other Chinook had a first salmon ceremony.

In the northern part of the salmon area there are two additions to be recorded.   On inquiry, Father Morice states that the Carrier, when the first salmon is caught, proclaim the news m a sort of chant which is taken up by all who hear it.   He adds that since the coming of the salmon is of great importance to these Indians, there may have been more ceremony before their culture disintegrated.[392]   On the basis of this slender evidence it is perhaps wiser to include the Carrier rather than to omit them, for even singing gives a ceremonial greeting to the salmon and from a tribe as simple in all their habits as the Carrier, one can scarcely expect more.

It has always seemed strange that the Haida and Tlingit, who have a rich ceremonial life, an abundance of salmon and the Salmon Boy myth which shows the reverential attitude toward the fish, should not have the ceremony.   There is only one slight clue among the Haida that points to a deviation from the regular fishing routine.   "When the first salmon were brought in, (from the fishing grounds to the village) it was customary to allow anyone to go down and take one."[393]   It is customary in many tribes, especially for hunters both of sea and land animals, to give freely of their bag.   Whether the Haida custom is related to this or whether it is an attenuated form of salmon ceremony is not clear.   For the purpose of this paper it will be arbitrarily classed as the latter.

Mr. Marius Barbeau states that he does not believe that the salmon ceremonies are as important among the northern tribes as they are further south.[394]   This will perhaps explain the absence of the ceremony from such groups as the Kaska and Tahltan.

On the map accompanying the earlier paper there are several errors.   The Makah are credited with a salmon ceremony which they do not have and the Tolowa who have a salmon dance like that of the Karok were unmarked. [139]

II ~ Relation to the Ceremonial Pattern

Ceremonies, like all other cultural traits, whether they are borrowed or developed within the group, are adjusted to the pattern evolved by the group for that kind of activity. This is true of the salmon ceremony. The relation of this ceremony to the local ceremonial pattern will be shown by analyzing the situation among several tribes, chosen for the divergence of the rite among them.

It is frequently found that a tribal group has more than one cycle of rituals.   The Tsimshian, for example, have an elaborate ceremonial life with the potlatch and secret societies as a nucleus and the acquisition of social prestige as a goal.   But scattered through the year, independent of these important rituals, are a series of minor ceremonies, connected with every incident of life.   The salmon ceremony is one of these.   Being outside of the great ritual cycle does not, however, relegate this ceremony to a position of unimportance. Quite the contrary: the

---

[390]   Boas, BBAE 20: 101-106.
[391]   Boas, BBAE 26: 45-49.
[392]   Morice, letter.
[393]   Swanton, Mem. AMNH 8: 69.
[394]   Barbeau, letter, November 4, 1927.

reason for the ceremony is to welcome the salmon, which is one of their principal foods, and therefore very important economically. All the shamans of the village assist in the performance.

Although there are two cycles of ceremonies current among the Tsimshian, the ritual pattern, the ceremonial paraphernalia and the acts which are considered ceremonial in character are largely the same. A careful analysis of the first salmon ceremony, as described by Boas from the mythology, will show that every step is derived from the regular ceremonial procedure of the tribe.

"When the first salmon has been caught, four old shamans are called to the fisherman's platform. They bring along a new cedar bark mat, bird's down, red ochre, and other paraphernalia belonging to a shaman."[395] There are four shamans because four is the ceremonial number of the Tsimshian. The shaman is present because he is the normal ceremonial leader. The use of a new mat may be traced to two customs: in the first fruits ceremonies of the Lillooet as well as their salmon ceremony new utensils are used; and furthermore, Tsimshian custom dictates that "when a visitor is led into a house, a good new mat is spread for him."[396]

"They spread the cedar-bark mat on the platform, and the shaman fisherman puts on his attire, holding the rattle in his right hand, the eagle tail in his left." In some accounts it is definitely stated that the shaman changes clothing with the fisherman. This change of clothing might be interpreted as an attempt to make the shaman and fisherman seem one. The eagle tail in the left hand and the rattle in the right is a typical position for a shaman at work.

"The shamans take up the mat at its four corners and carry up the salmon (in the same way as a guest is welcomed); the fisherman shaman going ahead of them, shaking his rattle and swinging his eagle tail." A person who is the [140] object of ceremony is carried in a blanket, the four corners held by four men. A bride is carried on an elkskin blanket to the house of the groom's father. Four men hold the corners of the blanket.[397] Also a bridegroom and his companions are carried into the bride's house when he comes to marry her.[398]

"The salmon is carried to the chief's house; and all the young people who are considered unclean are ordered to leave the house, while all the old people enter in front of the procession." It is appropriate that the ceremony should be conducted in the chief's house for all honored guests are received there. The taboo against young people is not derived from the ceremonial pattern but from the general attitude toward the salmon. Menstruating women, pregnant women, or those who have just given birth to children must not eat salmon or handle it. Only old women may work on salmon nets.

"All the shamans in the village dress up and come in, following the salmon." It is customary for the Tsimshian shamans to work in close cooperation. For instance: "When a person is sick, then the wife or the husband of the sick one will offer much property to the male shaman to treat the patient. Then the male shaman assembles all his shaman friends, sometimes ten or eighteen ...."[399] This cooperation among shamans is a peculiarly local trait, evidently not occurring among the Haida and Tlingit where the shaman is a solitary person, much feared by the laity. Again the Puget Sound shaman works independently except in such dramatic shamanistic performances as the *SbEtEtda'q* {*səbədaq*} or soul hunting expedition. There as many shamans work together as the person sponsoring the performance can afford to engage, but

---

[395] Boas, RBAE 31: 450. All subsequent quotations for this ceremony are from the same source.
[396] Boas, RBAE 31: 437.
[397] Boas, RBAE 31: 533.
[398] Boas, RBAE 31: 531.
[399] Boas, RBAE 31: 558.

they are independent. The reason for the many shamans in this instance is to display wealth, since one man can perform, as he does among the Klallam, just as well as the many.

"Inside [the house], the salmon is placed on a large cedar board, and the shamans march around it four times. Meanwhile the singers sit down in their proper places around the house, and the fisherman shaman calls two old women shamans to cut the salmon." Four, the ceremonial number appears again. The singers take the position they always occupy during rituals. The fact that the shaman calls two women shamans to cut the fish is borrowed directly from shamanistic procedure. Where a shaman attends a sick person his helper is always a female shaman.

"They take up their mussel-shell knives, while all the people keep quiet. They call the salmon by its honorary names — Chief Spring Salmon, Quartz Nose, Two Gills on Back, Lightning Following One Another, and Three Jumps." Honorific names are of great importance and significance. That the salmon should be addressed in this way while being cut up, shows very clearly that the ceremony is partly one of propitiation. The use of honorific names is important in a culture where names are high social privileges. The Bella Coola call the salmon by an archaic word for "salmon," a custom which [141] may be regarded as equivalent to this Tsimshian custom. Cutting the fish with musselshell knives lifts the act out of the daily routine, by using an implement which has been supplanted. This falls into a class with the use of the archaic word.

Throughout this ceremony the normal procedure in handling the salmon has been ritualized according to the ceremonial pattern of the Tsimshian. It has not been fitted into any one ceremonial pattern, but each ritual action has been drawn from the ceremonial behavior of the group. The ceremony belongs outside the important social rituals as do all the other first fruits ceremonies, but of this series the salmon ritual is the most elaborate, and probably of greatest significance to the group.

Among the Bella Coola the salmon ceremony is found in a similar situation. The Bella Coola are a Salish group, who after coming to the coast, adopted with avidity all the Kwakiutl ceremonial organization which they found around them. But the salmon ceremony, again, does not belong to this group of rituals. It may possibly be that they brought the ceremony with them, for there is not an act in the ritual which could not belong to the ceremonial complex of an Interior Salish group.

The Kwakiutl have several salmon rituals, each for a specific variety of salmon. This is a thoroughly Kwakiutl characteristic, for their life is exceptionally full of ritual acts. Here again, the salmon ceremony belongs to the minor rituals. It is not conducted by shamans as among the Tsimshian, but by the fisherman and his wife who have the appropriate family prayers. The procedure is as follows:

When the first dog salmon of the season is caught, the wife of the fisherman goes to meet him and prays to the salmon, "O Supernatural ones, O Swimmers, I thank you that you are willing to come to us. Don't let your coming be bad, for you come to be food for us. Therefore I beg you to protect me and the one who 'takes mercy on me, that we may not die without cause, Swimmers" The woman replies, "Yes," to herself. They go up the bank. When they finish cutting a speared salmon the woman gathers the refuse in a basket and pours it in the water at the mouth of a river, for various kinds of salmon come to life when the intestines are thrown in the water. The anal fin of a speared salmon must always be broken off at the intestines but when a salmon is caught with the hook, it is cut off lest the fisherman's line break. Those who clean salmon must be very careful about this.[400]

---

[400] Boas, RBAE 35: 609-610.

When the first four silver salmon have been caught by trolling, the wife of the fisherman meets him on the beach. She prays 'to the silver salmon and picking up the four with her finger, puts them on the beach in front of their house. She cuts the salmon with a fish knife so that the head and tail are left on the back bone. She sets up roasting tongs on the beach and puts the salmon on them so the eyes project on the tongs. After the refuse has been [142] thrown in the sea, the tongs with the eyes are taken to the fire in the house. As soon as they are blackened the fisherman calls his sept (*numaym*) to eat the roasted eyes for if they are kept in the house overnight the silver salmon would disappear from the sea. The guests sit in the rear of the fire. The housewife spreads new food mats and places the tongs with eyes before the guests. The person of highest rank prays to the food and after they have eaten, they drink water. They are careful not to wash their hands afterwards. The bones and pieces of skin are folded up in the food mat and thrown in the sea. The guests leave after eating.[401]

These are exceedingly simple, dignified rituals. Every significant act in the daily life of the Kwakiutl has a prayer connected with it. For instance, when a canoe-builder has almost felled the tree he is going to use he takes four chips of wood and throwing one behind the foot of the tree, he says, "O supernatural one! Now follow your supernatural power!" Throwing another, he says, "O friend! Now you see your leader, who says that you shall turn your head and fall there also." He throws a third chip and says, "O life-giver! Now you have seen which way your supernatural power went. Now go the same way." He throws the last one saying, "O friend, now you will go where your heartwood goes. You will lie on your face at the same place." After he says this he answers himself, saying, "Yes, I shall fall with my top there."[402]
When a woman cuts the roots of a young cedar tree she prays, "Look at me, friend! I come to ask for your dress, for you have come to take pity on us; for there is nothing for which you can not be used, because it is your way that there is nothing for which we cannot use you, for you are really willing to give us your dress. I come to beg you for this, long life-maker, for I am going to make a basket for lily roots out of you. I pray, friend, not to feel angry with me on account of what I am going to do to you, and I beg you, friend, to tell your friends about what I ask of you. Take care, friend! Keep sickness away from me, so that I may not be killed by sickness or in war, O friend!"[403]

The fisherman catches four silver salmon and the canoe-builder throws four chips behind the tree because the Kwakiutl, like the Tsimshian, have four as their ritual number. There is a very definite formula to these prayers. The animal or plant prayed to is called, "Friend, Supernatural One." It is thanked for giving of its substance. It is asked to keep illness and death from the devotee. The canoe-builder answers his prayer as does the wife of the salmon fisherman.

The ceremonial unit for rituals not controlled through the secret society, is the sept (*numaym*). The members of the fisherman's sept are called for the salmon ceremony. For larger feasts, members of the host's sept go as [143] messengers to Invite the guests. Minor feasts are prepared by the host and his wife. At the huckleberry feast the host's wife serves the guests who depart as soon as they have finished eating.[404] Guests are always seated behind the fire in order of rank. Finally, disposing of the refuse is one of the most widespread regulations regarding the salmon, based on the concept of their immortality.

---

[401] Boas, RBAE 35: 611-612.

[402] Boas, RBAE 35: 618.

[403] Boas, RBAE 35: 617.

[404] Boas, RBAE 35: 754.

Both the Tsimshian and the Kwakiutl have adopted the salmon ceremony into their set of minor rituals. This ceremony is one of the few performed by the Kwakiutl which does not add to the social prestige of the person giving it, but is for the good of the tribe. With the Tsimshian the salmon ceremony falls in a class with their first fruits rituals. These ceremonies being outside the great ceremonial cycle of these groups, they have taken on all the characteristics of their exoteric rituals.

The situation in Northwestern California is the reverse. It happens that among the Yurok the greatest salmon run comes in the fall, at the height of the ceremonial season. Here the salmon ceremony has been incorporated into the esoteric rituals of these groups and integrated most thoroughly with the ritual pattern of the group.

Kroeber has summarized very neatly the purpose of ceremonialism among the Yurok:

The major ceremonies of the Yurok reveal the following qualities:

1. The motive is to renew or maintain the established world. This purpose included bountiful wild crops, abundance of salmon, and the prevention of famine, earthquakes and flood. To a greater or less extent, the expression of these objects takes on the character of a new year's rite. This is particularly plain in the first salmon ceremony at Wetlkwan and the fish dam building at Kelpel.

2. The esoteric portion of the ceremony is the recitation of a long formula, narrating, mostly in dialogue, the establishment of the ceremony by the spirits of prehuman race and its immediate beneficial effects. This formula is spoken in sections before various rocks or spots that mark the abode of these spirits. The reciter is an old man, usually accompanied by an assistant; any prescribed symbolic acts are performed by them alone.

3. After the recitation of the formula or the major portion, a dance begins, and goes on every afternoon, or morning and afternoon for five, ten or more days.

4. The localization of these ceremonies is extreme. The formulas abound in place names. They are spoken at a series of places in and about the village which are exactly prescribed.[405]

The building of the salmon dam at Kelpel can be fitted exactly into Kroeber's characterization of the ceremonies at large. The formulist who is in charge of the ceremony fasts for a few days preceding the ceremony and visits sacred places. In the actual building of the dam a larger number of villagers participate than in other ceremonials where there is no material object to be accomplished. The labor of sixty men is required for ten days. [144]

The materials are secured at certain places and in specified ways, sanctity being attached to every action. In spite of the ceremonial character of the occasion there is merrymaking throughout, reaching its climax on the last day when the formulist's assistant "wearing a beard and impersonating a Karok who has eloped with another man's wife, pretends to be fleeing vengeance and allows his canoe to be capsized in midstream. He swims to Kelpel, crouches, and the mass of men, armed with long poles, clash them together over his head and lay them on his back until he is covered from sight." Before the dam is finished an imitation deer dance is held and the day the work is really completed the real dance is made. A few days later the people gather again and for twelve to sixteen days there is dancing.[406]

---

[405] Kroeber, BBAE 78: 53-54.
[406] Ibid, 58: 60.

In every feature this corresponds to the ritual pattern of the group. The same is true of the Karok and Hupa ceremonies. The ritual pattern resembles that of the Yurok to a great extent and the salmon ceremony has been thoroughly assimilated into that pattern. The ceremony in all three groups has been taken out of the hands of the people at large and carried out by a special group versed in the esoteric knowledge the ritual requires. Such a body of esoteric knowledge is built up here about all the rituals and clearly has developed by the efforts of this priestly class.

On the other hand, the neighbors of the Karok, the Shasta, had no community dances and very little ceremonial life. They knew the ceremonies of the people on the lower Klamath and believed that the Yurok at the mouth put medicine on the first salmon 'to bring the fish up the river', so they let it pass unmolested. After the first fish had passed, some were caught and hung up to dry. No salmon could be caught until this fish had been dried and a portion eaten by all who fished at that particular station.

It is interesting that these people are so poor ceremonially that they have to depend on another group for their "medicine." They knew the elaborate dances of the Karok and Yurok but made no attempt at imitation.[407] The concept of dancing for the good of the community or for world rejuvenation does not exist with them. Since there is nothing in their mythology that links up with the ceremony, we have here an instance of the diffusion of the ceremony to wholly unreceptive ground.

These instances of the salmon ceremonies will serve to show the extent to which these rites have been assimilated into the culture of the groups that practice them. Where there is a full ceremonial life, the ceremony partakes of this ritualistic wealth, whereas in simpler cultures it remains but a pause in the everyday routine. On the northwest coast where the ceremonial life clusters about the potlatch and the secret society rituals, the salmon ceremony, although following the local form of ritual, remains a thing apart. It is not a step in the all-important pursuit of wealth and social prestige. Quite to the contrary, [145] it is one of the few rites performed for the good of the whole group, to the social enhancement of no single individual. It might therefore be possible that this ceremony, together with the other first fruits ceremonies in the area, belongs to an older stratum of ceremonial life which existed before the elaborate superstructure of social rank and secret society organization developed. This supposition is also borne out by the fact that the salmon ceremony and first fruits rituals are quite uniformly among the people marginal to the Northwest Coast proper, especially in the Salish groups.

In Northwestern California the ceremony has been completely assimilated into the ritual life of the groups, even having a definite place in the ceremonial calendar. It has been endowed with a set of esoteric formulae and needs a formulist to repeat these to perform the ceremony. Of recent years the only person who knows the formula has refused on account of personal sorrow to repeat it, so it has been impossible for the Yurok to build the salmon dam and have the ritual. With her death even the possibility of having the ceremony will probably also disappear. [146]

---

[407] Kroeber, BBAE 78: 304.

TABLE I. RITUALIZATION OF NORMAL HANDLING OF SALMON

	Haida	Tsimshian	Carrier	Bella Coola	Kwakiutl	Cowichan	Songish	Klallam	Nootka	StsEllis	Lillooet
Caught by specified person	−	−	−	−	−	−	−	−	−	−	−
Carried in specified manner	−	+	+	+	+	+	+	+	−	+	+
Cut by specified person	−	+	−	−	+	+	−	−	−	−	−
Cut in ritual manner	−	+	−	−	+	+	+	+[8]	+	−	+
Cooked in ritual manner	−	−	−	+	+	+	+	+[8]	+	+	+
Eaten by: All present	[4]	−	−	−	+	+	−	[7][8]	−	+	−
Old men	−	−	−	−	−	−	−	−	−	−	−
Children	−	−	−	−	−	−	+	+	−	−	−
Ceremonial leader	−	−	−	−	−	−	−	−	−	−	−
Dance held	−	−	−	−	−	−	−	−	−	−	+
Prayers recited	−	−	−	−	+	+	−	−	−	+	−
Bones thrown in water	−	[1]	−	+	+	+	+	−	−	−	+

	Okanogan, Met-how, Nespelim, Wenatchee	Wishram	Upr. Chinook	Chinook proper	Kathlamet	Nisqualli	Puyallup	Snohomish	Quinault	Tillamook
Caught by specified person	−	−	−	−	−	−	−	−	−	−
Carried in specified manner	−	−	−	−	−	−	+	−	−	−
Cut by specified person	−	−	−	−	−	−	−	−	−	+
Cut in ritual manner	−	−	−	+	+	+	−	−	−	−
Cooked in ritual manner	−	+	−	−	+	−	−	+	−	+
Eaten by: All present	−	−	−	−	−	−	−	[7]	−	−
Old men	−	+	−	−	−	−	−	−	−	−
Children	−	−	+	−	−	−	−	−	−	−
Ceremonial leader	−	−	−	+	−	+	−	−	−	+
Dance held	−	−	−	−	−	−	−	−	−	+
Prayers recited	[3]	−	−	−	−	−	−	−	−	−
Bones thrown in water	−	−	−	[6]	−	−	−	−	[5]	[1]

	Alsea	Hupa	Lassik	Karok	Yurok	Tolowa	Klamath	Shasta	No. Maidu	Lemhi	Paviotso
Caught by specified person	−	+	−	+	+	−	−	−	+	−	−
Carried in specified manner	−	−	−	−	−	−	−	−	−	−	−
Cut by specified person	−	+	−	−	−	−	−	−	−	−	−
Cut in ritual manner	−	+	−	−	−	−	−	−	−	−	−
Cooked in ritual manner	+	+	+	−	+	−	+	+	+	−	−
Eaten by: All present	−	−	−	−	−	−	+	+	+	+	−
Old men	−	−	−	−	−	−	−	−	−	−	−
Children	−	−	−	−	−	−	−	−	−	−	−
Ceremonial leader	−	+	−	+	+	−	−	−	−	−	+
Dance held	−	+	−	−	+	+	−	−	−	−	−
Prayers recited	−	[2]	−	[2]	[2]	−	−	−	−	−	−
Bones thrown in water	−	−	−	−	−	−	−	−	−	−	−

[1] Bones thrown into fire.
[2] Formulae recited.
[3] Dream recited.
[4] First catch may be taken by anyone.
[5] Heart burned.
[6] Chanted when first salmon was caught.
[7] By all except host.
[8] Features belonging to Dungeness Klallam, others to Beecher Bay Klallam.

III ~ The Diffusion of the Ceremony

The salmon ceremony is not co-extensive with the salmon area, but in that part of the area where it is found, the distribution is almost continuous. The greatest discrepancy is found in the north where the fish runs in rivers north to the Yukon, while the Tsimshian on the Skeena and Nass Rivers are the most northerly to have the ceremony. The ritual also is not found as far inland as the salmon run. The Thompson and Shuswap on the eastern margin of the area of the ceremony depend largely on salmon, but do not celebrate its arrival. Farther south, the eastern outpost of the ceremony is among the Lemhi Shoshoni and the Paviotso of Pyramid Lake. Among the latter, incidentally, the run is that of whitefish or salmon trout in place of the true salmon. To the south there is nothing known of the treatment of the fish beyond the Northern Maidu. Roughly the distribution of the salmon is from Monterey Bay to Bering Strait, although a few are taken in the Salinas River, the most southerly stream of any size to flow into the Pacific. The salmon ceremony is therefore known from the Tsimshian on the north to the Northern Maidu on the south and as far inland as the Paviotso of Pyramid Lake.

Since the ceremony is not co-extensive with the salmon area, it cannot be held that it is in spontaneous reaction to the salmon. Throughout this area economic life varies but little, and salmon is an equally important item of food almost everywhere.

In other features of culture the groups performing this ceremony differ more widely, but rather in the degree of integration of the culture, than in fundamental structure. In the northernmost part of the area, along the coast, an elaborate social and ceremonial structure is built about the potlatch and social ranking. Marginal traces of these are found southward to the Columbia River. Northwestern California also has an elaborate ceremonial life, a social life based on wealth and the display of wealth. Beyond this point comes a real change. The Northern Maidu are typically central Californian, while such outposts as the Lemhi Shoshoni and the Paviotso have a Great Basin culture founded on entirely different principles. In view of the wide variations in ceremonial life, one would not expect to find this ceremony repeatedly developed in the several areas, and developed on precisely the same lines. This together with continuous distribution of the ceremony can point to only one explanation of its presence, namely through diffusion.

The distribution is not absolutely continuous but doubtless some gaps are due to lack of ethnographic knowledge,[408] while others occur in groups whose meagre ceremonial life would not point to the inclusion of the ritual. There are, however, enough contiguous groups to show that the ceremony spread over the area where it is now found. [147]

It was shown above that in every group where the ceremony was found it had been completely assimilated into the ritual pattern of the tribe. Then how much was diffused? Regardless of what ritual elaboration there has been, one feature is constant everywhere: what has been elaborated is the normal handling of the salmon. The fish is caught, carried ashore, cut, cooked and eaten normally. Every group, performing the ceremony, has taken several of these features and ritualized them according to its ceremonial pattern. The accompanying table uses as headings the normal handling of the salmon and shows the number of groups that have elaborated each step.

This tabulation shows clearly a surprising amount of divergence. If the details of the ceremony are considered this divergence becomes even greater. Comparing the ceremonies of two neighboring and culturally related tribes will show this. Both the Kwakiutl and Bella Coola do not detail any specified person to catch the first salmon, but once it is taken, it is carried ashore ceremonially, The Bella Coola keep the salmon under water until a mat is spread on skunk cabbage leaves to receive the fish. It may not touch the ground. The Kwakiutl fisherman's wife meets him on the beach and receives the salmon, she being the one who officiates at the cleaning and cooking of the fish. The Bella Coola do not delegate the cutting of the fish to any particular person, nor is the fish cut in a ritual manner. The Kwakiutl woman cuts the fish with a special knife and follows exact directions. The Kwakiutl set the salmon on roasting tongs so the eyes project on the tongs while the Bella Coola roast the fish in the usual manner. No statement is made about the eating of the fish in the Bella Coola ceremony, but for the Kwakiutl we know that the sept of the fisherman is invited.

These differences in the details of the ceremony are due to the fact that the handling of the fish has been ritualized in each group according to its own ceremonial pattern. This is also borne out in the discussion earlier in the paper of the relation of the ceremony to the ritual of each group.

In the development of this ceremony it is inevitable that there should be some details which coincide. It is difficult to decide whether these likenesses are due to local diffusion or whether they agree because of the ritualization of a common procedure based on common ceremonial habits. There are some instances of both processes.

Among the Lillooet, the salmon weir poles are decorated and a boy is sent out to pray at the fishing stations just before the salmon run is expected. Then when the fish appear the shaman in charge of the ceremony sends a man out to take the first fish. In Northwestern California the formulist who is in charge of the ceremony spends a number of days before the ritual praying at fishing stations and fasting. During the ceremonial period he catches the first salmon. The Northern Maidu shaman catches the first salmon and no one is allowed to catch any fish until he is successful. He then cooks the fish where it was caught and gives a piece to each person there.

It would be difficult to prove that these similarities are due to diffusion. [148] Beyond these preparatory rites there is no further agreement between the Lillooet and the Northwestern

---

[408] All judgments made here are on the basis of the scanty information available and might have to be altered materially if more data were obtained.

[22a] RBAE 31: 454.

Californian ceremonies, or between either of these and the Northern Maidu. Rather these likenesses are due to common ritual habits.

In the cutting of the fish there are a number of more exact correspondences, The Tsimshian specify that the tail must not be broken off, but cut with a mussel shell knife. The Kwakiutl woman breaks off the tail of a speared salmon, but cuts off that of one caught on the hook. The Cowichan cut off the tail also. Since all these people believe in the immortality of the salmon, this regulation against breaking off the tail may be a desire to prevent the splintering of the bone and thus losing some of the bones. In such an event, the salmon, according to their belief, would not fully revive. The Nisqualli and Chinook, on the other hand, require that the fish be cut lengthwise and not transversely. These two groups have very simple salmon ceremonies which are almost identical, so it is likely that these features are due to diffusion. In the northern group the ceremonies do not resemble one another to a great extent, yet the appearance of such definite details as these specifications as to the cutting of the fish, in tribes as close together as the Kwakiutl, Nootka and Cowichan would also point to the diffusion of these particular elements.

The ceremonial eating of the salmon is one feature that occurs in every form of the salmon rite. The particular group which partakes of it, however, varies greatly. In tribes where the ritual is performed by a shaman, a chief, or some other ceremonial leader, he either eats the first salmon himself or apportions it to those who may eat it. In Northwestern California, the Karok, Hupa or Yurok formulist together with his assistant eats the salmon. The Chinook and Nisqualli shamans eat the first fish. In both these groups the correspondence of these features may be due either to a local diffusion or to the similarity of ritual pattern. As was said before the Chinook-Nisqualli instance is probably one of the few cases where it seems feasible to assume that there has been actual diffusion of the ceremony.

There is another significant feature in the selection of those who may eat the first salmon. Only those who are ceremonially pure are allowed to partake of it, for the inclusion of others would offend the salmon and stop the run. Those excluded are generally persons who have recently had contact with death, parents of recently born children, menstruating women, and adolescents, Sometimes these are automatically excluded by allowing only children, as with the Songish, or very old people, as with the Wishram, to eat the fish. Even where theoretically the whole tribe eats the salmon, these groups are generally barred. This exclusion of the ceremonially impure is probably not due to diffusion but is based on the common belief that these people will offend the salmon, a taboo to be discussed more thoroughly later in this paper.

There are a few minor similarities that are not inherent in the normal treatment of the salmon. The Bella Coola wind red cedar bark about a stick [149] to which the line of the first salmon is attached. The Lower Lillooet decorate the weir poles with feathers. These two groups although not contiguous, are close enough to make it possible that this arbitrary act spread from one to the other. Both these tribes take great care that the first salmon does not touch the ground. The Songish and Cowichan carry the fish in the outstretched arms so their hands do not touch it, and the Tsimshian carry the fish on a mat. These also are arbitrary acts which have probably been transmitted.

On the whole, those cases are resolved as indicating diffusion, first, where the tribes sharing the custom are contiguous, and second, where the act is arbitrary and not inherent, in the special form, to handling the fish. It seems, however, that the greater part of the resemblances are due to the fact that these acts are the ceremonial stock in trade of the whole area. These acts have, therefore, not been diffused as part of the salmon ceremony, but in general, there was transmitted the attitude of reverence toward the salmon and the idea of ritualizing the handling of the first salmon.

Hence we are dealing here with the diffusion of a sentiment and a tendency toward ritualization, with later elaboration along the lines suggested by the ceremonial patterns of the groups, which are themselves largely common property in general nature, although they differ in details. [150]

IV ~ The Attitude Toward the Salmon
As Expressed in Beliefs and Taboos

The motive underlying the salmon ceremony belongs to a group of widespread beliefs attributing a conscious spirit to food plants and animals. Therefore, before it is safe to eat either the plant or animal this spirit must be propitiated by a ceremony or an offering. With agricultural people this gives rise to harvest festivals; with food gatherers, hunters and fisherman the first gathering or catch of the season is the occasion for ceremony.

Since the plant or animal is endowed with a conscious spirit, it can either present itself in abundance or not appear at all. Hence a second motivation for ceremony: an appeal for abundance. Coupled with that, especially in hunting and fishing, is the petition for luck.

It will be shown later that the salmon ceremony as practiced on the North Pacific Coast is related to the sporadic first fruits ceremonies found in North America. In this area the general attitude toward salmon is developed in a specific manner.[22a] Throughout, there exists the feeling that the salmon is a person, living a life very similar to that of the people who catch him. The salmon have a chief who leads them up the streams during the run. In performing the ceremony over the one actually caught first, they believe that they are honoring the chief of the salmon. The Tsimshian concept illustrates this point very well. They believe the earth to be flat and surrounded by an ocean, beyond which there are several countries, one being that of the spring salmon. The cottonwood leaves which have fallen into the river are "salmon" for these salmon people- In the spring they send out scouts to see if the leaves have fallen or "if the salmon are in the river." As soon as the salmon scouts find them, the salmon people start on their journey to the Skeena River. On their way the spring salmon, who are regarded as the leaders, tell the other varieties when they are to start out.[409]

This conception is carried out in the belief that a Tsimshian shaman can see what is going on in the village of the spring salmon and when he sees them starting up the Skeena River, he knows they will arrive eight days after the breaking of the ice. Being able to see into the salmon world is a very important function of the Tsimshian shaman.[410]

The Cowichan of the Fraser River Delta believe that the salmon country is toward the sunset. Their chief sees that the rules regarding the salmon are obeyed.[411]

Linked with this idea is the concept of the immortality of food plants and animals. Therefore, if the bones and refuse are properly disposed of, the animal [151] will revive and return another season. This idea is spread far beyond the salmon area and also applied to other animals. The salmon bones and refuse are generally disposed of by throwing them into the water, where they revive and return to the salmon country, but in a few instances they are thrown into the fire. This is done by the Tsimshian and Tillamook,[412] two peoples so far apart that one can scarcely claim diffusion, especially because the other practice is found quite consistently between them. Very little is known of the Tillamook, so the custom cannot be explained by relating it to similar

---

[409] See appendix.

[410] Boas, RBAE 31: 474.

[411] Boas, BAAS 1894: 463.

[412] Boas, RBAE 31: 449. Boas, UCal 20: 9.

practices in regard to other animals, but this is possible for the Tsimshian. The bones and unused parts of mountain goats are burned, for until this is done the mountain goat spirit is sick.[413] Similarly porcupine bones are thrown in the fire to protect the animal from sickness.[414]

The tribes who throw the bones of salmon into the water are: Bella Bella, Kwakiutl, Nootka, Bella Coola, Cowichan, Songish, Lillooet.[415] This group forms a compact, continuous distribution within the larger area of the salmon ceremony.

Related fundamentally to the same idea is the custom of not breaking the salmon bones. This is specifically stated for the Bella Coola, Siciatl and Tsimshian, while the Chinook and Quinault take great care that the heart of the salmon shall not be eaten by a dog or otherwise mutilated.[416] They either roast and eat the heart or bum it, but never throw it into the water. On the diminishing of the Chinook tribe the salmon ceremony was no longer performed, but the heart of the first salmon was always disposed of, for if it were mutilated the fishing would be spoiled.[417]

Another custom may be associated with these practices, namely that the first salmon must be eaten before sun down or may not be taken home. The Kwakiutl believe that if the roasted eyes of the silver salmon are kept in the house over-night, the fish will disappear.[418] The Chinook always eat the first catch before sunset.[419] The Klamath gave the alternative custom relative to the sucker when questioned about a salmon ceremony. At one spot on the banks of the Sprague River, the first sucker is roasted to ashes so that many will come. Those which follow cannot be taken home but must be roasted there on the [152] bank. If they are taken home the fish will not come any longer.[420] The Puyallup are cautioned to kill only as much dog salmon as they need, for the salmon will take the soul of a wasteful person. When the salmon reaches his home in the ocean the person will die.[421] All these taboos can be traced to the idea that the salmon is regarded as a person who allows himself to be caught and on reviving returns to his own country.

In Northwestern California these concepts of personality and immortality for the salmon are also current. The first salmon said, "I will not be caught," and he deposited his scales in the fish nets and they became salmon. The first salmon then went back to the ocean.[422] In their formulae repeated at the salmon ceremony, the coming of the great salmon leader from the miraculous country across the ocean, is recounted.

In the salmon ceremony the fish may usually be eaten only by those who are ceremonially clean. This excludes menstruating women, those who have had recent contact with the dead, parents of recently born children, and youths who have not reached puberty. For

---

[413] Boas. RBAE 31: 448.

[414] Boas, RBAE 31: 449.

[415] Bella Bella, Boas, RBAE 31: 886-887; Kwakiutl, Boas, RBAE 33: 611-612; Nootka, Boas, BAAS 1890: 599; Bella Coola, Boas, Mem AMNH 2: 77; Cowichan, Boas, BAAS 1894: 461; Songish, Boas, BAAS 1890: 569; Lillooet, Teit, Mem AMNH 4: 280-281.

[416] Bella Coola, Mem AMNH 2: 77; Siciatl, Hill-Tout, JAT 34: 33; Tsimshian, RBAE 31: 206; Chinook, Swan, 107; Quinault, Cobb, Pacific Salmon Fisheries, 23.

[417] Swan, 107-108.

[418] Boas, RBAE 35: 611.

[419] Franchere, 260.

[420] Spier, notes.

[421] Arthur Ballard, personal communication.

[422] Kroeber, BBAE 78: 68.

example, the Cowichan prohibit widows, widowers, menstruating women and youths from eating at the ceremony.[423] Their neighbors, the Lillooet, do not allow an unmarried adult woman, a menstruating woman, orphan, widow or widower to eat of the first fish, for the run would be poor if they did.[424] When the procession with the first salmon approaches the chief's house, the Tsimshian shaman orders all young people who are unclean to leave the house.[425] In many other instances it is specified that only the old men or only the children eat of the first catch, thus eliminating this undesirable group.

Not only is the first catch taboo to the ceremonially unclean, but at any time those who have had contact with birth, death or puberty are prohibited from eating fresh salmon. The parents of a newborn child are prohibited from eating fresh salmon among the Songish and Snanaimuq,[426] while the Yurok specify that the father of the child must eat apart and touch no fresh salmon or meat for five or six days, with the same prescription of fifty days for a normal birth and sixty after a still birth, on the part of the mother.[427]

The immediate survivors of the dead are similarly restrained from eating salmon. The Songish not only will not allow a widow or widower to eat salmon, but they must keep away from the water for fear that their presence will drive away the fish.[428] The Lillooet claim that salmon are particularly susceptible to the influence of dead bodies, so all recently bereaved must avoid [153] eating the fresh fish. Elderly persons can shorten the period of taboo.[429] The Siciatl like the Songish do not allow the survivors of dead relatives to go near a creek in which the salmon run during the early part of the season; neither may they eat fresh fish.[430] The Wishram do not allow the father of a still born child or one that dies in early infancy to go near a fishing station, otherwise the run would stop. The bereaved parents may not eat salmon for five days and must go into a sweatlodge every day to purify themselves. The same taboo holds if a man's wife dies.[431]

Those prohibitions against eating of fresh salmon by mourners and women who have recently born children or are in the menstrual period are widely spread. In most groups the same taboo holds for fresh meat. It is almost universal for the immediate relatives of the dead to fast either during the burial period or for a brief mourning period. In groups where the custom is not outright fasting there is at least a restriction of diet, this generally being the elimination of fresh meat and fish. The rationalization of these taboos is twofold. Some peoples believe that eating meat or fish at this time will cause illness; others maintain that the animal or fish will be offended at being brought in contact with death. With the salmon, it would seem to be the second of these reasons which underlies the taboos. In almost every instance the reason given for prohibiting mourners from eating fresh salmon is that the fish will be offended and cease to run in that locality. These taboos connected with mourning are found consistently throughout the salmon area and beyond. Possibly the puberty and menstrual customs are the most widespread.

In the salmon area the person who is ceremonially unclean not only does not eat salmon, but may not approach the waters where the salmon run, with the same idea that their presence

---

[423] Boas, BAAS 1894: 461.
[424] Teit, Mem AMNH 4: 280.
[425] Boas RBAE 31: 450.
[426] Boas, BAAS 1890: 21; Boas, AA 1889: 321.
[427] Kroeber, BBAE 78: 45.
[428] Boas, BAAS 1890: 24.
[429] Hill-Tout, JAI 35: 139.
[430] Hill-Tout, JAI 34: 33.
[431] Spier, notes.

would offend the fish so that they would no longer come. A Bella Coola or Tsimshian girl at puberty may not eat fresh salmon or go near the sea or the rivers for one year.[432] Among the Klamath where the salmon taboos are transferred to the sucker, a girl at puberty and during menstrual periods may not eat fresh fish or meat, because if she did she would get "consumption" and die. This instance and that of the Northern Shoshoni, both on the very margin of the salmon area, are the only ones listed where the person transgressing the taboo may be injured, elsewhere it is always the fish or game that will be offended.[433]

In defining these customs for the Ute of the Great Basin, Lowie draws the following conclusions:

It is clear that a family likeness pervades the Shoshonean menstrual customs and that the abstention from flesh is the most persistent trait in the complex. This is a point of great comparative value, for this taboo seems to be practically always associated with the puberty usages of California tribes and extends with the qualification that fresh meat or fish is forbidden, as far north as Tahltan territory.[434] [154]

This area could be extended even further. At least one instance of similar taboos is on record for the Southeast. The Creeks prohibit a woman in her menstrual period or after confinement from eating fish or venison or anointing herself with bear grease. Also after attending a burial a person abstained from eating fish.[435] These taboos, it will be remembered, are found in an area where there are first fruits ceremonies and where first catches of fish and game are especially treated. It cannot be claimed that these two sets of behavior always travel together, for without doubt, the dietary restrictions are much more widespread, but their occurrence together in such widely divergent areas is not without interest.

Among the salmon fishing peoples there generally exists a taboo against the use of salmon and game at the same time. This prohibition against using together two kinds of food obtained from different sources is widespread and sporadic among primitive people. The rational basis for these taboos is frequently that the two seasons do not coincide. In fact it is only for a brief transitional period when the two products are available, that the taboo is effective. An excellent example of this taboo is the rigid distinction made by the Eskimo between land and sea products. The Nootka do not eat salmon and venison at the same time. The Yurok do not use salmon or any other fish at the same time with bear meat, grouse eggs or acorns blackened by prolonged soaking.[436] This taboo is, then, another expression of the desire not to offend game.

The most important of the remaining taboos is the relation between twins and salmon. This is peculiar to the North Pacific Coast and there limited to a fairly compact group, the Tsimshian, Kwakiuti, Nootka, Makah and Klallam. In most of these instances, the relation is expressed in a different manner.

Among the Tsimshian twins have supernatural power to call the salmon and olachen. The Kwakiutl twins of the same sex were salmon before their birth. Their father dances for four days after their birth swinging a large square rattle. By swinging the same rattle the twins can

---

[432] Boas, BAAS 1889: 838.

[46a] See appendix.

[433] Lowie, PaAMNH 20: 274.

[434] Swanton, BBAE 73: 384-385.

[435] Kroeber, BBAE 78: 69.

[436] Sapir in Hastings, Encyclopedia of Religion and Ethics, 594.

produce favorable weather, or cure disease. Both the Nootka twins and their father have close connection with the salmon. The father of twins is regarded as an instrument of the salmon world and during the fishing season devotes all his time to singing songs and performing secret rituals to give his tribesmen a maximum catch. The birth of twins forebodes an unusually big salmon run. It is likely that there may be some idea among the Nootka corresponding to the Kwakiutl conception that twins are salmon before birth, for if a Nootkan twin child sees a salmon mistreated he involuntarily bursts into tears.[437]

Swan relates of the Makah that when twins were born during the fishing season on Tatoosh Island, the parents were sent back to the mainland and prohibited from eating any sort of fish.[438] The Klallam follow the same procedure. [155]

The parents of twins are required to move away from the shore into the woods as soon after the birth as the mother can walk. They are not allowed near the water for one year and the father may not hunt or fish. During this time they may not eat fresh fish or meat.[51a]

Beyond this area there is evidently no such association. At least it is disclaimed by the Wishram and Klamath,[62] and not mentioned for the Yurok, all rather typical tribes of the southern salmon area. Although there are few primitive groups who do not pay some attention to twins, this association of twins and salmon seems to be restricted to this very small group within the salmon area.

All these taboos which are practiced toward the salmon are not limited to this particular area; neither are they practiced even there exclusively toward the salmon. Many of these groups believe just as firmly in the immortality of other animals but it happens that no set of rites has crystallized around the beaver or deer, for example. The Lillooet, Thompson and Shuswap throw beaver and deer bones in the water, while a Yurok does not wash his hands in running water after eating venison because the deer would drown.

We find therefore that the ceremony and the various taboos related to the salmon are based on the same 'fundamental concept, the immortality and conscious personality of the animal, and the desire not to offend it so that it may come in abundance. [156]

V ~ Relation To Other First Fruits Ceremonies And The Bear Cult

In North America there is a sporadic occurrence of first fruits ceremonies, a ritual feature generally associated with the Old World. There are two distinct areas of distribution of these ceremonies, one east of the Mississippi River where the most significant ritual of this kind is held for the corn, and the other in scattered groups along the Pacific Coast where the ritual is always performed for wild products. Although the complete distribution of the first fruits ceremonies of the east is not given here, the groupings obtained are sufficient to assume that they are connected. The ceremony is a harvest festival, conducted before it is permissible to eat of the new crop. The ceremonial eating in the southern part of the area is generally preceded by the taking of an emetic to purify the participants. The event not only celebrates the ripening of the corn but in many places marks the beginning of a new year, and at this time the village is thoroughly cleaned, the people make new clothing and household goods, and new fires are lighted.

---

[437] Swan, Smith. Cont. Know. 16: 82.

51a See appendix.

[438] Spier, notes.

This harvest ceremony in the Southeast sets a ritual pattern which the Creeks, at least, have carried over to other traits. The first acorns or fruits gathered were not eaten, neither was the first fish caught in a new fish weir, nor corn from a newly broken field.[439] Hunters gave the first deer killed to the shaman who had helped them through repeating formulae.

On the Pacific Coast there are two distinct groups of tribes, celebrating first fruits ceremonies and then a wide scattering of peoples who share the custom to a limited degree. The compact groups center about the lower Fraser River and in northwestern California. In the Northwestern Caltfomian group there is an echo of the concept found in the Southeast, namely, the coincidence of the first fruits rituals and the opening of the new year. This is true for the Hupa and Karok especially, and shared to a lesser degree by the Yurok.[440] In this area the first fruits ritual is localized and performed for a particular product in each place. The Hupa catch the first salmon at Haslinding while the lamprey ceremony is performed in another part of the valley.[441] In autumn the first acorns are treated in a similar way. The acorn ceremony is also performed by the Yuki who catch salmon but have no ritual for it.[442]

In this area there can be no doubt but that the salmon ceremony has been completely assimilated into the ritual pattern and has become one of these first fruits ceremonies, the most important rituals of the year.

Going northward from these groups the salmon ceremony alone is to be found through Oregon and southern Washington except among the Chehalis, [157] who have a lamprey ceremony. On Puget Sound there are again some first fruits ceremonies, but of a much simpler nature than those of California. The Snohomish have a simple feast at which all the guests, but not the host, eat of the piece de resistance, when the first salmon or deer are caught and when the first berries are picked.[443] This tribe is the southernmost outpost of the second group of first fruits rituals. Among the Interior Salish both m Washington and British Columbia and along the Lower Fraser to the coast there is a compact area of these ceremonies. The Interior Salish of Washington, together with the Sahaptian {no, Salish} Methow and Wenatchee {Sahaptin name for psk^{w}aws}, have a salmon ritual and a deer ritual following the same pattern, the former performed in the spring, the latter when the first snow had fallen.[444] It is especially mentioned for the Okanagon, but probably applies also to the others of this group, that first berries are eaten ceremonially in the manner current in the Plateau of British Columbia.[445] The Thompson and Lillooet, both typically tribes of this area, have ceremonies for the first berries. "When half the berry crop is ripe, the Lillooet chief calls the people to pick them. The people paint all exposed parts of their bodies red and are seated before the chief. He holds up a birch bark tray with the various kinds of berries to the mountain and says, "Qailus, we tell you, we are going to eat fruit." He addresses each mountain, and walking sunwise gives each person present a berry to eat. Then the women gather berries, but only enough for one day's meals, for to keep them overnight would be unlucky.[446] There are other first fruits ceremonies of the same pattern performed by the

---

[439] Swanton, BRAE 73: 383-384.

[440] Kroeber, BBAE 78: 53.

[441] Kroeber, BBAE 78: 134.

[442] Kroebcr, BBAE 78: 188.

[443] Haeberlin-Gunther, ZE 1924: 17.

[444] Curtis, 7: 78.

[445] Hill-Tout, JAI 41: 132.

[446] Teit, Mem AMNH 4: 282.

Thompson, the Stspelis and other Cowichan of the Fraser Delta. The berry ceremony does not occur again between this group and the Tsimshian, whose ritual is similar to that of the Interior Salish.

The other first fruits ceremonies of the coast are sporadic rituals connected with fishing, especially with olachen fishing.[60a] The Tlingit handle the first olachen carefully, address it as chief and give a festival in his honor. Then the fishing proceeds in the usual way.[447] The Tsimshian roast the first olachen ceremonially and pray for plenty of fish.[448]

All these western examples of the first fruits ceremony occur in the salmon area. In Northwestern California, the salmon ceremony is shared by all who have the other first fruits ceremonies, except the Yuki. The Interior Salish tribes who depend so largely on salmon, curiously enough do not all perform the ceremony. The Lower Lillooet have an elaborate ritual and show great reverence for the salmon, but the upper division of the tribe does not share it. Neither do their close neighbors, the Thompson and Shuswap.

It is clear that the salmon ceremony in Northwestern California belongs to the first fruit complex there, but with the North Pacific Coast this is not so obvious. While the Thompson, Shuswap and Upper Lillooet have other first [158] fruits ceremonies and no salmon ritual there are other groups in the vicinity for whom the reverse is true. It is impossible to prove that one or the other is earlier, but it is obvious that the ritual pattern of both ceremonies is the same. The same attitude underlies the ceremonies. There is always a propitiation and a supplication for abundance.

The attitude at the basis of the salmon ceremony is also shown toward the bear. From eastern Siberia to the Atlantic shores of North America there is spread a series of customs turning on veneration of the supernatural power attributed to the bear. To some extent the area of the salmon ceremony coincides with this wider distribution, especially in the north. But more interesting than the overlapping of this distribution is the fact that the ritual pattern of the two ceremonies is largely alike. There are prayers of propitiation to the bear, the animal is butchered in a certain fashion, only a particular group is allowed to eat of the animal, the refuse is especially disposed of. All these are features of the salmon rites and agree even in the specific way of doing them. One of the most widespread taboos in regard to the bear is that the bones must be kept away from dogs which is the same reason given for burning the salmon heart or throwing the bones in the water. The Kwakiutl treat the bear much as they do the salmon, as an honored guest. Those who are ceremonially unclean may not partake of the bear, just as they are forbidden to eat of the salmon.[449]

Again the bear and the salmon are not alone in being the object of these taboos. They concern other animals in the same areas, but they have not been so thoroughly crystallized into a set of rites. The Interior Salish Thompson, Shuswap and Lillooet also throw deer and beaver bones into the water. The Skaulits always throw sturgeon bones into the water.[450] The refuse from butchering a mountain goat is carefully disposed of by the Tsimshian and Lillooet. The Ten' a throw goose, duck and swan feathers into the river that they may change back to birds; fish bones into the water and animal bones into the forest.[451] In every instance there is attributed some supernatural power to these animals and the effort is made not to offend them by being careless with their bodies so that they will come abundantly.

[60a] See appendix.

[447] Dall, 413.

[448] Boas, BAAS 1889: 747.

[449] Hallowell, AA., n.s, 28, 1-175.

[450] Hill-Tout, JAI 34: 339.

[451] Reed and Parsons, 339.

These concepts and the specific ways of expressing them are found over a wide area of northern North America. In some instances they have crystallized into rituals, elsewhere they remain taboos individually observed. On analyzing the situations where the ceremonies have developed, it will be found that almost invariably it has been in connection with a seasonal animal or product. The dramatic and spectacular arrival of the salmon, the ripening of the berries which have been watched from the time they blossom in the spring, the harvesting of the corn, the gathering of the acorns, are all seasonal events. There is a definite occasion which presents itself for celebration. That the seasonal occurrence of game intensifies the ceremonial response is clear. On the [159] other hand where game is available at all times, but the hunt is set at a definite time, there is also this tendency toward ceremony. The bear could be hunted throughout the summer and fall, but instead he is attacked in the spring when he emerges from hibernation or even driven from his lair. The intensive whale rituals are performed only by those tribes who go out to sea on whale hunts, which are conducted at a definitely determined time. Contrarywise the beaver, the deer, the porcupine and the mountain goat, although perhaps better and more easily obtainable at certain seasons, are hunted casually and so present no occasion for a ritual.

DISTRIBUTION OF FIRST SALMON, BEAR, AND FIRST FRUIT RITES WITH
REFERENCES TO SOURCES

	SALMON	BEAR	FIRST FRUITS
1	Achomawi, BBAE 78:313		
2		Algonkin, Hallowell 139	
3	Alsea, U Cal 20:9		
4		Assiniboin, Hallowell 71	
5	Bella Coola, Mem AMNH 2:78		
6	Carrier, Morice letter Sept. 28, 1927	Carrier, Hallowell 141	
7			Cherokee, Trans. AES 3:75
8			Chickasaw, JAFL 20:50
9		Chilcotin, Hallowell 142	
10	Chinook, CNAE 1:196 Swan 107 Franchère 260 Bancroft 1:233		
11	Cowichan, BAAS 1894:461		Cowichan, BAAS 1894:461
12			Creek, Adair 96-111
68		Eastern Cree, Hallowell 139	
72		Forest Potawatomi, Hallowell 140	
67	Haida, Mem AMNH 8:69		
13			Huron, Summary Report 10
14	Hupa, U Cal 1:23		Hupa, BBAE 78:134
15			Iroquois, Summary Report 471
16	Karok, BBAE 78:104		Karok, BBAE 78:102
17		Kaska, Hallowell 141	
18	Klallam, U W 1:202		
19	Klamath, Spier ms.		
20	Kwakiutl, RBAE 35:609, 611, 1318 BAAS 1890:614	Kwakiutl, Hallowell 74	
21		Lenape, Hallowell	Lenape, Indian Notes 144
22	Lillooet (Lower), Mem AMNH 4:280	Lillooet, Hallowell 142	Lillooet, Mem AMNH 4:282
23		Malecite, Hallowell 68	
24		Menominee, Hallowell 140	Menominee, AA 13:556
25	Methow, Curtis 7:78		Methow, Curtis 7:78
26		Miami, Hallowell 72	
27		Micmac, Hallowell 68	
71		Mistassini, Hallowell 66	
28		Miwok, Hallowell 76	
29			Mohegan, Pa AMNH 3:194
30		Montagnais, Hallowell 137	
31		Naskapi, Hallowell 137	
32			Natchez, BBAE 43:113
33	Nisqualli, CNAE 1:196		

Distribution of First Salmon, Bear, and
First Fruit Rites with References to Sources [159-60]

#	SALMON	BEAR	FIRST FRUITS
34	Nootka, BAAS 1890:599	Nootka, Hallowell 74	
35	No. Maidu, BAMNH 17:198		
36	No. Shoshoni, Pa AMNH 2:218		
37			Ojibway, RBAE 19:1091
38	Okanagon, Curtis 7:78		Okanagon, Curtis 7:78
39			Osage, Trans U P 2:171
40	Paviotso, Pa AMNH 20:306		
41		Penobscot, Hallowell 67	
42		Plains Cree, Hallowell 70	
43		Plains Ojibway, Hallowell 139	
44	Puyallup, Ballard letter		
45	Quinault, Olson ms.		
46		Saulteaux, Hallowell 138	
47			Seminole, RBAE 5:522
48	Shasta, BAMNH 17:430 RBAE 78:294		
49		Shuswap, Hallowell 142	
50	Snohomish, ZE 1924:72		Snohomish, ZE 1924:17
51	Songish, BAAS 1890:569		Songish BAAS 1890:596
52	StsEe'lis, JAI 34:330		StsEe'lis, JAI 34:330
53		Tahltan, Hallowell 141	
54		Ten'a, Hallowell 144	
69		Tete de Boule, Hallowell 142	
55		Thompson, Hallowell 142	Thompson, Mem AMNH 2:349
56	Tillamook, U Cal 20:10		
57		Tlingit, Hallowell 74	Tlingit, Dall 413
70		Timiskaming Algonkin, Hallowell 139	
58	Tolowa, CNAE 3:67		
59	Tsimshian, RBAE 31:450	Tsimshian, Hallowell 60	Tsimshian, BAAS 1889:847
60		Wailaki, Hallowell 76	
61	Wenatchee, Curtis 7:78		Wenatchee, Curtis 7:78
62			Winnebago, RBAE 37:384
63	Wishram, PAES 2:183 Spier ms.		
64			Yuchi, U P 1:112-131
65			Yuki, BBAE 78:183
66	Yurok, BBAE 78:60 CNAE 3:56		Yurok, BBAE 78:53

NOTE: The figures preceding the tribal names refer to the numbers on the map.

VI ~ The Relation of the Ceremony To Mythology

It [161] has been shown that the salmon ceremony has been thoroughly integrated with the ritual life in the various groups which practice it and that the fundamental attitude on which it is based is expressed also in a series of taboos and beliefs. In other words, this attitude of veneration of the salmon is an integral part of the culture of these groups. It is then to be expected that there should be some reflection of this in the mythology.

Throughout the area where the ceremony is performed and even in the groups which do not have the ritual there are myths about the salmon. These myths show a striking uniformity, dealing invariably with salmon taboos and beliefs, often giving the local variant of these customs. This is often indirectly done, especially if there is a well built novelistic plot to the tale. Generally these myths fall into the cultural divisions of the area, with one type centering about the Kwakiutl speaking groups on Vancouver Island and the mainland opposite, another about Puget Sound, and a third among the Interior Salish and southward to California.

These myths readily fall into four major groups:

1. Raven and the salmon
    a. Raven carves a salmon out of wood
    b. Raven marries Salmon Woman
2. The Salmon Boy Myth
3. Salmon origin tales
4. Miscellaneous tales
    a. Taboo and belief tales
    b. Novelistic tales

The first group with very few exceptions is found only in the northern part of the area and belongs to the Raven cycle. The tales either appear independently or the two incidents are told in sequence as one story. In the first episode (A of the table, page 164) Raven carves a salmon of wood and finds that it has no soul, or it is tough or cannot swim. So he goes to the salmon country to get whatever the fish lacks. The second tale (B of the table) relates the marriage of Raven and Salmon Woman (a variant being that he abducts the daughter of the salmon chief) who produces salmon by magical means. Raven's hair catches on the drying salmon, he insults them, and Salmon Woman leaves him, taking all the fish with her.

The first episode alone is found only in two Kwakiutl speaking groups, the River's Inlet and Newetee, and among the Bella Coola, almost contiguous groups. The second tale has a much wider distribution, occurring in the three groups mentioned above, then inland from the Bella Coola to the Chilcotin and Lillooet and northward to the Tsimshian, Haida and Tlingit. The two episodes combined into one tale (AB of the table) is again found [162] in the first mentioned groups, where both episodes occur among the Chilcotin who do not tell the first episode alone.

These tales have nothing in common with the ceremony except that the disappearance of the fish after Raven insults them stresses the need for reverence toward the salmon.

The myth of Salmon Boy has a more direct connection with the ceremony in that it describes the ritual for the first salmon. The plot varies but little. A boy is taken to the salmon country, where he is told to club a child when he wants food, eat and throw its bones into the water. The child revives immediately. The boy returns to his father's village in the salmon run and is caught by his father. He teaches his people how to treat the salmon.

This tale (C of the table) is found in thirteen tribes of whom five have the ceremony. It cannot be said that this myth dictates the ritual or determines its presence, but it is, no doubt, explanatory. The pattern of this story occurs again in a Lillooet tale about the mountain goat. A young hunter treats the mountain goat he kills disrespectfully so their chief's daughters lure him to their camp. The chief sends out two boys and sends the hunter out for goats. He shoots the boys and they are carefully brought in and butchered; the blood is soaked up with leaves and offal are thrown in the lake. The hunter later skins a goat and hides the cartilege. The goat has a bleeding nose. When the hunter returns to his people he instructs them in butchering mountain goats.[452] The Skaulits have a similar myth about the sturgeon.[453]

Salmon origin tales take on a very definite pattern among the Interior Salish tribes. Coyote is the culture hero-trickster of these groups and the coming of salmon is always due to his efforts. The typical version is that Coyote transforms himself into a plank, a dish or a baby, floats into a salmon trap and is cared for by the two women who own it. In their absence he breaks their dam and liberates the salmon. This version is found in Kutenai, Thompson, Shuswap, Lillooet, Flathead, Nez Perce, Okanagon, Sanpoil, Seshelt, Snohomish, Wishram.[454] All these groups tell this story in their sequence of Coyote adventures. From the Wishram southward the tale is attached to the culture hero who brings the salmon from the place where it is hidden by its owner. The Klamath variant is an interesting transition. The culture hero (*Kemukumps*, Old One) made a dam where the people could fish. The people above got no fish at all, so they hired Loon to break the dam, with the approval of the culture hero.[455]

---

[452] Hill-Tout, JAI 33: 195, 196.

[453] Hill-Tout, JAI 34: 365.

[454] Boas, BBAE 59: 301, except Snohomish, Haeberlin, JAFL 37: 404.

[455] Spier, ms.

In Northwestern California the Hupa, Yurok and Wiyot[456] have a tale clearly connected with the Coyote tales and the Klamath version. The culture hero deceives the woman who owns the salmon and liberates them by breaking a dam. [163]

This continuity of distribution from the Plateau of British Columbia to northwestern California may be indicative of other cultural affiliations. The Lillooet and the Hupa and Yurok are the only groups who have preparatory rites before the salmon ceremony. In the light of this, the prophesying dreams of the Wenatchee, Methow, Okanagon and Nespelim may be considered as an expression of this same idea. This salmon origin tale has the widest distribution and the most consistent of any one salmon story. On the other hand, since to a large extent, it is so firmly woven into the Coyote cycle, the interest in the salmon is probably an incidental matter.

The miscellaneous group of salmon tales includes a variety of stories that explain taboos and beliefs related to the salmon. They are largely minor tales in the mythologies that include the more important salmon stories. The Tlingit tell the tale of a man who found a salmon on the beach during a famine. The salmon told the man to put him back in the water. Then plenty of fish came- Later another salmon told the man to eat him and put his bones under his pillow. The man finds two babies, one of whom becomes a hero.[457]

Faintly resembling this is the Sk!qomic tale of the father of twins who dreams that he should put the bones of all the fish in the river in a box. After he does this he dies and no more fish come until another man in a trance discovers this. The Tsimshian Salmon Boy myth emphasizes the same belief in the incident of the salmon chief's illness due to keeping dried salmon more than one season.

The StsEe'lis, Sk!qomic and Lillooet have an interesting tale. Two children develop out of the roe of salmon and proceed to adventures characteristic of the mythology of this region.[458]

In Puget Sound, especially the southern end, from the Snuqualmi to the Puyallup, there are numerous short tales each expressing some salmon taboo, as not ridiculing the humpback for his appearance (Snuqualmi), or doubting the return of the salmon (Skokomish), or the quarrel among the varieties of salmon over the use of a stream and the agreement to run at a certain season (Puyallup).[459]

The Chinook and Kathlamet[460] have in their Coyote stories the establishment of local salmon taboos as Coyote moves upstream and fishes in each place. This localizing, so typical of northwestern California, is found also in the Klamath myths. The Tillamook have two salmon stories, dealing with behavior toward the salmon.[461] These tales resemble more closely the Pugef Sound type than the Kathlamet, Klamath or Califomian variety. The Snohomish and Chinook[462] have tales of remarkable likeness, A chief offers his daughter to the one who can split elkhorn. Salmon succeeds and is killed by [164] the wolves who in turn are killed by his son. These tales involve no taboos or beliefs and are purely novelistic with the salmon as a character.

The tribal distribution of the tales discussed here has been. plotted in the accompanying table. It shows clearly several definite distributions that overlap only to a slight degree. The Raven tales are segregated in the north, the salmon origin tales thru the Interior. The miscellaneous tales are limited to groups that have no definite cycles of stories. In these

---

456 Kroeber, BBAE 78: 73, 119.

457 Swanton, BBAE 39: 196.

458 Hill-Tout, JAI 34: 342; Hill-Tout, BAAS 1900: 541; Hill-Tout, JAI 35: 185-189.

459 Ballard.

460 Boas, BBAE 20: 101-106; Boam BBAE 26: 45-49.

461 Boas, JAFL 11: 24, 142.

462 Haeberlin, JAFL 37: 384; Boas ,BBAE 20: 77.

mythologies salmon is not a character, except in a few novelistic tales where his exploits are in no way contingent on his usual supernatural attributes. It would seem rather that in these various groups, a local type of myth has become explanatory of the salmon taboos and beliefs. The only exception to this is the Salmon Boy myth which has a definite pattern of its own that it retains throughout its distribution.

This salmon mythology occurs much more widely in the salmon area than the ceremony. Where the two occur together it is clear that the mythology does not determine the ritual, but in some instances is explanatory of it. The ceremony and the mythology are based on the same fundamental attitude toward the salmon and may be regarded as interrelated cultural traits, but it cannot be claimed that one is determined by the other; at most the mythology is explanatory.

TABLE II. Distribution of Salmon Myths

Tlingit		B		C
Haida				
Masset		B		
Skidegate		B		C
Kaigani				C
Tsimshian		B		C
Nass		B		
Kwakiutl		B		
River's Inlet	A	B	AB	
Newette	A	B	AB	
Bella Bella				C
Bella Coola	A	B	AB	C
Chilcotin		B	AB	C
Shuswap		B		C
StEelis				C
Sk!qomic				C
Nootka				C
Siciatl				C
Quinault				C

REFERENCES FOR THE SALMON MYTH IN TABLE

Tlingit

    (B) Swanton BBAE 39: 108.
    (C) BBAE 39: 301.

Haida

  Masset   (B) Swanton Mem AMNH 14: 303,330.
  Skidegate   (B) Swanton BBAE 29: 26.
              (C) BBAE 29: 7-14. [165]

Kagani	(C) Swanton MemAMNH 8: 243.
Tsimshian	(B) Boas RBAE 31: 76.
	(C) RAE 31: 192.
Nass	(B) Boas BBAE 27: 32.
Kwakiutl	(B) Boas, Sagen 159; Boas CUCA 2: 49.
	(AB) Boas CUCA 2: 169;Boas MemAMNH 5: 330
Rivers Inlet	(A) Boas, Sagen 209.
	(B) Boas RBAE 31: 669.
	(AB)Boas, Sagen 210; RBAE 31: 669.
Newette	(A) Sagen, 174.
	(B) Sagen, 174.
	(AB) Sagen, 175.
Bella Bella	(C) RBAE 31: 886. {Heiltsuk}
Bella Coola	(A) Sagen, 242. {Nuxalk}
	(B) Boas MemAMNH 2: 94; Sagen, 246.
	(AB) Sagen, 242; MemAMNH 2: 94.
	(C) MemAMNH 2: 73.
Chilcotin	(B) Farrand MemAMNH 4: 18.
	(AB) Ibid.
	(C) MemAMNH 4: 24.
Shuswap	(B) Teit MemAMNH 4: 637,
	(C) MemAMNH 4: 690.
StsEe'lis	(C) Hill-Tout JAI 34: 331.
Sklqomic	(C) Hill-Tout BAAS 1900: 520-522.
Siciatl	(C) Hill-Tout JAI 34: 46.
Nootka	(C) Boas RBAE 31: 919.
Quinault	(C) Farrand MemAMNH 4: 112.

VII ~ Summary

It [166] has been shown that on the North Pacific Coast and inland, as far as the salmon ascend the streams, there is a ceremony performed when the first salmon is caught. The distribution of this ceremony is not as wide as the occurrence of salmon but spread over a fairly continuous area. In every tribe where the ceremony is performed, the ritual has been integrated with the ceremonial pattern of the group, being simple or elaborate according to that pattern. The specific similarities between the ceremonies are due to likeness of ritual pattern of the tribes involved and not due to diffusion of this ceremony. In no case did the ceremony itself spread from one group to another, but the idea of ritualizing the taboos toward the salmon, which were already present, was diffused.

This attitude of veneration which is ritualized in the ceremony is also expressed in other practices and taboos. The concepts underlying this attitude of veneration are the belief in the immortality of the salmon and the conscious will of the fish in allowing himself to be caught. These concepts are also held toward other animals, as well as toward plants. This is expressed in the first fruits ceremonies found in the same area. It is also expressed in the bear cult. The area of the salmon ceremony is entirely within the territory covered by the bear cult, which spreads from eastern Siberia through northern North America. Generally it was found that while this attitude is held toward many animals and expressed in special behavior toward them, wherever the animal or plant makes a definitely periodic appearance this attitude is intensified and frequently becomes the basis of a group ceremonial.

The mythologies of the tribes practicing the salmon ceremony contain some tales explanatory of the taboos and beliefs regarding the salmon, but it cannot be claimed that these myths determine the presence of the ceremony or its ritual. The majority of these myths are part of the cycles of tales centering about Raven or Coyote and it seems that the salmon episodes are only incidental.

The attitude of veneration toward certain game animals of which the salmon ceremony is one ritualistic expression is highly developed only in north-western North America. It is the basis of the widespread bear cult and the first fruits ceremonies of the Pacific Coast. Its linkage with the belief In the immortality of game and its conscious will to be caught gives rise to a set of propitiatory rites that are exceptional in North America culture. The harvest festivals of the Southeast and eastern Woodlands are feasts of thanksgiving for the abundance of crops and do not seem to have the same underlying attitude. In every salmon ritual it is clear that the welfare of the animal is most important and the taboos regulate conduct that his spirit may not be offended.

In this complex there are two features of almost universal distribution: the first fruits ritual and a definite relationship toward animals. Among primitive [167] people there is frequently the belief that a new thing is sacred and requires a ritual to remove the taboo. This is done through the ceremonial eating of the product or through sacrifice to the dead or to the chief. These expressions do not involve the attitude toward the plant itself which is so characteristic of northwestern North America. When first fruits are given to the chief or sacrificed to the dead, it is to honor him, more than to honor the thing which is being given. A feeling of definite relationship toward food animals is most strongly developed in Australia. But there the behavior is prompted by an attitude of coercion rather than conciliation as in our American instance.

It would seem then, that in northwestern North America we have a definitely local interpretation of two widespread cultural features, which is an isolated example in the New World. [168]

Bibliography

The following abbreviations are used:

AA	American Anthropologist.
BAAS	Reports, British Association for the Advancement of Science,
BBAE	Bulletin, Bureau of American Ethnology.
CNAE	Contributions to North American Ethnology.
CUCA	Columbia University Contributions to Anthropology.
Indian Notes	Indian Notes and Monographs, Museum of the American Indian, Heye Foundation.
JAFL	Journal of American. Folklore.
JAI	Journal of the Royal Anthropological Institute.
Mem AMNH	Memoirs, American Museum of Natural History.
Pa AMNH	Anthopological Papers, American Museum of Natural History.
RBAE	Report, Bureau of American Ethnology.
Sagen	Boas, Indianische Sagen.

Smith. Cont. Know.	Smithsonian Contributions to Knowledge.
Summary Report	Summary Report of the Anthropological Division, Geological Survey of Canada.
TransAES	Transactions of the American Ethnological Society.
TransUP	Transactions, Department of Archaeology, University of Pennsylvania.
U Cal	University of California Publications in American Archaeology and Ethnology.
UP	University of Pennsylvania, Anthropological Publications, University Museum.
UW	University of Washington Publications in Anthropology.
ZE	Zeitschrift fur Ethnologic.

ADAIR, JAMES *History of the American Indians* (London, 1775).

BALLARD, ARTHUR *Some Tales of the Southern Puget Sound Salish* (UW, 2, 1927, 57-81).

BANCROFT, HUBERT HOWE Native Races of the Pacific States of North America (San Francisco, 1875).

BARBEAU, C.M *On Huron Work, 1911* (Summary Report for 1911).

BARTRAM, WILLIAM *Observations on the Creek and Cherokee Indians* (Trans AES, 3, part 3, 1853).

BOAS, FRANZ *Chinook Texts* (BBAE 20, 1894).

 Ethnology of the Kwakiutl (RBAE 35, 1921).

 Fifth Report on the Northwestern Tribes of Canada (BAAS 1889, 797-893). [169]

 *Indianische Sagen von der Nord-Pacifischen Kuste Amerika*s (Berlin, 1895).

 Kwakiutl Tales (CUCA 2, 1910).

 Mythology of the Bella Coola (Mem AMNH 2, part 2, 1898, 25-127).

 Ninth Report on the Northwestern Tribes of Canada (BAAS 1894, 453-463).

 Notes on the Snanaimuq (AA 1889, 321-328).

 Notes on the Tillamook (U Cal, 20, 1923, 3-16).

 Sixth Report on the Northwestern Tribes of Canada (BAAS 1890, 553-715, reprint pp. 1-162).

 Tsimshian Mythology (RBAE 31, 1909).

 Tsimshian Texts (BBAE 27, 1902).

BOAS, FRANZ and HUNT, GEORGE *Kwakiutl Texts*, I (Mem AMNH 5, 1902).

COBB, JOHN *Pacific Salmon Fisheries* (Bureau of Fisheries Document, no. 902, 1921).

CURTIS, EDWARD S. *The North American Indian* (Cambridge, 1907-1924).

DALL, W. *Alaska and its Resources* (Boston, 1870).

DIXON, ROLAND B. *The Northern Maldu* (BAMNH 17, 1905, 119-346).

 The Shasta (BAMNH 17, 1907, 381-498).

FARRAND, LIVINGSTON *Traditions of the Chilcotin Indians* (Mem AMNH 4, part 1, 3-54).

 Traditions of the Quinault (Mem AMNH 4, part 3, 1902),

FRANCHERE, GABRIEL *Narrative of a Voyage to the Northwest Coast of America* (New York, 1854).

GIBBS, GEORGE *Tribes of Western Washington and Northwestern Oregon* (CNAE 1, 1877, 157-219).

GODDARD, PLINY EARLE *The Life and Culture of the Hupa* (U Cal 1, 1903, 3-88).

GOLDENWEISER, A.A. *On Iroquois Work, 1912* (Summary Report for 1912).

GUNTHER, ERNA *An Analysis of the First Salmon Ceremony* (AA, n.s, 28, 1926, 605-617).

Klallam Ethnography (UW, 1, 1927, 171-314).

HAEBERLIN, HERMANN *Mythology of Puget Sound* (JAFL 37, 1924, 341-438).

HAEBERLIN, HERMANN und GUNTHER, ERNA *Ethnographische Notizen liber die Indianer des Puget Sundes* (ZE, 1924, 1-74).

HALLOWELL, A. IRVING *Bear Ceremonialism in the Northern Hemisphere* (AA, n.s, 28, 1926, 1-175).

HARRINGTON, M.R *Religion and Ceremonies of the Lenape* (Indian Notes, 1921).

HILL-TOUT, CHARLES *Ethnological Report on the StsEe'lis and Skaulits Tribes of the Halokmɛlɛn Division of the Salish of British Columbia* (JAI 34, 1904, 311-376). [170]

Notes on the Sk!qomic of British Columbia, a Branch of the Great Salish Stock of North America (BAAS 1900, 472-549).

Report on the Ethnology of the Siciatl of British Columbia, a Coast Division of the Salish Stock (JAI 34, 1904, 20-91).

Report on the Ethnology of the StlatlumH of British Columbia (JAI 35, 1905, 126-218).

JENKS, A.B *Wild Rice Gatherers of the Upper Lakes* (RBAE 19, 1900).

KROEBRR, A.L *Handbook of the Indians of California* (BBAE 78, 1925).

MACCAULEY, C. *Seminole Indians of Florida* (RBAE 5, 1887).

LOWIE, ROBERT H. *Ceremonialism in North America* (AA, n.s, 16, 1914, 239-260).

The Northern Shoshone (PaAMNH 2, 1909, 165-306).

Notes on Shoshonean Ethnography (PaAMNH 20, 1924, 185-314).

POWERS, STEPHEN *Tribes of California* (CNAE 3, 1877).

RADIN, PAUL *The Winnebago Tribe* (RBAE 37, 1923).

REED, T.B, and PARSONS, ELSIE CLEWS *Cries-For-Salmon* (in *American Indian Life*, E.C Parsons, ed, New York, 1922).

SAPIR, EDWARD *Indians of Vancouver Island* (in Hastings, *Encyclopedia of Religion and Ethics*, vol. 12, 591-595. Edinburgh and New York, 1921).

Wishram Texts (PAES 2, 1909, 1-314).

SKINNER, ALANSON B. *Comparative Sketch of the Menominee* (AA, n.s, 13, 1911).

SPECK, FRANK G. *Ethnology of the Yuchi* (UP 1, part 1, 1909).

The Mohegan Indians (PaAMNH 3, 1909).

Notes on Chickasaw Ethnology and Folklore (JAFL 20: 1920, 50-58).

Notes on Osage Ethnology (Trans UP 2, part 2, 1907).

SPIER, LESLIE *Klamath and Wishram Notes*, ms.

SWAN, JAMES G. *The Indians of Cape Flattery* (Smith.Cont.Know. 16, 1870, 1-105).

The Northwest Coast (New York, 1857).

SWANTON, JOHN R. *Contribution to the Ethnology of the Haida* (Mem AMNH 8, part 1, 1905).

Haida Texts — Masset Dialect (Mem AMHN 14, part 2, 1908).

Haida Texts and Myths (BBAE 29, 1905).

Indian Tribes of the Lower Mississippi Valley (BBAE 43, 1911).

Tlingit Myths and Texts (BBAE 39, 1909).

TEIT, JAMES *The Lillooet Indians* (Mem AMNH 4, part 5, 1906, 193-300).

The Shuswap (Mem AMNH 4, part 7, 1909, 449-789). [171]

Appendix

The information added here was received too late to incorporate in the paper. The Wishram notes were contributed by Doctor Edward Sapir, the Kwakiutl information by Professor Franz Boas, and the Bella Coola {Nuxalk} notes by Mr. T.F McIlwraith.

Additional Description Of
A Wishram First Salmon Ceremony

When the first single fish comes in spring (especially Chinook salmon) and is caught, it is roasted and all old people are called and they eat this first fish. This gives good luck for that season, particularly for that fishing place where the first fish was caught. Before the fish is eaten, there used to be lots of talk.[3a]

Bella Coola Attitude Toward Salmon

The Bella Coola undoubtedly consider that all living creatures are, in a sense, supernatural. This does not imply that they are superior to humans, but rather that they belong to a different plane, sometimes superior, sometimes inferior. The salmon, probably owing to their great economic value, figure prominently. For instance, the older people have no doubt concerning the immortality of the fish. When the latter "die" they are merely freed from the flesh and return the following year.[22a]

Bella Coola Taboos

In former times, adult women were not allowed on the river bank during the early part of the salmon run. This prohibition was discontinued when the sun's shadow cast a diagonal scar on a certain mountain, which took place about the first of August. One of the jealously guarded prerogatives is that of enforcing prohibitions with regard to the river during the salmon run. No refuse must be thrown in the river; no freshly hewn planks can be set afloat; a new canoe must be kept for ten days before launching and no widow or widower of less than a year's standing can embark at the village. Infringement of any of these prohibitions was punished by ducking or beating although it is unlikely that anyone dared intentionally to err.[46a]

Bella Coola Attitude Toward Twins

Salmon are responsible for the birth of twins, although no explanation of this belief is offered. It is believed that twins formerly could understand the speech of birds, animals and fish, and that many of them could assume salmon form at will. The corpse of a twin was formerly deposited, in its coffin, in the crotch of a tree in the river valley. Thenceforth the river cut into this bank from year to year until it undermined the tree, afterward keeping to a single channel. Before an adult woman can eat salmon, the sticks on which it has been exposed to the flames must be removed. If this is omitted, she will bear twins.[51a] [172]

Vita of Erna Gunther

Born November 9, 1896 at Brooklyn, New York of Alsace Lorraine (Grand Est) stock, fluent in German, French, and English. Attended New York City public schools. A.B., Barnard College, 1919. Graduate study of anthropology, Columbia University, 1919-1921; University of California, 1925; University of Washington, 1924-1926. A.M, Columbia University, 1920. Assistant in Anthropology, Barnard College, 1919-1921. Associate in Anthropology, University of Washington, 1923, ethnographic field work among the Havasupai (Arizona), 1921; among the tribes of Puget Sound (Washington and British Columbia), 1921-1927. Preparation of a concordance of the mythology of southwestern United States for the American Folklore Society, 1927 to date.

Bibliography

1924   Haeberlin, Hermann and Gunther, Erna   *Ethnographische Notizen liber die Indianer des Puget Sundes* (Zeitschrift für Ethnologic, bd. 26, pp. 1-80).

1925   *Klallam Folk Tales* (University of Washington Publications in Anthropology, vol. 1, pp. 113-170).

1926   *An Analysis of the First Salmon Ceremony* (American Anthropologist, n.s 28, pp. 605-617).

1927   *Klallam Ethnography* (University of Washington Publications in Anthropology, vol. 1, pp. 171-314).

1928   *Accretion in American Indian Folk Tales* (Folklore, London). In press.

* = key entry
f = span of 5 pages, mostly forward
#0 = span of 10 pages

Please report typo-gnomes so they can be zapped away
Corrections & Suggestions Welcome

Sold @ Amazon.com

New Fire 1947 Maps

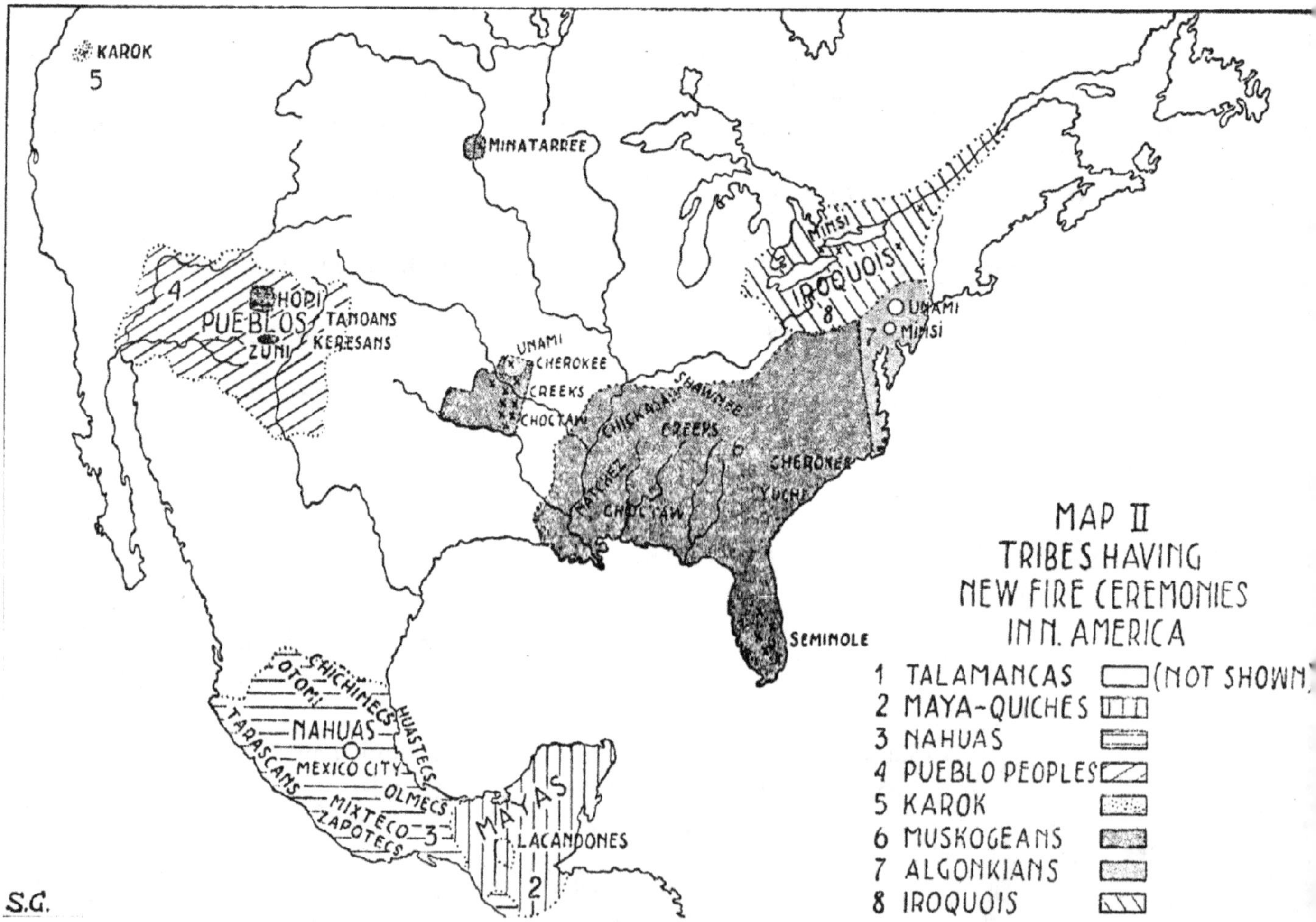

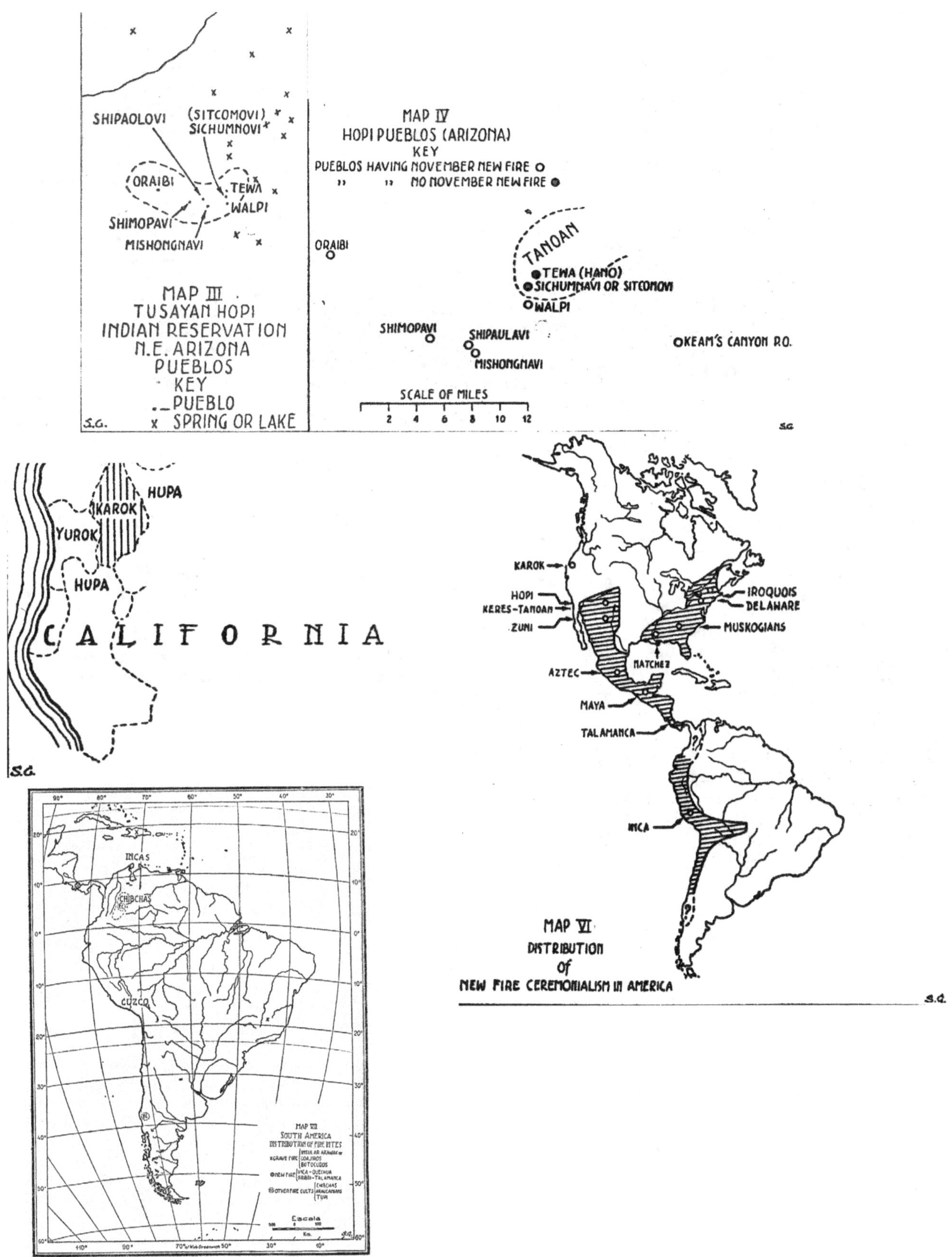

SHIPAOLOVI
(SITCOMOVI)
SICHUMNOVI
ORAIBI
TEWA
WALPI
SHIMOPAVI
MISHONGNAVI
MAP III
TUSAYAN HOPI
INDIAN RESERVATION
N.E. ARIZONA
PUEBLOS
KEY
PUEBLO
SPRING OR LAKE
S.G.
MAP IV
HOPI PUEBLOS (ARIZONA)
KEY
PUEBLOS HAVING NOVEMBER NEW FIRE
NO NOVEMBER NEW FIRE
TANOAN
TEWA (HANO)
SICHUMNAVI OR SITCOMOVI
WALPI
ORAIBI
SHIMOPAVI
SHIPAULAVI
MISHONGNAVI
OKEAM'S CANYON P.O.
SCALE OF MILES
2 4 6 8 10 12
S.G.
HUPA
KAROK
YUROK
HUPA
CALIFORNIA
S.G.
KAROK
HOPI
KERES-TANOAN
ZUNI
AZTEC
NATCHEZ
MAYA
TALAMANCA
INCA
IROQUOIS
DELAWARE
MUSKOGIANS
MAP VI
DISTRIBUTION
of
NEW FIRE CEREMONIALISM IN AMERICA
S.G.
INCAS
CHIBCHAS
CUZCO
MAP VII
SOUTH AMERICA
DISTRIBUTION OF FIRE RITES
GRAVE FIRE
NEW FIRE
OTHER FIRE CULTS
Escala
Km.

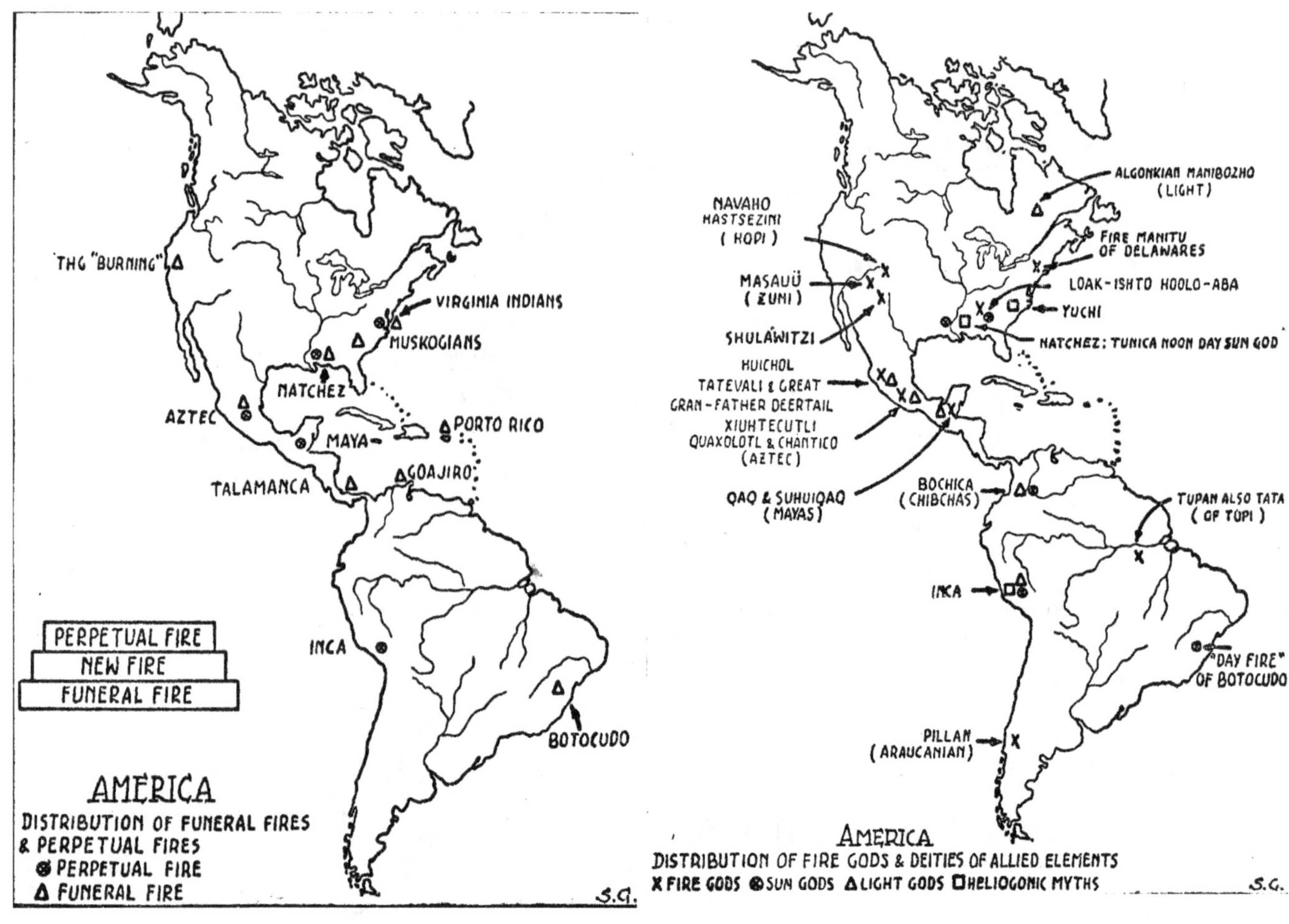
THE "BURNING"
VIRGINIA INDIANS
MUSKOGIANS
NATCHEZ
AZTEC
MAYA
PORTO RICO
TALAMANCA
GOAJIRO
INCA
BOTOCUDO
PERPETUAL FIRE
NEW FIRE
FUNERAL FIRE
AMERICA
DISTRIBUTION OF FUNERAL FIRES & PERPETUAL FIRES
PERPETUAL FIRE
FUNERAL FIRE
S.G.
ALGONKIAN MANIBOZHO (LIGHT)
NAVAHO HASTSEZINI (HOPI)
FIRE MANITU OF DELAWARES
MASAUÜ (ZUNI)
LOAK-ISHTO HOOLO-ABA
YUCHI
SHULÁWITZI
NATCHEZ: TUNICA NOON DAY SUN GOD
HUICHOL
TATEVALI & GREAT GRAN-FATHER DEERTAIL
XIUHTECUTLI QUAXOLOTL & CHANTICO (AZTEC)
QAQ & SUHUIQAQ (MAYAS)
BOCHICA (CHIBCHAS)
TUPAN ALSO TATA (OF TUPI)
INCA
PILLAN (ARAUCANIAN)
"DAY FIRE" OF BOTOCUDO
AMERICA
DISTRIBUTION OF FIRE GODS & DEITIES OF ALLIED ELEMENTS
X FIRE GODS SUN GODS LIGHT GODS HELIOGONIC MYTHS
S.G.